SPIKEware Base Rapid Decision Support™ SAS Macro Package

Usage Guide

Version 4.0

© 2006, 2017 Paul D. McDonald, MBA

SPIKEware Consulting

Overland Park, KS

http://www.spikeware.net/

Table of Contents

Introduction 8

Functions 9
 %ABS 9
 %AIRY 9
 %ARCOS 10
 %ARSIN 11
 %ATAN 12
 %BAND 12
 %BETAINV 13
 %BIG 14
 %BLSHIFT 15
 %BNOT 15
 %BOR 16
 %BRSHIFT 17
 %BXOR 18
 %BYTE 19
 %CDF 19
 %CEIL 21
 %CEXIST 21
 %CHARACTER 22
 %CINV 23
 %CNONCT 23
 %COLLATE 24
 %COMB 25
 %COMMAND 26
 %COMPOUND 27
 %CONSTANT 27
 %COS 29
 %COSH 29
 %CSS 30
 %CURRENTPATH 31
 %CV 31
 %DACCDB 32
 %DACCDBSL 33
 %DACCSL 33
 %DACCSYD 34
 %DAIRY 35
 %DATA 35
 %DATAMEM 36

%DATAPATH	37
%DATE	38
%DATETIME	38
%DEPDB	39
%DEPDBSL	40
%DEPSL	40
%DEPSYD	41
%DEQUOTE	42
%DIGAMMA	42
%DOSPATH	43
%E	44
%ERF	44
%ERFC	45
%EULER	46
%EXIST	46
%EXP	47
%FACT	48
%FEXIST	48
%FILEDT	49
%FILEEXIST	50
%FILEREAD	51
%FILESCAN	52
%FINV	53
%FIPNAME	54
%FIPNAMEL	55
%FIPSTATE	56
%FLOOR	57
%FNONCT	58
%FREAD	59
%FUZZ	59
%GAMINV	60
%GAMMA	61
%GETVAR	61
%GETVARC	62
%GETVARN	63
%IBESSEL	64
%IEFBR14	64
%INDEXC	65
%INDEXW	66
%INFO	67
%INT	68
%INTCK	69
%INTNX	69
%INTRR	70
%IRR	71
%JBESSEL	72

%KURTOSIS	73
%LIBREF	73
%LGAMMA	74
%LOG	76
%LOG10	76
%LOG2	77
%LOGPDF	77
%LOGSDF	79
%MACEPS	81
%MAX	81
%MEAN	82
%MEM	83
%MIN	84
%MORT	84
%MPUT	85
%N	87
%NAME	87
%NETPV	89
%NEXTDATA	90
%NMISS	90
%NORMAL	92
%NPV	92
%NUMERIC	93
%OBSCNT	94
%ORDINAL	94
%PFD	95
%PERM	96
%PI	97
%POISSON	97
%PREFIX	98
%PROBBETA	99
%PROBBNML	99
%PROBBNRM	100
%PROBCHI	101
%PROBF	102
%PROBGAM	103
%PROBHYPR	103
%PROBIT	104
%PROBNEGB	105
%PROBNORM	105
%PROBT	106
%RANBIN	107
%RANBINARY	108
%RANCAU	108
%RANEXP	109
%RANGAM	110

%RANGE	111
%RANK	111
%RANNOR	112
%RANPOI	113
%RANTRI	114
%RANUNI	114
%RECCNT	115
%REPEAT	116
%REVERSE	117
%ROUND	118
%SAVING	118
%SDF	119
%SIGN	120
%SIN	121
%SINH	122
%SKEWNESS	122
%SLEEP	123
%SMALL	124
%SORTLIST	125
%SQRT	126
%SQRTBIG	126
%SQRTMACEPS	127
%SQRTSMALL	127
%STD	128
%STDERR	129
%STFIPS	129
%STNAME	130
%STNAMEL	131
%STRING	132
%SUFFIX	133
%SUM	133
%SYSMSG	134
%TAN	135
%TANH	135
%TIME	136
%TODAY	137
%TRANSLATE	137
%TRANWRD	138
%TRIGAMMA	139
%UNIQUE	140
%USS	141
%VAR	141
%VARCNT	142
%VARFMT	143
%VARINFMT	143
%VARLABEL	144

%VARLEN	145
%VARLIST	146
%VARNUM	146
%VARTYPE	147
%WAKEUP	148
%WORDCNT	149
%ZIPFIPS	150
%ZIPNAME	151
%ZIPNAMEL	151
%ZIPSTATE	152

Macros 154
%BIGSORT	154
%BREAKOUT	155
%CHECKALL	157
%CHECKREC	159
%COMPARE	161
%CONTENTS	165
%DATANOTE	169
%DECRYPT	170
%DIRECTORY	171
%DOCUMENT	173
%DOCUMENT_RTF	174
%DOUBLES	175
%ENCRYPT	178
%EXCEPTION	180
%FILECAT	182
%FILEIN	182
%FILENOTE	184
%FILEOUT	185
%FINDFILE	187
%FORMAT	188
%GOOD2BAD	190
%HTML2TXT	192
%LFOOT	193
%LINESOFCODE	195
%MAKETITLE	203
%MANIFEST	206
%OUTLIER	208
%PARETO	214
%PGMTEST	218
%POPOPTS	219
%POPTITLE	220
%PUSHOPTS	223
%PUSHTITLE	224
%SAMPLE	227

%SAS2XLS	228
%SAS2XML	230
%SCRAMBLE	231
%SHUFFLE	232
%SLIDE	233
%SORTALL	237
%STEMLEAF	238
%SYSVARS	239
%TIMENOTE	241
%TRIMFILE	243
%UNIV	251
%WORDWRAP	252
%XLS2SAS	253
%XML2SAS	256

Methods 257

%_AGE	257
%_C2F	257
%_CITY	258
%_F2C	259
%_PCTCHANGE	260
%_PROPERNAME	261
%_STATE	262
%_ZIP	263

FAQ 265

General Questions	265
Installation/Usage	265
Licensing	265
Applications	266
Non-SAS Components	266

Introduction

This document is the Usage Guide for the SPIKEware Base Rapid Decision Support™ SAS Macro package Version 4.0. Additional information, examples, and support can be found at http://www.spikeware.net/.

Rapid Decision Support™ (RDS™) v4.0 is a collection of 233 SAS Macros, 8 SAS® Programs, and other selected supporting tools and utilities designed specifically for functioning with The SAS Software System®. While a few are designed specifically to work in Microsoft Windows® and others specifically in UNIX®, most of the components are designed for any operating system using SAS Software v8.x or above. RDS consists of over 32,000 lines of code developed over 10 years time.

Many of the macros are simply the "SAS Macro Language" equivalent of a SAS data step function (such as %cos, %kurtosis, %sum). Others also operate as a function but complete "macro-related" operations (%data, %sortlist, %varcnt, %wordcnt). Another group (identified with the first character as an "_" underscore) is designed specifically to function inside a data step (%_c2f, %_state, %_propername). And finally the remaining macros are "procedure-style" because they generate a report, modify a data set, or complete some other such function (%exception, %outlier, %stemleaf).
In addition to the documentation on the website, each macro comes with a "DEMO" program at the bottom of the file. This program shows how the macro should work. You will also find the comments in the source code to be very descriptive and helpful.

Two macros of special note are %xls2sas and %pareto. These macros replace functions that are normally only available in other SAS "add-on" products--SAS\QC using PROC PARETO and SAS\Access for PC File Formats using PROC IMPORT. While the SAS products will complete the tasks in question faster, they do require additional licensing fees.

One other macro worthy of special note is %DOSPATH. This macro utilizes the Windows XP batch file "dospath.bat" (which, in turn, uses "choice.exe"). These files (and other Windows batch files) are available for free from our website.

Installation: It is very simple to install these macros. Simply create a location for the macros (such as !SASROOT\macro*.sas for Microsoft Windows environments, other similar locations depending on your operating system) and use the included "autoexec.sas" program in the root directory. You may need to modify the autoexec program to match your site requirements.

Page Breaks, Line Breaks, etc: To paraphrase the icon Forrest Gump, "Page breaks is as page breaks does." In the interest of saving paper, page breaks in this document are kept to a minimum.

Contact Information: Questions and comments are welcomed at SPIKEware. Visit our website to contact us – http://www.spikeware.net/

Credits
RDS, Rapid Decision Support, and its components are the property of SPIKEware, Inc. in Overland Park, KS
Microsoft Windows and its components are the property of Microsoft Corporation in Redmond, WA http://www.microsoft.com/.
SAS, The SAS Software System, and its components are property of the SAS Institute, Inc. in Cary, NC http://www.sas.com/.
UNIX and its components are the property of The Open Group in San Francisco, CA http://www.unix.org/.
Other programs and components that may have been inadvertently not listed are the property of their respective companies.

Special thanks to the following people: Pat McDonald, Ryan Carr, Joseph Murphy, Jim Christine, Robert Patten, Laura Tuttle, Russell Seybert, Steve Warnock, and Rob van der Woude for their contributions, assistance, and ideas.

Functions

%ABS

Purpose
ABS macro function similar to the ABS data step function. Returns the Absolute Value of an input string, or returns a missing value if the input is non-numeric.

Syntax
%abs(argument)

> *ARGUMENT* is numeric.

Example

Sample Program
```
%put abs = %abs(-5) ;
%put abs = %abs(5) ;
%put abs = %abs(0) ;
%put abs = %abs(2.45) ;
%put abs = %abs ;
%let abschar = %abs(abc) ;
```

SAS Log
```
1          %put abs = %abs(-5) ;
abs = 5
2          %put abs = %abs(5) ;
abs = 5
3          %put abs = %abs(0) ;
abs = 0
4          %put abs = %abs(2.45) ;
abs = 2.45
5          %put abs = %abs ;
NOTE:  Argument 1 to macro function %ABS is missing or out of range.
abs = .
6          %let abschar = %abs(abc) ;
NOTE:  Invalid numeric data abc in Argument 1 for macro function %ABS.
```

SAS Listing
This sample program does not have any listing output.

%AIRY

Purpose
AIRY macro function similar to the AIRY data step function. It returns the value of the AIRY function [Abramowitz, M. and Stegun, I (1964), Handbook of Mathematical Functions with Formulas, Graphs, and Mathematical Tables—National Bureau of Standards Applied Mathematics Series #55, Washington, DC: U.S. Government Printing Office.]

Syntax

%airy(argument)

> *ARGUMENT* is numeric

Example

Sample Program

```
%put airy=%airy(2) ;
%put airy=%airy(-2) ;
%put airy=%airy(A) ;
```

SAS Log

```
1          %put airy=%airy(2) ;
airy=0.03492413042327
2          %put airy=%airy(-2) ;
airy=0.22740742820168
3          %put airy=%airy(A) ;
NOTE:  Invalid numeric data A in Argument 1 for macro function %AIRY.
airy=.
```

SAS Listing

This sample program does not have any listing output.

%ARCOS

Purpose

ARCOS macro function similar to the ARCOS data step function. Returns the ArcCosine or Inverse Cosine value.

Syntax

%arcos(argument)

> *argument* is numeric [range between -1 and 1]

See Also

%ARCOS, %ARSIN, %ATAN, %COS, %COSH, %SIN, %SINH, %TAN, %TANH

Example

Sample Program

```
%put ARCOS(0.1) = %arcos(0.1) ;
%put ARCOS(-1) = %arcos(-1) ;
%put ARCOS(1) = %arcos(1) ;
%put ARCOS(100) = %arcos(100) ;
%put ARCOS(ABC) = %arcos(ABC) ;
```

SAS Log

```
1          %put ARCOS(0.1) = %arcos(0.1) ;
ARCOS(0.1) = 1.47062890563333
2          %put ARCOS(-1) = %arcos(-1) ;
```

```
ARCOS(-1) = 3.14159265358979
3          %put ARCOS(1) = %arcos(1) ;
ARCOS(1) = 0
4          %put ARCOS(100) = %arcos(100) ;
NOTE:  Argument 1 to macro function %ARCOS is missing or out of range.
ARCOS(100) = .
5          %put ARCOS(ABC) = %arcos(ABC) ;
NOTE:  Invalid numeric data ABC in Argument 1 for macro function %ARCOS.
ARCOS(ABC) = .
```

SAS Listing

This sample program does not have any listing output.

%ARSIN

Purpose

ARSIN macro function similar to the ARSIN data step function. returns the ArcSine or Inverse Sine value.

Syntax

%arsin(argument)

argument is numeric [range between -1 and 1]

See Also

%ARCOS, %ARSIN, %ATAN, %COS, %COSH, %SIN, %SINH, %TAN, %TANH

Example

Sample Program

```
%put ARSIN(0.1) = %arsin(0.1) ;
%put ARSIN(-1) = %arsin(-1) ;
%put ARSIN(1) = %arsin(1) ;
%put ARSIN(100) = %arsin(100) ;
%put ARSIN(ABC) = %arsin(ABC) ;
```

SAS Log

```
1          %put ARSIN(0.1) = %arsin(0.1) ;
ARSIN(0.1) = 0.10016742116155
2          %put ARSIN(-1) = %arsin(-1) ;
ARSIN(-1) = -1.57079632679489
3          %put ARSIN(1) = %arsin(1) ;
ARSIN(1) = 1.57079632679489
4          %put ARSIN(100) = %arsin(100) ;
NOTE:  Argument 1 to macro function %ARSIN is missing or out of range.
ARSIN(100) = .
5          %put ARSIN(ABC) = %arsin(ABC) ;
NOTE:  Invalid numeric data ABC in Argument 1 for macro function %ARSIN.
ARSIN(ABC) = .
```

SAS Listing

This sample program does not have any listing output.

%ATAN

Purpose

ATAN macro function similar to the ATAN data step function. It returns the ArcTangent or Inverse Tangent value.

Syntax

%atan(argument)

    argument is numeric [range between -1 and 1]

See Also

%ARCOS, %ARSIN, %ATAN, %COS, %COSH, %SIN, %SINH, %TAN, %TANH

Example

Sample Program

```
%put ATAN(0.1) = %atan(0.1) ;
%put ATAN(100) = %atan(100) ;
%put ATAN(-0.1) = %atan(-0.1) ;
%put ATAN(ABC) = %atan(ABC) ;
%put ATAN() = %atan() ;
```

SAS Log

```
1          %put ATAN(0.1) = %atan(0.1) ;
ATAN(0.1) = 0.09966865249116
2          %put ATAN(100) = %atan(100) ;
ATAN(100) = 1.56079666010823
3          %put ATAN(-0.1) = %atan(-0.1) ;
ATAN(-0.1) = -0.09966865249116
4          %put ATAN(ABC) = %atan(ABC) ;
NOTE:  Invalid numeric data ABC in Argument 1 for macro function %ATAN.
ATAN(ABC) = .
5          %put ATAN() = %atan() ;
NOTE:  Argument 1 to macro function %ATAN is missing or out of range.
ATAN() = .
```

SAS Listing

This sample program does not have any listing output.

%BAND

Purpose

BAND macro function similar to the BAND data step function. It returns the BITWISE LOGICAL AND of two arguments. Accepts HEX values.

Syntax

%band(argument-1, argument-2)

    argument-1 and *argument-2* are numeric, non-negative, and non-missing.

See Also
%BXOR, %BRSHIFT, %BOR, %BNOT, %BLSHIFT, %BAND

Example

Sample Program
```
%put BAND(1,2) = %band(1,2) ;
%put BAND(0,2) = %band(0,2) ;
%put BAND(1,) = %band(1,) ;
%put BAND(1,-2) = %band(1,-2) ;
%put BAND(1,B) = %band(1,B) ;
%put HEX: BAND(0Fx,05x) = %band(0Fx,05x) ;
%put HEX: BAND(1,05x) = %band(1,05x) ;
%put HEX: BAND(0Fx,2) = %band(0Fx,2) ;
```

SAS Log
```
1          %put BAND(1,2) = %band(1,2) ;
BAND(1,2) = 0
2          %put BAND(0,2) = %band(0,2) ;
NOTE:  Argument 1 to macro function %BAND is missing or out of range.
BAND(0,2) = .
3          %put BAND(1,) = %band(1,) ;
NOTE:  Argument 2 to macro function %BAND is missing or out of range.
BAND(1,) = .
4          %put BAND(1,-2) = %band(1,-2) ;
NOTE:  Argument 2 to macro function %BAND is missing or out of range.
BAND(1,-2) = .
5          %put BAND(1,B) = %band(1,B) ;
NOTE:  Invalid numeric data B in argument 2 for macro function %BAND.
BAND(1,B) = .
6          %put HEX: BAND(0Fx,05x) = %band(0Fx,05x) ;
HEX: BAND(0Fx,05x) = 5
7          %put HEX: BAND(1,05x) = %band(1,05x) ;
HEX: BAND(1,05x) = 1
8          %put HEX: BAND(0Fx,2) = %band(0Fx,2) ;
HEX: BAND(0Fx,2) = 2
```

SAS Listing
This sample program does not have any listing output.

%BETAINV

Purpose
BETAINV macro function similar to the BETAINV data step function. The BETAINV function returns the pth quantile from the beta distribution with shape parameters a and b. The probability that an observation from a beta distribution is less than or equal to the returned quantile is p. BETAINV is the inverse of the PROBBETA function.

Syntax
%betainv(p,a,b)

> *p* is a numeric probability. Range: $0 <= p <= 1$
>
> *a* is a numeric shape parameter. Range: $a > 0$
>
> *b* is a numeric shape parameter. Range: $b > 0$

Example

Sample Program
```
%put BETAINV(0.001,2,4) = %betainv(0.001,2,4) ;
%put BETAINV(10,2,4) = %betainv(10,2,4) ;
%put BETAINV(10,-2,4) = %betainv(10,-2,4) ;
%put BETAINV(10,A,4) = %betainv(10,A,4) ;
%put BETAINV(10,,4) = %betainv(10,,4) ;
```

SAS Log
```
1          %put BETAINV(0.001,2,4) = %betainv(0.001,2,4) ;
BETAINV(0.001,2,4) = 0.01010178788373
2          %put BETAINV(10,2,4) = %betainv(10,2,4) ;
NOTE:  Argument 1 to macro function %BETAINV is missing or out of range.
BETAINV(10,2,4) = .
3          %put BETAINV(10,-2,4) = %betainv(10,-2,4) ;
NOTE:  Argument 1 to macro function %BETAINV is missing or out of range.
BETAINV(10,-2,4) = .
4          %put BETAINV(10,A,4) = %betainv(10,A,4) ;
NOTE:  Invalid numeric data A in argument 2 for macro function %BETAINV.
BETAINV(10,A,4) = .
5          %put BETAINV(10,,4) = %betainv(10,,4) ;
NOTE:  Argument 2 to macro function %BETAINV is missing or out of range.
BETAINV(10,,4) = .
```

SAS Listing
This sample program does not have any listing output.

%BIG

Purpose
Returns the largest double-precision number

Syntax
%big

See Also
%CONSTANT

Example

Sample Program
```
%put BIG=%big ;
```

SAS Log
```
1          %put BIG=%big ;
BIG=1.7976931348623E308
```

SAS Listing
This sample program does not have any listing output.

%BLSHIFT

Purpose
BLSHIFT macro function similar to the BLSHIFT data step function. It returns the bitwise logical left shift of two arguments. It accepts HEX values.

Syntax
%blshift(argument-1, argument-2)

>*argument-1* and *argument-2* are numeric, nonnegative, and nonmissing. Range: 0 to the largest 32-bit unsigned integer

See Also
%BXOR, %BRSHIFT, %BOR, %BNOT, %BLSHIFT, %BAND

Example

Sample Program
```
%put BLSHIFT(1,2) = %blshift(1,2);
%put BLSHIFT(07x,2) = %blshift(07x,2);
%put BLSHIFT(1,32) = %blshift(1,32);
%put BLSHIFT(1,A) = %blshift(1,A);
```

SAS Log
```
1          %put BLSHIFT(1,2) = %blshift(1,2);
BLSHIFT(1,2) =s 4
2          %put BLSHIFT(07x,2) = %blshift(07x,2);
BLSHIFT(07x,2) = 28
3          %put BLSHIFT(1,32) = %blshift(1,32);
NOTE:  Argument 2 to macro function %BLSHIFT is missing or out of range.
BLSHIFT(1,32) = .
4          %put BLSHIFT(1,A) = %blshift(1,A);
NOTE:  Invalid numeric data A in argument 2 for macro function %BLSHIFT.
BLSHIFT(1,A) = .
```

SAS Listing
This sample program does not have any listing output.

%BNOT

Purpose
BNOT macro function similar to the BNOT data step function. It returns the bitwise logical NOT of an argument. It accepts HEX values.

Syntax
%bnot(argument)

>*argument* is numeric, nonnegative, and nonmissing. Range: 0 to the largest 32-bit unsigned integer

See Also
%BXOR, %BRSHIFT, %BOR, %BNOT, %BLSHIFT, %BAND

Example

Sample Program
```
%put BNOT(10) = %bnot(10) ;
%put BNOT(0Fx) = %bnot(0Fx) ;
%put BNOT(A) = %bnot(A) ;
%put BNOT() = %bnot() ;
%put BNOT(-5) = %bnot(-5);
```

SAS Log
```
1          %put BNOT(10) = %bnot(10) ;
BNOT(10) = 4294967285
2          %put BNOT(0Fx) = %bnot(0Fx) ;
BNOT(0Fx) = 4294967280
3          %put BNOT(A) = %bnot(A) ;
NOTE:  Invalid numeric data A in argument 1 for macro function %BNOT.
BNOT(A) = .
4          %put BNOT() = %bnot() ;
NOTE:  Argument 1 to macro function %BNOT is missing or out of range.
BNOT() = .
5          %put BNOT(-5) = %bnot(-5);
NOTE:  Argument 1 to macro function %BNOT is missing or out of range.
BNOT(-5) = .
```

SAS Listing
This sample program does not have any listing output.

%BOR

Purpose
BOR macro function similar to the BOR data step function. It returns the bitwise logical OR of two arguments.

Syntax
%bor(argument-1, argument-2)

> *argument-1* and *argument-2* are numeric, non-negative, and nonmissing. Separate the arguments with a comma. Range: 0 to the largest 32-bit unsigned integer.

See Also
%BXOR, %BRSHIFT, %BOR, %BNOT, %BLSHIFT, %BAND

Example

Sample Program
```
%put BOR(01x,0F4x) = %bor(01x,0F4x) ;
%put BOR(1,0F4x) = %bor(1,0F4x) ;
%put BOR(-1,5) = %bor(-1,5) ;
%put BOR(1,A) = %bor(1,A) ;
%put BOR(1,) = %bor(1,) ;
```

SAS Log

```
1          %put BOR(01x,0F4x) = %bor(01x,0F4x) ;
BOR(01x,0F4x) = 245
2          %put BOR(1,0F4x) = %bor(1,0F4x) ;
BOR(1,0F4x) = 245
3          %put BOR(-1,5) = %bor(-1,5) ;
NOTE:  Argument 1 to macro function %BOR is missing or out of range.
BOR(-1,5) = .
4          %put BOR(1,A) = %bor(1,A) ;
NOTE:  Invalid numeric data A in argument 2 for macro function %BOR.
BOR(1,A) = .
5          %put BOR(1,) = %bor(1,) ;
NOTE:  Argument 2 to macro function %BOR is missing or out of range.
BOR(1,) = .
```

SAS Listing

This sample program does not have any listing output.

%BRSHIFT

Purpose

BRSHIFT macro function similar to the BRSHIFT data step function. It returns the bitwise logical right shift of two arguments and can accept HEX values.

Syntax

%brshift(argument-1, argument-2)

> *argument-1* is numeric, nonnegative, and nonmissing. Range: 0 to the largest 32-bit unsigned integer.
>
> *argument-2* is numeric, nonnegative, and nonmissing. Range: 0 to 31, inclusive.

See Also

%BXOR, %BRSHIFT, %BOR, %BNOT, %BLSHIFT, %BAND

Example

Sample Program

```
%put BRSHIFT(01Cx,2) = %brshift(01Cx,2) ;
%put BRSHIFT(1,2) = %brshift(1,2) ;
%put BRSHIFT(-1,2) = %brshift(-1,2) ;
%put BRSHIFT(1,ABC) = %brshift(1,ABC) ;
%put BRSHIFT(,2) = %brshift(,2) ;
%put BRSHIFT(1,35) = %brshift(1,35) ;
```

SAS Log

```
1          %put BRSHIFT(01Cx,2) = %brshift(01Cx,2) ;
BRSHIFT(01Cx,2) = 7
2          %put BRSHIFT(1,2) = %brshift(1,2) ;
BRSHIFT(1,2) = 0
3          %put BRSHIFT(-1,2) = %brshift(-1,2) ;
NOTE:  Argument 1 to macro function %BRSHIFT is missing or out of range.
BRSHIFT(-1,2) = .
4          %put BRSHIFT(1,ABC) = %brshift(1,ABC) ;
NOTE:  Invalid numeric data ABC in argument 2 for macro function %BRSHIFT.
```

```
BRSHIFT(1,ABC) = .
5          %put BRSHIFT(,2) = %brshift(,2) ;
NOTE:  Argument 1 to macro function %BLSHIF is missing or out of range.
BRSHIFT(,2) = .
6          %put BRSHIFT(1,35) = %brshift(1,35) ;
NOTE:  Argument 2 to macro function %BRSHIFT is missing or out of range.
BRSHIFT(1,35) = .
```

SAS Listing

This sample program does not have any listing output.

%BXOR

Purpose

BXOR macro function similar to the BXOR data step function. It returns the bitwise logical EXCLUSIVE OR of two arguments and can accept HEX values.

Syntax

%bxor(argument-1, argument-2)

>*argument-1* and *argument-2* are numeric, nonnegative, and nonmissing. Separate the arguments with a comma. Range: 0 to the largest 32-bit unsigned integer.

See Also

%BXOR, %BRSHIFT, %BOR, %BNOT, %BLSHIFT, %BAND

Example

Sample Program

```
%put BXOR(03x,01x) = %bxor(03x,01x) ;
%put BXOR(-1,50) = %bxor(-1,50) ;
%put BXOR(A,10) = %bxor(A,10) ;
%put BXOR(,01x) = %bxor(,01x) ;
```

SAS Log

```
1          %put BXOR(03x,01x) = %bxor(03x,01x) ;
BXOR(03x,01x) = 2
2          %put BXOR(-1,50) = %bxor(-1,50) ;
NOTE:  Argument 1 to macro function %BXOR is missing or out of range.
BXOR(-1,50) = .
3          %put BXOR(A,10) = %bxor(A,10) ;
NOTE:  Invalid numeric data A in argument 1 for macro function %BXOR.
BXOR(A,10) = .
4          %put BXOR(,01x) = %bxor(,01x) ;
NOTE:  Argument 1 to macro function %BXOR is missing or out of range.
BXOR(,01x) = .
```

SAS Listing

This sample program does not have any listing output.

%BYTE

Purpose
BYTE macro function similar to the BYTE data step function. It returns one character in the ASCII or the EBCDIC collating sequence.

Syntax
%byte(n)

    n specifies an integer that represents a specific ASCII or EBCDIC character. Range: 0-255

See Also
%BYTE, %COLLATE, %RANK

Example

Sample Program
```
%put BYTE(40) = %byte(40) ;
%put BYTE(A)  = %byte(A) ;
%put BYTE()   = %byte() ;
%put BYTE(350) = %byte(350) ;
```

SAS Log
```
1          %put BYTE(40) = %byte(40) ;
BYTE(40) = (
2          %put BYTE(A)  = %byte(A) ;
NOTE: Argument 1 to macro function %BYTE is missing or out of range.
BYTE(A) = .
3          %put BYTE() = %byte() ;
NOTE: Argument 1 to macro function %BYTE is missing or out of range.
BYTE() = .
4          %put BYTE(350) = %byte(350) ;
NOTE: Argument 1 to macro function %BYTE is missing or out of range.
BYTE(350) = .
```

SAS Listing
This sample program does not have any listing output.

%CDF

Purpose
CDF macro function similar to the CDF data step function. It computes cumulative distribution functions.

Syntax
%CDF (dist,quantile,parm-1, . . . ,parm-k)

    dist is a character string that identifies the distribution. Valid distributions are as follows:
- Bernoulli - BERNOULLI
- Beta - BETA
- Binomial – BINOMIAL

- Cauchy - CAUCHY
- Chi squared - CHISQUARED
- Exponential - EXPONENTIAL
- F - F
- Gamma – GAMMA
- Geometric GEOMETRIC
- Hypergeometric - HYPERGEOMETRIC
- LaPlace - LAPLACE
- Logistic - LOGISTIC
- Lognormal – LOG NORMAL
- Negative binomial - NEGBINOMIAL
- Normal - NORMAL GAUSS
- Pareto - PARETO
- Poisson - POISSON
- T - T
- Uniform - UNIFORM
- Wald (inverse Gaussian) - WALD IGAUSS
- Weibull - WEIBULL

Note: Except for T and F, any distribution can be minimally identified by its first four characters. To keep with the spirit of the data step function CDF, the DIST option can be quoted or unquoted (unquoted is preferred). quantile is a numeric random variable.

parm-1, . . . ,parm-k are shape, location, or scale parameters appropriate for the specific distribution. See the description for each distribution in Details under the HELP library for the data step function CDF for complete information about these parameters.

See Also
%CDF, %LOGCDF, %PDF, %SDF, %LOGSDF

Example

Sample Program
```
%put CDF=%cdf(POISSON, 2, 1) ;
%put CDF=%cdf('POISSON', 2, 1) ;
%put CDF=%cdf("POISSON", 2, 1) ;
%put CDF=%cdf(POISSON) ;
%put CDF=%cdf(POISSON, 2) ;
```

SAS Log
```
1          %put CDF=%cdf(POISSON, 2, 1) ;
CDF=0.9196986029286
2          %put CDF=%cdf('POISSON', 2, 1) ;
CDF=0.9196986029286
3          %put CDF=%cdf("POISSON", 2, 1) ;
CDF=0.9196986029286
4          %put CDF=%cdf(POISSON) ;
NOTE:  Argument 2 to macro function %CDF is missing or out of range.
CDF=.
5          %put CDF=%cdf(POISSON, 2) ;
NOTE:  Argument 3 to macro function %CDF is missing or out of range.
CDF=.
```

SAS Listing
This sample program does not have any listing output.

%CEIL

Purpose
CEIL macro function similar to the CEIL data step function. It returns the smallest integer that is greater than or equal to the argument.

Syntax
%ceil(argument)

> *argument* is numeric.

Example

Sample Program
```
%put CEIL(3.14159) = %ceil(3.14159) ;
%put CEIL(ABC) = %ceil(ABC) ;
```

SAS Log
```
1          %put CEIL(3.14159) = %ceil(3.14159) ;
CEIL(3.14159) = 4
2          %put CEIL(ABC) = %ceil(ABC) ;
NOTE: Argument 1 to macro function %CEIL is missing or out of range.
CEIL(ABC) = .
```

SAS Listing
This sample program does not have any listing output.

%CEXIST

Purpose
Verifies the existence of a SAS catalog or SAS catalog entry and returns a value

Syntax
CEXIST(entry, U)

> *entry* - specifies a SAS catalog, or the name of an entry in a catalog. If the entry value is a one- or two-level name, then it is assumed to be the name of a catalog. Use a three or four-level name to test for the existence of an entry within a catalog.
>
> *U* - (optional) tests whether the catalog can be opened for updating

See Also
%CEXIST, %EXIST, %FEXIST, %FILEEXIST, %LIBREF

Notes

CEXIST returns 1 if the SAS catalog or catalog entry exists, or 0 if the SAS catalog or catalog entry does not exist.

Example

Sample Program

```
%put CEXIST = %cexist (work.sasmacr.data.macro) ;
%put CEXIST = %cexist (work.sasmac1.data.macro) ;
```

SAS Log

```
1          %put CEXIST = %cexist (work.sasmacr.data.macro) ;
CEXIST = 1
2          %put CEXIST = %cexist (work.sasmac1.data.macro) ;
CEXIST = 0
```

SAS Listing

This sample program does not have any listing output.

%CHARACTER

Purpose

Returns a list of all character variables in a given SAS data set

Syntax

%character (data)

> *data* is a valid SAS data set name. The data set must exist.

See Also

%CHARACTER, %NUMERIC, *CHARACTER*, *NUMERIC*, *ALL*

Notes

If no CHARACTER variables are found in the data set, a NULL STRING is returned. This can be used to get a specific list of CHARACTER variables when the automatic variable *CHARACTER* cannot be used. To create a list of all variables, use both of the macros %CHARACTER and %NUMERIC to build a list.

Example

Sample Program

```
%put Character variables in SASHELP.SHOES: %character(sashelp.shoes) ;
```

SAS Log

```
1          %put Character variables in SASHELP.SHOES: %character(sashelp.shoes) ;
Character variables in SASHELP.SHOES: Region Product Subsidiary
```

SAS Listing

This sample program does not have any listing output.

%CINV

Purpose

CINV macro function similar to the CINV data step function. It returns a quantile from the chi-squared distribution.

Syntax

%cinv(p, df, nc)

    p is a numeric probability. Range: $0 <= p < 1$

    df is a numeric degrees of freedom parameter. Range: $df > 0$

    nc is a numeric non-centrality parameter. Range: $nc >= 0$ (NOTE: NC is not required in the data step function, but is required in the macro function.)

Example

Sample Program

```
%put CINV(0.95, 3, 0) = %cinv(0.95, 3, 0) ;
%put CINV(0.95, 3.5, 4.5) = %cinv(0.95, 3.5, 4.5) ;
%put CINV(AAA, 3.5, 4.5) = %cinv(AAA, 3.5, 4.5) ;
%put CINV(-1, 3.5, 4.5) = %cinv(-1, 3.5, 4.5) ;
```

SAS Log

```
1          %put CINV(0.95, 3, 0) = %cinv(0.95, 3, 0) ;
CINV(0.95, 3, 0) = 7.81472790325117
2          %put CINV(0.95, 3.5, 4.5) = %cinv(0.95, 3.5, 4.5) ;
CINV(0.95, 3.5, 4.5) = 17.5045821169631
3          %put CINV(AAA, 3.5, 4.5) = %cinv(AAA, 3.5, 4.5) ;
NOTE:  Argument 1 to macro function %CINV is missing or out of range.
CINV(AAA, 3.5, 4.5) = .
4          %put CINV(-1, 3.5, 4.5) = %cinv(-1, 3.5, 4.5) ;
NOTE:  Argument 1 to macro function %CINV is missing or out of range.
CINV(-1, 3.5, 4.5) = .
```

SAS Listing

This sample program does not have any listing output.

%CNONCT

Purpose

CNONCT macro function similar to the CNONCT data step function. It returns the non-centrality parameter from a chi-squared distribution.

Syntax

%cnonct(x, df, prob)

x is a numeric random variable. Range: x ge 0

df is a numeric degrees of freedom parameter. Range: df > 0

prob is a probability. Range: 0 < prob < 1

Notes

The CNONCT function returns the nonnegative non-centrality parameter from a noncentral chi-square distribution whose parameters are x, df and nc. If prob is greater than the probability from the central chi-square distribution with the parameters x and df, a root to this problem does not exist. In this case a missing value is returned. A Newton-type algorithm is used to find a nonnegative root nc of the equation. If the algorithm fails to converge to a fixed point, a missing value is returned.

Example

Sample Program

```
%put CNONCT(.5, .5, .5) = %cnonct (.5, .5, .5) ;
%put CNONCT(-1, .5, .5) = %cnonct (-1, .5, .5) ;
%put CNONCT(10, .5, A) = %cnonct (10, .5, A) ;
```

SAS Log

```
1          %put CNONCT(.5, .5, .5) = %cnonct (.5, .5, .5) ;
CNONCT(.5, .5, .5) = 0.96804184061199
2          %put CNONCT(-1, .5, .5) = %cnonct (-1, .5, .5) ;
NOTE:  Argument 1 to macro function %CNONCT is missing or out of range.
CNONCT(-1, .5, .5) = .
3          %put CNONCT(10, .5, A) = %cnonct (10, .5, A) ;
NOTE:  Invalid numeric data A in Argument 3 for macro function %CNONCT.
CNONCT(10, .5, A) = .
```

SAS Listing

This sample program does not have any listing output.

%COLLATE

Purpose

COLLATE macro function similar to the COLLATE data step function. It returns an ASCII or EBCDIC collating sequence character string.

Syntax

%collate(start-position, end-position)

> *start-position* specifies the numeric position in the collating sequence of the first character to be returned. Interaction: If you specify only start-position, COLLATE returns consecutive characters from that position to the end of the collating sequence or up to 255 characters, whichever comes first.
>
> *end-position* specifies the numeric position in the collating sequence of the last character to be returned. The maximum end-position for the EBCDIC collating sequence is 255. For ASCII collating sequences, the characters that correspond to end-position values between 0 and 27 represent the standard character set. Other ASCII characters that correspond to end-position values between 128 and 255 are available

on certain ASCII operating environments, but the information those characters represents varies from host environment. Tip: end-position must be larger than start-position.

See Also
%BYTE, %COLLATE, %RANK

Notes
The DATA STEP FUNCTION allows for a third parameter, LENGTH. This macro does not utilize that feature.

Example

Sample Program
```
%put COLLATE(15, 25) = %collate (15, 25) ;
%put COLLATE(-1, -5) = %collate (-1, -5) ;
%put COLLATE(AA, 22) = %collate (AA, 22) ;
```

SAS Log
```
1          %put COLLATE(15, 25) = %collate (15, 25) ;
COLLATE(15, 25) = &%'"()+-*/<
2          %put COLLATE(-1, -5) = %collate (-1, -5) ;
NOTE:  Argument 1 to macro function %COLLATE is missing or out of range.
COLLATE(-1, -5) =
3          %put COLLATE(AA, 22) = %collate (AA, 22) ;
NOTE:  Invalid numeric data AA in Argument 1 for macro function %COLLATE.
COLLATE(AA, 22) =
```

SAS Listing
This sample program does not have any listing output.

%COMB

Purpose
COMB macro function similar to the COMB data step function. It computes the number of combinations of n elements taken r at a time and returns a value

Syntax
%comb(n, r)

    n is a positive integer that represents the total number of elements from which the sample is chosen.

    r is a positive integer less than or equal to n that represents the number of chosen elements.

Example

Sample Program
```
%put COMB(2456, 17) = %comb(2456, 17) ;
%put COMB(10, 10) = %comb(10, 10) ;
%put COMB(A, 15) = %comb(A, 15) ;
%put COMB(10, -1) = %comb(10, -1) ;
```

SAS Log
```
1          %put COMB(2456, 17) = %comb(2456, 17) ;
COMB(2456, 17) = 1.1447502046759E43
2          %put COMB(10, 10) = %comb(10, 10) ;
COMB(10, 10) = 1
3          %put COMB(A, 15) = %comb(A, 15) ;
NOTE: Invalid numeric data A in Argument 1 for macro function %COMB.
COMB(A, 15) = .
4          %put COMB(10, -1) = %comb(10, -1) ;
NOTE: Argument 2 to macro function %COMB is missing or out of range.
COMB(10, -1) = .
```

SAS Listing
This sample program does not have any listing output.

%COMMAND

Purpose
This macro returns to SAS the value of an operating system command. It only returns the FIRST LINE returned by the OS. Any additional lines returned after the first line are ignored.

Syntax
%command (command)

COMMAND is any valid operating system command.

See Also
%COMMAND, %DOSPATH, %DIRECTORY, %CURRENTPATH, %FINDFILE, %SYSVARS, %DATAPATH, %DATAMEM, %MEM

Notes
This macro has not been tested in any operating system outside of Microsoft Windows XP.

Example

Sample Program
```
%put COMMAND=%command(time /t) ;
%put COMMAND=%command(date /t) ;
%put COMMAND=%command ;
%put COMMAND=%command(NotACommand) ;
```

SAS Log
```
1          %put COMMAND=%command(time /t) ;
COMMAND=03:47 PM
2          %put COMMAND=%command(date /t) ;
COMMAND=Fri 06/30/2006
3          %put COMMAND=%command ;
NOTE: Argument 1 to macro function %COMMAND is missing or out of range.
COMMAND=.
4          %put COMMAND=%command(NotACommand) ;
COMMAND=.
```

SAS Listing
This sample program does not have any listing output.

%COMPOUND

Purpose
COMPOUND macro function similar to the COMPOUND data step function. It returns values of compound interest calculations.

Syntax
%compound(a,f,r,n)

    a = non-negative numeric, the initial amount. Range: a >= 0
    f = non-negative numeric, the future amount (at the end of n periods). Range: f >= 0
    r = non-negative numeric, the periodic interest rate expressed as a fraction. Range: r >= 0
    n = non-negative integer, the number of compounding periods.

See Also
%SAVING, %COMPOUND, %MORT

Example

Sample Program
```
%put future = %compound(2000,.,0.09/12,30) ;
```

SAS Log
```
1          %put future = %compound(2000,.,0.09/12,30) ;
future = 2502.54352764667
```

SAS Listing
This sample program does not have any listing output.

%CONSTANT

Purpose
Computes some machine and mathematical constants and returns a value

Syntax
    CONSTANT(constant<, parameter>)
- CONSTANT is a character string that identifies the constant. Valid constants are (quoted or unquoted): The natural base - E
- Euler constant - EULER
- Pi - PI
- Exact integer - EXACTINT <,nbytes>
- The largest double precision number - BIG
- The log with respect to base of BIG - LOGBIG <,base> The square root of BIG - SQRTBIG

- The smallest double precision number - SMALL
- The log with respect to base of SMALL - LOGSMALL <,base>
- The square root of SMALL - SQRTSMALL
- Machine precision constant - MACEPS
- The log with respect to base of MACEPS - LOGMACEPS <,base>
- The square root of MACEPS - SQRTMACEPS

PARAMETER is an optional numeric parameter. Some of the constants specified in constant have an optional argument that alters the functionality of the CONSTANT function.

See Also

%E, %EULER, %PI, %BIG, %SQRTBIG, %SMALL, %SQRTSMALL, %MACEPS, and %SQRTMACEPS

Notes

For LOGBIG, LOGSMALL, and LOGMACEPS, the PARAMETER value must be greater than 1 + MACEPS. For EXACTINT, PARAMETER must be between 2 and 8 inclusive.

Example

Sample Program

```
%put CONSTANT=%constant(e) ;
%put CONSTANT=%constant(big) ;
%put CONSTANT=%constant(LOGMACEPS, 10) ;
%put CONSTANT=%constant('LOGMACEPS', 1.000000015) ;
%put CONSTANT=%constant('LOGMACEPS', 1.1) ;
%put CONSTANT=%constant(EXACTINT, 3) ;
%put CONSTANT=%constant(EXACTINT, 1) ;
%put CONSTANT=%constant('LOGMACEPS', 1.0000000075) ;
%put CONSTANT=%constant(badvalue) ;
```

SAS Log

```
1          %put CONSTANT=%constant(e) ;
CONSTANT=2.71828182845904
2          %put CONSTANT=%constant(big) ;
CONSTANT=1.7976931348623E308
3          %put CONSTANT=%constant(LOGMACEPS, 10) ;
CONSTANT=-15.653559774527
4          %put CONSTANT=%constant('LOGMACEPS', 1.000000015) ;
CONSTANT=-2402910258.56658
5          %put CONSTANT=%constant('LOGMACEPS', 1.1) ;
CONSTANT=-378.172126661769
6          %put CONSTANT=%constant(EXACTINT, 3) ;
CONSTANT=8192
7          %put CONSTANT=%constant(EXACTINT, 1) ;
NOTE:   Argument 2 to macro function %CONSTANT is missing or out of range.
CONSTANT=.
8          %put CONSTANT=%constant('LOGMACEPS', 1.0000000075) ;
NOTE:   Argument 2 to macro function %CONSTANT is missing or out of range.
CONSTANT=.
9          %put CONSTANT=%constant(badvalue) ;
NOTE: Argument 1 to macro function %CONSTANT is invalid.
NOTE: The first argument of the %CONSTANT macro function can be one of the following:
NOTE: E, EULER, PI, EXACTINT, BIG, LOGBIG, SQRTBIG, SMALL, LOGSMALL, SQRTSMALL,
MACEPS, LOGMACEPS, or SQRT
CONSTANT=.
```

SAS Listing

This sample program does not have any listing output.

%COS

Purpose

COS macro function similar to the COS data step function. It returns the COSINE value.

Syntax

%cos(argument)
  argument is numeric and is specified in radians.

See Also

%ARCOS, %ARSIN, %ATAN, %COS, %COSH, %SIN, %SINH, %TAN, %TANH

Example

Sample Program

```
%put COS(PI) = %cos(%pi) ;
%put COS(.3) = %cos(.3) ;
```

SAS Log

```
1          %put COS(PI) = %cos(%pi) ;
COS(PI) = -1
2          %put COS(.3) = %cos(.3) ;
COS(.3) = 0.9553364891256
```

SAS Listing

This sample program does not have any listing output.

%COSH

Purpose

COSH macro function similar to the COSH data step function. It returns the Hyperbolic Cosine value.

Syntax

%cosh(argument)
  argument is numeric

See Also

%ARCOS, %ARSIN, %ATAN, %COS, %COSH, %SIN, %SINH, %TAN, %TANH

Example

Sample Program
```
%put COSH(PI) = %cosh(%pi) ;
%put COSH(3) = %cosh(3) ;
```

SAS Log
```
1          %put COSH(PI) = %cosh(%pi) ;
COSH(PI) = 11.5919532755214
2          %put COSH(3) = %cosh(3) ;
COSH(3) = 10.0676619957777
```

SAS Listing
This sample program does not have any listing output.

%CSS

Purpose
CSS macro function similar to the CSS data step function. It returns the Corrected Sum of Squares.

Syntax
%css (argument, argument, . . .)
   argument is numeric. At least two arguments are required.

See Also
%CSS, %VAR, %N, %NMISS, %SUM, %SKEWNESS, %KURTOSIS, %RANGE, %CV, %USS, %STD, %STDERR, %MIN, %MAX

Example

Sample Program
```
%put CSS=%css(1,2,3,4,5) ;
%put CSS=%css(1,2,A,4,5) ;
%put CSS=%css ;
%put CSS=%css(1) ;
```

SAS Log
```
1          %put CSS=%css(1,2,3,4,5) ;
CSS=10
2          %put CSS=%css(1,2,A,4,5) ;
NOTE:  Invalid numeric data A in argument 3 for macro function %CSS.
CSS=.
3          %put CSS=%css ;
NOTE:  Argument 1 to macro function %CSS is missing or out of range.
CSS=.
4          %put CSS=%css(1) ;
NOTE:  Argument 2 to macro function %CSS is missing or out of range.
CSS=.
```

SAS Listing
This sample program does not have any listing output.

%CURRENTPATH

Purpose
This macro function returns the full operating system path of the current path.

Syntax
%currenpath

See Also
%COMMAND, %DOSPATH, %DIRECTORY, %CURRENTPATH, %FINDFILE, %SYSVARS, %DATAPATH, %DATAMEM, and %MEM

Example

Sample Program
```
%let path=%currentpath ;
%put path=&path ;

x cd .. ;
%let path2=%currentpath ;
%put path2=&path2 ;

x cd "&path" ;
%put DOSPATH=%dospath(%currentpath) ;
```

SAS Log
```
1         %let path=%currentpath ;
2         %put path=&path ;
path=C:\Perl\bin
4         x cd ..
4         !            ;
5         %let path2=%currentpath ;
6         %put path2=&path2 ;
path2=C:\Perl
8         x cd "&path"
8         !            ;

10        %put DOSPATH=%dospath(%currentpath) ;
DOSPATH=C:\Perl\bin
```

SAS Listing
This sample program does not have any listing output.

%CV

Purpose
CV macro function similar to the CV data step function. It returns the coefficient of variation.

Syntax
%cv (argument, argument, . . .)
    argument is numeric. At least two arguments are required.

See Also
%CSS, %VAR, %N, %NMISS, %SUM, %SKEWNESS, %KURTOSIS, %RANGE, %CV, %USS, %STD, %STDERR, %MIN, %MAX

Example

Sample Program
```
%put CV=%cv(1,2,3,4,5) ;
%put CV=%cv(1,2,A,4,5) ;
%put CV=%cv ;
%put CV=%cv(1) ;
```

SAS Log
```
1          %put CV=%cv(1,2,3,4,5) ;
CV=52.704627669473
2          %put CV=%cv(1,2,A,4,5) ;
NOTE:  Invalid numeric data A in argument 3 for macro function %CV.
CV=.
3          %put CV=%cv ;
NOTE:  Argument 1 to macro function %CV is missing or out of range.
CV=.
4          %put CV=%cv(1) ;
NOTE:  Argument 2 to macro function %CV is missing or out of range.
CV=.
```

SAS Listing
This sample program does not have any listing output.

%DACCDB

Purpose
DACCDB macro function similar to the DACCDB data step function. It returns the accumulated declining balance depreciation.

Syntax
%daccdb(p,v,y,r)

> *p* is numeric, the period for which the calculation is to be done. For non-integer p arguments, the depreciation is prorated between the two consecutive time periods that precede and follow the fractional period.
> *v* is numeric, the depreciable initial value of the asset.
> *y* is numeric, the lifetime of the asset. Range: $y > 0$
> *r* is numeric, the rate of depreciation expressed as a decimal. Range: $r > 0$

Example

Sample Program
```
%put depreciation = %daccdb(10,1000,15,2) ;
%put depreciation = %daccdb(10,1000,15,0) ;
```

SAS Log

```
1          %put depreciation = %daccdb(10,1000,15,2) ;
depreciation = 760.9322839449
2          %put depreciation = %daccdb(10,1000,15,0) ;
NOTE: Argument 4 to macro function %DACCDB is missing or out of range.
depreciation = .
```

SAS Listing

This sample program does not have any listing output.

%DACCDBSL

Purpose

DACCDBSL macro function similar to the DACCDBSL data step function. It returns the accumulated declining balance with conversion to a straight-line depreciation.

Syntax

%daccdbsl(p,v,y,r)

p = numeric, the period for which the calculation is to be done. For non-integer p arguments, the depreciation is prorated between the two consecutive time periods that precede and follow the fractional period.
v = numeric, the depreciable initial value of the asset.
y = numeric, the lifetime of the asset. Range: y > 0
r = numeric, the rate of depreciation expressed a s a decimal. Range: r > 0

Example

Sample Program

```
%put depreciation = %daccdbsl(10,1000,15,2) ;
%put depreciation = %daccdbsl(10,1000,15,0) ;
```

SAS Log

```
1          %put depreciation = %daccdbsl(10,1000,15,2) ;
depreciation = 772.653270868987
2          %put depreciation = %daccdbsl(10,1000,15,0) ;
NOTE: Argument r to macro function %DACCDBSL is missing or out of range.
depreciation = .
```

SAS Listing

This sample program does not have any listing output.

%DACCSL

Purpose

DACCSLSL macro function similar to the DACCSL data step function. It returns the accumulated straight-line depreciation.

Syntax

%daccsl(p,v,y)

> *p* is numeric, the period for which the calculation is to be done. For non-integer p arguments, the depreciation is prorated between the two consecutive time periods that precede and follow the fractional period.
>
> *v* is numeric, the depreciable initial value of the asset.
>
> *y* is numeric, the lifetime of the asset. Range: y > 0

Example

Sample Program

```
%put depreciation = %daccsl(1.75,1000,10) ;
%put depreciation = %daccsl(1.75,1000, 0) ;
```

SAS Log

```
1          %put depreciation = %daccsl(1.75,1000,10) ;
depreciation = 175
2          %put depreciation = %daccsl(1.75,1000, 0) ;
NOTE: Argument 3 to macro function %DACCSL is missing or out of range.
depreciation = .
```

SAS Listing

This sample program does not have any listing output.

%DACCSYD

Purpose

DACCSYDSL macro function similar to the DACCSYD data step function. It returns the accumulated sum-of-years-digits depreciation.

Syntax

%daccsyd(p,v,y)

> *p* is numeric, the period for which the calculation is to be done. For non-integer p arguments, the depreciation is prorated between the two consecutive time periods that precede and follow the fractional period.
>
> *v* is numeric, the depreciable initial value of the asset.
>
> *y* is numeric, the lifetime of the asset. Range: y > 0

Example

Sample Program

```
%put depreciation = %daccsyd(1.75,1000,10) ;
%put depreciation = %daccsyd(1.75,1000, 0) ;
```

SAS Log
```
1          %put depreciation = %daccsyd(1.75,1000,10) ;
depreciation = 304.545454545454
2          %put depreciation = %daccsyd(1.75,1000, 0) ;
NOTE: Argument 3 to macro function %DACCSYD is missing or out of range.
depreciation = .
```

SAS Listing
This sample program does not have any listing output.

%DAIRY

Purpose
DAIRY macro function similar to the DAIRY data step function. It returns the derivative of the airy function.

Syntax
%dairy(x)

> *x* is any numeric value

Notes
The DAIRY function returns the value of the derivative of the airy function (Abramowitz and Stegun 1964- Amos, Daniel, and Weston 977).

Example

Sample Program
```
%put DAIRY(10) = %dairy(10) ;
```

SAS Log
```
1          %put DAIRY(10) = %dairy(10) ;
DAIRY(10) = -3.5206336767389E-10
```

SAS Listing
This sample program does not have any listing output.

%DATA

Purpose
This macro is used to make notes in the sas log more clear. It takes an input string (a dataset name) and checks the format. If it is a first level dataset name (i.e. TEMP) the macro turns the value into a second level dataset name (i.e. WORK.TEMP.) If the input string is already a two level it does not add the WORK. string in front of the value. In either case, it returns the value as uppercase text.

Syntax
%data (data)

> *data* is a SAS data set name. The data set need not be present.

Notes

If no value is given, the value of the automatic macro variable SYSLAST will be used. If no SAS data sets have been created in the SAS session, the value will be WORK._NULL_

Example

Sample Program
```
%put workdata=%data(workdata) ;
%put libname.data=%data(libname.data) ;
%put SYSLAST=%data ;
```

SAS Log
```
1          %put workdata=%data(workdata) ;
workdata=WORK.WORKDATA
2          %put libname.data=%data(libname.data) ;
libname.data=LIBNAME.DATA
3          %put SYSLAST=%data ;
SYSLAST=WORK._NULL_
```

SAS Listing
This sample program does not have any listing output.

%DATAMEM

Purpose
This macro returns the physical file address of a given SAS data set

Syntax
%datamem (data)

>   *DATA* is a valid SAS data set name. The data set must exist.

See Also
%COMMAND, %DOSPATH, %DIRECTORY, %CURRENTPATH, %FINDFILE, %SYSVARS, %DATAPATH, %DATAMEM, %MEM

Notes
This macro assumes that the SAS data set physical file will have a value of *.sas7bdat for SAS versions 7+ and *.sc2 for all others. It does NOT check if you are using a different ENGINE for a libname such as declaring a libname with an engine of V6 while running in SAS9 or 8.x. See references in %DATAPATH for further details. The macro will also not function if a data library has more than one path for the libname (such as SASHELP at most sites).

%DOSPATH and %DATAPATH are required for operation (included in the RDS™ package). %DOSPATH also requires the Windows batch file DOSPATH.BAT.

Example

Sample Program
```
%put The physical file size of data set TEMP is %datamem(sashelp.shoes) bytes. ;
%put The physical file size of data set TEMP2 is %datamem(sashelp.vcolumn) bytes. ;
%put The physical file size of data view VIEW1 is %datamem(nodata) bytes. ;
```

SAS Log
```
1          %put The physical file size of data set TEMP is %datamem(sashelp.shoes) bytes. ;
The physical file size of data set TEMP is 41984 bytes.
2          %put The physical file size of data set TEMP2 is %datamem(sashelp.vcolumn) bytes. ;
The physical file size of data set TEMP2 is 5120 bytes.
3          %put The physical file size of data view VIEW1 is %datamem(nodata) bytes. ;
WARNING: File WORK.NODATA.DATA does not exist.
The physical file size of data view VIEW1 is . bytes.
```

SAS Listing
This sample program does not have any listing output.

%DATAPATH

Purpose
This macro returns the physical file address of a given SAS data set

Syntax
%datapath (data)

>   *DATA* is a valid SAS data set name. The data set must exist.

See Also
%COMMAND, %DOSPATH, %DIRECTORY, %CURRENTPATH, %FINDFILE, %SYSVARS, %DATAPATH, %DATAMEM, %MEM

Notes
This macro assumes that the SAS data set physical file will have a value of *.sas7bdat for SAS versions 7+ and *.sc2 for all others. It does NOT check if you are using a different ENGINE for a libname such as declaring a libname with an engine of V6 while running in SAS9 or 8.x.

Example

Sample Program
```
%put datapath = %datapath(sashelp.shoes) ;
%put datapath = %datapath(sashelp.vcolumn) ;
%put datapath = %datapath(nodata) ;
```

SAS Log
```
1          %put datapath = %datapath(sashelp.shoes) ;
datapath = c:\sasv8\core\sashelp\SHOES.sas7bdat
2          %put datapath = %datapath(sashelp.vcolumn) ;
```

```
datapath = c:\sasv8\base\sashelp\VCOLUMN.sas7bvew
3          %put datapath = %datapath(nodata) ;
WARNING: Data set WORK.NODATA does not exist.
datapath =
```

SAS Listing

This sample program does not have any listing output.

%DATE

Purpose

Returns the current date as DATE9. format.

Syntax

%DATE

See Also

%DATETIME, %FILEDT, %TODAY, %DATE, %TIME

Notes

This macro function is the same as %TODAY. It differs from the &SYSDATE automatic macro variable because it evaluates the CURRENT DATE and not the DATE AT STARTUP.

Example

Sample Program

```
%put DATE=%date ;
```

SAS Log

```
1          %put DATE=%date ;
DATE=30JUN2006
```

SAS Listing

This sample program does not have any listing output.

%DATETIME

Purpose

This macro returns the current date and time in text format.

Syntax

%datetime

See Also

%DATETIME, %FILEDT, %TODAY, %DATE, %TIME

Notes

There are no options on this macro

Example

Sample Program
```
%put The current date and time is %datetime ;
```

SAS Log
```
1          %put The current date and time is %datetime ;
The current date and time is June 30, 2006 at 15:48:14
```

SAS Listing
This sample program does not have any listing output.

%DEPDB

Purpose
DEPDB macro function similar to the DEPDB data step function. It returns the declining balance depreciation.

Syntax
%depdb(p,v,y,r)

> p is numeric, the period for which the calculation is to be done. For non-integer p arguments, the depreciation is prorated between the two consecutive time periods that precede and follow the fractional period.
>
> v is numeric, the depreciable initial value of the asset.
>
> y is numeric, the lifetime of the asset. Range: $y > 0$
>
> r is numeric, the rate of depreciation expressed as a decimal. Range: $r > 0$

Example

Sample Program
```
%put DEPDB(10,1000,15,2) = %depdb(10,1000,15,2) ;
```

SAS Log
```
1          %put DEPDB(10,1000,15,2) = %depdb(10,1000,15,2) ;
DEPDB(10,1000,15,2) = 36.7796486238614
```

SAS Listing
This sample program does not have any listing output.

%DEPDBSL

Purpose

DEPDBSL macro function similar to the DEPDBSL data step function. It returns the declining balance with conversion to a straight-line depreciation.

Syntax

%depdbsl(p,v,y,r)

>p is numeric, the period for which the calculation is to be done. For non-integer p arguments, the depreciation is prorated between the two consecutive time periods that precede and follow the fractional period.
>
>v is numeric, the depreciable initial value of the asset.
>
>y is numeric, the lifetime of the asset. Range: $y > 0$
>
>r is numeric, the rate of depreciation expressed as a decimal. Range: $r > 0$

Example

Sample Program

```
%put DEPDBSL(10,1000,15,2) = %depdbsl(10,1000,15,2) ;
```

SAS Log

```
1          %put DEPDBSL(10,1000,15,2) = %depdbsl(10,1000,15,2) ;
DEPDBSL(10,1000,15,2) = 45.4693458262025
```

SAS Listing

This sample program does not have any listing output.

%DEPSL

Purpose

DEPSL macro function similar to the DEPSL data step function. It returns the straight-line depreciation.

Syntax

%depsl(p,v,y)

>p is numeric, the period for which the calculation is to be done. For non-integer p arguments, the depreciation is prorated between the two consecutive time periods that precede and follow the fractional period.
>
>v is numeric, the depreciable initial value of the asset.
>
>y is numeric, the lifetime of the asset. Range: $y > 0$

Example

Sample Program
```
%put depreciation = %depsl(1.75,1000,10) ;
%put depreciation = %depsl(1.75,1000, 0) ;
```

SAS Log
```
1          %put depreciation = %depsl(1.75,1000,10) ;
depreciation = 100
2          %put depreciation = %depsl(1.75,1000, 0) ;
NOTE:  Argument 3 to macro function %DEPSL is missing or out of range.
depreciation = .
```

SAS Listing
This sample program does not have any listing output.

%DEPSYD

Purpose
DEPSYD macro function similar to the DEPSYD data step function. It returns the sum-of-years-digits depreciation.

Syntax
%depsyd(p,v,y)

> *p* is numeric, the period for which the calculation is to be done. For non-integer p arguments, the depreciation is prorated between the two consecutive time periods that precede and follow the fractional period.
>
> *v* is numeric, the depreciable initial value of the asset.
>
> *y* is numeric, the lifetime of the asset. Range: y > 0

Example

Sample Program
```
%put depreciation = %depsyd(1.75,1000,10) ;
%put depreciation = %depsyd(1.75,1000, 0) ;
```

SAS Log
```
1          %put depreciation = %depsyd(1.75,1000,10) ;
depreciation = 168.181818181818
2          %put depreciation = %depsyd(1.75,1000, 0) ;
NOTE:  Argument 3 to macro function %DEPSYD is missing or out of range.
depreciation = .
```

SAS Listing
This sample program does not have any listing output.

%DEQUOTE

Purpose
DEQUOTE macro function similar to the DEQUOTE data step function. It removes quotation marks from a character value.

Syntax
%dequote(string)

    STRING is any character string.

Example

Sample Program
```
%put string=%dequote ("c:\mystring\text.txt") ;
%put string=%dequote ('c:\mystring\text.txt') ;
```

SAS Log
```
1          %put string=%dequote ("c:\mystring\text.txt") ;
string=c:\mystring\text.txt
2          %put string=%dequote ('c:\mystring\text.txt') ;
string=c:\mystring\text.txt
```

SAS Listing
This sample program does not have any listing output.

%DIGAMMA

Purpose
DIGAMMA macro function similar to the DIGAMMA data step function. Returns the value of the DIGAMMA function.

Syntax
%digamma(argument)

    argument is numeric

Example

Sample Program
```
%put DIGAMMA(10) = %digamma(10) ;
```

SAS Log
```
1          %put DIGAMMA(10) = %digamma(10) ;
DIGAMMA(10) = 2.25175258906672
```

SAS Listing
This sample program does not have any listing output.

%DOSPATH

Purpose
This macro returns a DOS FILE PATH from a given WINDOWS FILE PATH. The input file specification can be quoted or unquoted, but it will always return an unquoted string.

Syntax
%dospath (file-specification)

FILE-SPECIFICATION is a valid File Specification. It can be quoted or unquoted.

See Also
%COMMAND, %DOSPATH, %DIRECTORY, %CURRENTPATH, %FINDFILE, %SYSVARS, %DATAPATH, %DATAMEM, %MEM

Notes
This macro requires the batch file DOSPATH.BAT, which in turn will require the executable file CHOICE.EXE. These files are included in the RDS package. One additional requirement: the file given must exist. The macro can honor OS wildcards PROVIDED the file is given in quoted form. Unquoted wildcards will produce unreliable results.

Example

Sample Program
```
%put path=%dospath(C:\SASV8\SAS.exe) ;
%put path=%dospath(C:\SASV8\sas.exe) ;
%put path=%dospath(C:\*.txt) ;
%put path=%dospath(C:\junk.txt) ;
%put path=%dospath ;
```

SAS Log
```
1    %put path=%dospath(C:\SASV8\SAS.exe) ;
path=C:\sasv8\sas.exe
2    %put path=%dospath(C:\SASV8\sas.exe) ;
path=C:\sasv8\sas.exe
3    %put path=%dospath(C:\*.txt) ;
path=C:\version.txt
4    %put path=%dospath(C:\junk.txt) ;
WARNING: Physical file does not exist, C:\junk.txt
NOTE: The given argument will be returned by the function (unquoted).
path=C:\junk.txt
5    %put path=%dospath ;
NOTE:  Argument 1 to macro function %DOSPATH is missing or out of range.
path=.
```

SAS Listing
This sample program does not have any listing output.

%E

Purpose
Returns the natural number E

Syntax
%e

See Also
%CONSTANT

Example

Sample Program
```
%put E=%e ;
```

SAS Log
```
1          %put E=%e ;
E=2.71828182845904
```

SAS Listing
This sample program does not have any listing output.

%ERF

Purpose
ERF macro function similar to the ERF data step function. It returns the value of the (normal) error function.

Syntax
%erf(argument)

    argument is numeric

See Also
%ERF, %ERFC

Notes
You can use the ERF to find the probability (p) that a normally distributed random variable with mean 0 and standard deviation will take on a value less than X. For example, the quantity that is given by the following statement is equivalent to PROBNORM(X): $p = 0.5 + 0.5*erf(x/sqrt(2))$.

Example

Sample Program
```
%put ERF(10) = %erf(10) ;
%put ERF(1) = %erf(1) ;
```

```
%put ERF(-1) = %erf(-1) ;
```

SAS Log
```
1          %put ERF(10) = %erf(10) ;
ERF(10) = 1
2          %put ERF(1) = %erf(1) ;
ERF(1) = 0.84270079294971
3          %put ERF(-1) = %erf(-1) ;
ERF(-1) = -0.84270079294971
```

SAS Listing
This sample program does not have any listing output.

%ERFC

Purpose
ERFC macro function similar to the ERFC data step function. It returns the value of the complementary (normal) error function.

Syntax
%erfc(argument)

argument is numeric

See Also
%ERF, %ERFC

Notes
The ERFC function returns the complement to the ERF function (that is, 1 - ERF(argument)).

Example

Sample Program
```
%put ERFC(10) = %erfc(10) ;
%put ERFC(1)  = %erfc(1) ;
%put ERFC(-1) = %erfc(-1) ;
```

SAS Log
```
1          %put ERFC(10) = %erfc(10) ;
ERFC(10) = 2.0884875837625E-45
2          %put ERFC(1)  = %erfc(1) ;
ERFC(1)  = 0.15729920705028
3          %put ERFC(-1) = %erfc(-1) ;
ERFC(-1) = 1.84270079294971
```

SAS Listing
This sample program does not have any listing output.

%EULER

Purpose
Returns the EULER constant

Syntax
%euler

See Also
%CONSTANT

Example

Sample Program
```
%put EULER=%euler ;
```

SAS Log
```
1          %put EULER=%euler ;
EULER=0.57721566490153
```

SAS Listing
This sample program does not have any listing output.

%EXIST

Purpose
Verifies the existence of a SAS data library member

Syntax
%EXIST(member-name, member-type)

> *member-name* specifies the SAS data library member. If member-name is blank or a null string, EXIST uses the member specified by the system variable *LAST*.
>
> *member-type* specifies the type of SAS data library member:
> - ACCESS - an access descriptor for SAS/ACCESS software
> - CATALOG - a SAS catalog or catalog entry
> - DATA - a SAS data file (default)
> - VIEW - a SAS data view

See Also
%CEXIST, %EXIST, %FEXIST, %FILEEXIST, %LIBREF

Notes

EXIST returns 1 if the library member exists, or 0 if member-name does not exist or member-type is invalid. Use CEXIST to verify the existence of an entry in a catalog.

Example

Sample Program

```
%put EXIST=%exist(sashelp.shoes) ;
%put EXIST=%exist(sashelp.shoes, data) ;
%put EXIST=%exist(sashelp.shoes, 'data') ;
%put EXIST=%exist(doesnot.exist) ;
%put EXIST=%exist(sashelp.shoes, wiggly) ;
```

SAS Log

```
1          %put EXIST=%exist(sashelp.shoes) ;
EXIST=1
2          %put EXIST=%exist(sashelp.shoes, data) ;
EXIST=1
3          %put EXIST=%exist(sashelp.shoes, 'data') ;
EXIST=1
4          %put EXIST=%exist(doesnot.exist) ;
EXIST=0
5          %put EXIST=%exist(sashelp.shoes, wiggly) ;
NOTE: Argument 2 in macro function %EXIST is missing or out of range.
Expecting DATA, CATALOG, VIEW, or
EXIST=0
```

SAS Listing

This sample program does not have any listing output.

%EXP

Purpose

EXP macro function similar to the EXP data step function. It Returns the value of the exponential function.

Syntax

%exp(argument)

       argument is a numeric value

Notes

The EXP function returns the complement to the ERF function (that is, 1 - ERF(argument)).

Example

Sample Program

```
%put EXP(10) = %exp(10) ;
%put EXP(1)  = %exp(1) ;
%put EXP(-1) = %exp(-1) ;
```

SAS Log

```
1          %put EXP(10) = %exp(10) ;
```

```
EXP(10) = 22026.4657948067
2          %put EXP(1)  = %exp(1) ;
EXP(1)  = 2.71828182845904
3          %put EXP(-1) = %exp(-1) ;
EXP(-1) = 0.36787944117144
```

SAS Listing

This sample program does not have any listing output.

%FACT

Purpose

FACT macro function similar to the FACT data step function. It returns the value of the factorial function.

Syntax

%fact(argument)

> *argument* is a non-negative integer must be <= 170 for current SAS software

Example

Sample Program

```
%put FACT(10) = %fact(10) ;
%put FACT(1)  = %fact(1) ;
%put FACT(-1) = %fact(-1) ;
%put FACT(170) = %fact(170) ;
%put FACT(171) = %fact(171) ;
```

SAS Log

```
1          %put FACT(10) = %fact(10) ;
FACT(10) = 3628800
2          %put FACT(1)  = %fact(1) ;
FACT(1)  = 1
3          %put FACT(-1) = %fact(-1) ;
NOTE: Argument 1 to macro function %FACT is missing or out of range.
FACT(-1) = .
4          %put FACT(170) = %fact(170) ;
FACT(170) = 7.257415615308E306
5          %put FACT(171) = %fact(171) ;
NOTE: Argument 1 to macro function %FACT is missing or out of range.
FACT(171) = .
```

SAS Listing

This sample program does not have any listing output.

%FEXIST

Purpose

Verifies the existence of an external file associated with a fileref and returns a value

Syntax

FEXIST(fileref)

fileref specifies the fileref assigned to an external file. Restriction: The fileref must have been previously assigned.

See Also
%CEXIST, %EXIST, %FEXIST, %FILEEXIST, %LIBREF

Notes
FEXIST returns 1 if the external file that is associated with the fileref exists, and 0 if the file does not exist. You can assign filerefs by using the FILENAME statement or the FILENAME external file access function. In some operating environments, you can also assign filerefs by using system commands. FEXIST checks for the actual physical existance of the file. If the physical file does not exist, but a filename is associated with it the function will return a value of 0.

Example

Sample Program
```
filename autoexec '!sasroot\autoexec.sas' ;
%put FEXIST=%fexist(autoexec) ;

filename autoexec clear ;
%put FEXIST=%fexist(autoexec) ;
```

SAS Log
```
1          filename autoexec '!sasroot\autoexec.sas' ;
2          %put FEXIST=%fexist(autoexec) ;

FEXIST=1
4          filename autoexec clear ;
NOTE: Fileref AUTOEXEC has been deassigned.
5          %put FEXIST=%fexist(autoexec) ;
FEXIST=0
```

SAS Listing
This sample program does not have any listing output.

%FILEDT

Purpose
This macro returns the current date and time in a text format that is suitable for a unique date-time stamp of a filename.

Syntax
%filedt (secdec)

> *SECDEC* can be the value 0, 1, 2, or 3 representing the number of decimal places for the SECONDS component of the output.

See Also
%DATETIME, %FILEDT, %TODAY, %DATE, %TIME

Notes

The function outputs the date-time stamp in the following format: 01NOV2005@h11m18s13.395 -- DDMONCCYY@hHRmMNsSS.SSS

Example

Sample Program

```
%put The current date and time is %filedt ;
%put The current date and time is %filedt(3) ;
%put The current date and time is %filedt(0) ;
%put The current date and time is %filedt(-1) ;
%put The current date and time is %filedt(1.3) ;
%put The current date and time is %filedt(7) ;
%put The current date and time is %filedt(a) ;
```

SAS Log

```
1          %put The current date and time is %filedt ;
The current date and time is 30JUN2006_h15m48s43
2          %put The current date and time is %filedt(3) ;
The current date and time is 30JUN2006_h15m48s43.493
3          %put The current date and time is %filedt(0) ;
The current date and time is 30JUN2006_h15m48s44
4          %put The current date and time is %filedt(-1) ;
NOTE: Argument 1 to macro function %FILEDT is missing or out of range.
The default value 0 (zero) will be
The current date and time is 30JUN2006_h15m48s44
5          %put The current date and time is %filedt(1.3) ;
NOTE: Argument 1 to macro function %FILEDT is missing or out of range.
The default value 0 (zero) will be
The current date and time is 30JUN2006_h15m48s44
6          %put The current date and time is %filedt(7) ;
NOTE: Argument 1 to macro function %FILEDT is missing or out of range.
The maximum value 3 (three) will be
The current date and time is 30JUN2006_h15m48s43.503
7          %put The current date and time is %filedt(a) ;
NOTE: Invalid numeric data a in argument 1 for macro function %FILEDT.
The default value 0 (zero) will be
The current date and time is 30JUN2006_h15m48s44
```

SAS Listing

This sample program does not have any listing output.

%FILEEXIST

Purpose

Verifies the existence of an external file by its physical name and returns a value

Syntax

FILEEXIST(filename)

>   *FILENAME* specifies a fully qualified physical filename of the external file in the operating environment. Can be quoted or unquoted.

See Also
%CEXIST, %EXIST, %FEXIST, %FILEEXIST, %LIBREF

Notes
FILEEXIST returns 1 if the external file exists and 0 if the external file does not exist. The specification of the physical name for file-name varies according to the operating environment. Although your operating environment utilities may recognize partial physical filenames, you must always use fully qualified physical filenames with FILEEXIST.

Example

Sample Program
```
%put FILEEXIST=%fileexist('!SASROOT\autoexec.sas') ;
%put FILEEXIST=%fileexist(!SASROOT\autoexec.sas) ;
%put FILEEXIST=%fileexist(nofile.sas) ;
%put FILEEXIST=%fileexist ;
```

SAS Log
```
1          %put FILEEXIST=%fileexist('!SASROOT\autoexec.sas') ;
FILEEXIST=1
2          %put FILEEXIST=%fileexist(!SASROOT\autoexec.sas) ;
FILEEXIST=1
3          %put FILEEXIST=%fileexist(nofile.sas) ;
FILEEXIST=0
4          %put FILEEXIST=%fileexist ;
NOTE: Argument 1 in macro function %FILEEXIST is missing or out of range.
FILEEXIST=0
```

SAS Listing
This sample program does not have any listing output.

%FILEREAD

Purpose
Retrieves and returns the Nth record of a given file specification

Syntax
%fileread (file-spec, record, length)

    FILE-SPEC is the OS File Specification. Can be quoted or unquoted

    RECORD is the record number to retrieve

    LENGTH (optional/max=256) is the length to retrieve

See Also
%FREAD, %FILEREAD

Notes
If the given file specification does not exist, the function returns a null string.

Example

Sample Program
```
%put read=%fileread ('!SASROOT\license.txt', 7) ;
```

SAS Log
```
1    %put read=%fileread ('!SASROOT\license.txt', 7) ;
read=BEFORE YOU CLICK ON THE "ACCEPT" BUTTON. BY CLICKING ON THE "ACCEPT" BUTTON YOU ARE
```

SAS Listing
This sample program does not have any listing output.

%FILESCAN

Purpose
This macro scans an input file for occurrences of all variable names in a given SAS dataset. It is designed to scan a SAS program to determine if there are any variables in a SAS dataset that are not used by that program. If so, the macro prints a report. If not, a note is put in the log.

Syntax
```
%filescan (data = SAS-data-set,                    [required]
           file = _SAS_program_file_to_scan_,      [required]
           <,DEBUG = YES | Y | NO | N>)
```

Example

Sample Program
```
filename saspgm temp ;

data _null_ ;
   file saspgm ;
   put 'data test1 ;' ;
   put '   set prod.data ;' ;
   put '   if id = 12345 then id = 54321 ;' ;
   put 'run ;' ;
run ;

data check ;
   id = 'anything' ;
   myvar = 'anything else' ;
run ;

%filescan (data=check, file=saspgm)
```

SAS Log
```
1     filename saspgm temp ;
2
3     data _null_ ;
4        file saspgm ;
5        put 'data test1 ;' ;
6        put '   set prod.data ;' ;
7        put '   if id = 12345 then id = 54321 ;' ;
8        put 'run ;' ;
9     run ;
```

```
NOTE: The file SASPGM is:
      File Name=C:\DOCUME~1\q727909\LOCALS~1\Temp\SAS Temporary Files\_TD3248\#LN00009,
      RECFM=V,LRECL=256

NOTE: 4 records were written to the file SASPGM.
      The minimum record length was 5.
      The maximum record length was 34.
NOTE: DATA statement used:
      real time           0.01 seconds
      cpu time            0.01 seconds


10
11   data check ;
12      id = 'anything' ;
13      myvar = 'anything else' ;
14   run ;

NOTE: The data set WORK.CHECK has 1 observations and 2 variables.
NOTE: DATA statement used:
      real time           0.01 seconds
      cpu time            0.01 seconds


15
16   %filescan (data=check, file=saspgm)
NOTE: Macro FILESCAN printed a report of variables in WORK.CHECK not found in file saspgm.
NOTE: The MACRO %FILESCAN used:
      real time           0.62 seconds
      cpu time            unknown
```

SAS Listing

```
                                    The SAS System
--------------------------------- Found in File?=NO ---------------------------------

                                Input        SAS Source
                    Variable    Dataset      Code File
                    Name        Name         Scanned

                    id          WORK.CHECK   saspgm

--------------------------------- Found in File?=YES --------------------------------

                                Input        SAS Source
                    Variable    Dataset      Code File
                    Name        Name         Scanned

                    myvar       WORK.CHECK   saspgm
```

%FINV

Purpose

FINV macro function similar to the FINV data step function. It returns a quantile from the F distribution.

Syntax

%finv(p, ndf, ddf, nc)

p is the numeric probability. Range: $0 \le p < 1$

ndf is the numeric numerator degrees of freedom parameter. Range: ndf > 0

ddf is the numeric denominator degrees of freedom parameter. Range: ddf > 0

nc is the numeric non-centrality parameter. Range: nc >= 0

Notes

In the data step function, the value NC is optional but it is NOT OPTIONAL in the macro function. The FINV function returns the pth quantile from the F distribution with numerator degrees of freedom ndf, denominator degrees of freedom ddf, and non-centrality parameter nc. The probability that an observation from the F distribution is less than the quantile is p.

This function accepts noninteger degrees of freedom parameters ndf and ddf. The non-centrality parameter nc is defined such that if X and Y are normal random variables with means mu and 0, respectively, and variance 1, then x^2/y^2 has a noncentral F distribution with nc = mu^2.

CAUTION: For large values of nc, the algorithm could fail-in that case, a missing value is returned. FINV is the inverse of the PROBF function.

Example

Sample Program
```
%put FINV(.95,2,10.3,2) = %finv(.95,2,10.3,2) ;
```

SAS Log
```
1          %put FINV(.95,2,10.3,2) = %finv(.95,2,10.3,2) ;
FINV(.95,2,10.3,2) = 7.58376602401988
```

SAS Listing
This sample program does not have any listing output.

%FIPNAME

Purpose
FIPNAME macro function similar to the FIPNAME data step function. It converts FIPS codes to upper case state names.

Syntax
%fipname(FIPS)

FIPS is the numeric state FIPS code.

See Also
%FIPNAME, %FIPNAMEL, %FIPSTATE, %STFIPS, %STNAME, %STNAMEL, %ZIPFIPS, %ZIPNAME, %ZIPNAMEL, %ZIPSTATE

Notes

At the time of this writing, valid FIPS codes are between 0 and 95 inclusive. This macro ensures that only such values are used and all other FIPS input return the string INVALID CODE. Several other values between 0 and 95 also return INVALID CODE.

Example

Sample Program

```
%put state = %fipname(22) ;
%put state = %fipname(0) ;
%put state = %fipname(65) ;
%put state = %fipname(97) ;
%put state = %fipname(NC) ;
%put state = %fipname(200) ;
```

SAS Log

```
1          %put state = %fipname(22) ;
state = LOUISIANA
2          %put state = %fipname(0) ;
state =
3          %put state = %fipname(65) ;
state = INVALID CODE
4          %put state = %fipname(97) ;
NOTE: Argument 1 to macro function %FIPNAME is missing or out of range.
state = INVALID CODE
5          %put state = %fipname(NC) ;
NOTE: Invalid numeric data NC in Argument 3 for macro function %FIPNAME.
state = INVALID CODE
6          %put state = %fipname(200) ;
NOTE: Argument 1 to macro function %FIPNAME is missing or out of range.
state = INVALID CODE
```

SAS Listing

This sample program does not have any listing output.

%FIPNAMEL

Purpose

FIPNAMEL macro function similar to the FIPNAMEL data step function. It converts FIPS codes to mixed case state names.

Syntax

%fipnamel(FIPS)

> *FIPS* is the numeric FIPS code.

See Also

%FIPNAME, %FIPNAMEL, %FIPSTATE, %STFIPS, %STNAME, %STNAMEL, %ZIPFIPS, %ZIPNAME, %ZIPNAMEL, %ZIPSTATE

Notes

At the time of this writing, valid FIPS codes are between 0 and 95 inclusive. This macro ensures that only such values are used and all other FIPS input return the string INVALID CODE. Several other values between 0 and 95 also return INVALID CODE.

Example

Sample Program

```
%put state = %fipnamel(22) ;
%put state = %fipnamel(0) ;
%put state = %fipnamel(65) ;
%put state = %fipnamel(97) ;
%put state = %fipnamel(NC) ;
%put state = %fipnamel(200) ;
```

SAS Log

```
1          %put state = %fipnamel(22) ;
state = Louisiana
2          %put state = %fipnamel(0) ;
state =
3          %put state = %fipnamel(65) ;
state = Invalid Code
4          %put state = %fipnamel(97) ;
NOTE:  Argument 1 to macro function %FIPNAMEL is missing or out of range.
state = Invalid Code
5          %put state = %fipnamel(NC) ;
NOTE:  Invalid numeric data NC in Argument 3 for macro function %FIPNAMEL.
state = Invalid Code
6          %put state = %fipnamel(200) ;
NOTE:  Argument 1 to macro function %FIPNAMEL is missing or out of range.
state = Invalid Code
```

SAS Listing

This sample program does not have any listing output.

%FIPSTATE

Purpose

FIPSTATE macro function similar to the FIPSTATE data step function. It converts FIPS codes to two character postal codes.

Syntax

%fipstate(FIPS)

>   *FIPS* is the numeric FIPS code.

See Also

%FIPNAME, %FIPNAMEL, %FIPSTATE, %STFIPS, %STNAME, %STNAMEL, %ZIPFIPS, %ZIPNAME, %ZIPNAMEL, %ZIPSTATE

Notes

At the time of this writing, valid FIPS codes are between 0 and 95 inclusive. This macro ensures that only such values are used and all other FIPS input return the string INVALID CODE. Several other values between 0 and 95 also return INVALID CODE.

Example

Sample Program
```
%put state = %fipstate(22) ;
%put state = %fipstate(0) ;
%put state = %fipstate(65) ;
%put state = %fipstate(97) ;
%put state = %fipstate(NC) ;
%put state = %fipstate(200) ;
```

SAS Log
```
1          %put state = %fipstate(22) ;
state = LA
2          %put state = %fipstate(0) ;
state =
3          %put state = %fipstate(65) ;
state = --
4          %put state = %fipstate(97) ;
NOTE: Argument 1 to macro function %FIPSTATE is missing or out of range.
state = Invalid Code
5          %put state = %fipstate(NC) ;
NOTE: Invalid numeric data NC in Argument 3 for macro function %FIPSTATE.
state = Invalid Code
6          %put state = %fipstate(200) ;
NOTE: Argument 1 to macro function %FIPSTATE is missing or out of range.
state = Invalid Code
```

SAS Listing
This sample program does not have any listing output.

%FLOOR

Purpose
FLOOR macro function similar to the FLOOR data step function. It returns the smallest integer that is less than or equal to the argument.

Syntax
%floor(argument)

argument is numeric.

Example

Sample Program
```
%put FLOOR(3.14159) = %floor(3.14159) ;
%put FLOOR(ABC) = %floor(ABC) ;
```

SAS Log

```
1          %put FLOOR(3.14159) = %floor(3.14159) ;
FLOOR(3.14159) = 3
2          %put FLOOR(ABC) = %floor(ABC) ;
NOTE:  Argument 1 to macro function %FLOOR is missing or out of range.
FLOOR(ABC) = .
```

SAS Listing

This sample program does not have any listing output.

%FNONCT

Purpose

FNONCT macro function similar to the FNONCT data step function. It returns the value of the noncentrality parameter of an F distribution.

Syntax

%fnonct(x, ndf, ddf, prob)

    x is a numeric random variable. Range: x ge 0 (integer)

    ndf is a numeric numerator degrees-of-freedom parameter (integer) Range: df > 0

    ddf is a numeric denominator degrees of freedom parameter (integer) Range: df > 0

    prob is a probability. Range: 0 < prob < 1

Notes

Although it does not state it in the original SAS Institute documentation for the regular functions, X, NDF and DDF must be integers.

Example

Sample Program

```
%put FNONCT(5, 5, 5, .5) = %fnonct (5, 5, 5, .5) ;
%put FNONCT(-1, .5, .5, .5) = %fnonct (-1, .5, .5, .5) ;
%put FNONCT(10, .5, .5, A) = %fnonct (10, .5, .5, A) ;
```

SAS Log

```
1          %put FNONCT(5, 5, 5, .5) = %fnonct (5, 5, 5, .5) ;
FNONCT(5, 5, 5, .5) = 17.914424482347
2          %put FNONCT(-1, .5, .5, .5) = %fnonct (-1, .5, .5, .5) ;
NOTE:  Argument 1 to macro function %FNONCT is missing or out of range.
FNONCT(-1, .5, .5, .5) = .
3          %put FNONCT(10, .5, .5, A) = %fnonct (10, .5, .5, A) ;
NOTE:  Invalid numeric data A in Argument 4 for macro function %FNONCT.
FNONCT(10, .5, .5, A) = .
```

SAS Listing

This sample program does not have any listing output.

%FREAD

Purpose
Retrieves and returns the Nth record of a given file declared by a FILENAME reference

Syntax
%fread (filename, record, length)

    FILENAME is the SAS Filename

    RECORD is the record number to retrieve

    LENGTH (optional/max=256) is the length to retrieve

See Also
%FREAD, %FILEREAD

Notes
If the given filename does not exist, the function returns a null string.

Example

Sample Program
filename autoexec '!SASROOT\autoexec.sas' ;

%put read=%fread (autoexec, 5) ;

SAS Log
```
17   filename autoexec '!SASROOT\autoexec.sas' ;
18   %put read=%fread (autoexec, 5) ;
read= | Purpose  Initialization of the SAS Software System.  This program runs every  |
```

SAS Listing
This sample program does not have any listing output.

%FUZZ

Purpose
FUZZ macro function similar to the FUZZ data step function. It returns the nearest integer if the argument is within 1E-12.

Syntax
%fuzz(argument)

    argument is a numeric value

Example

Sample Program
```
%put FUZZ(5.9999999999999) = %fuzz(5.9999999999999) ;
%put FUZZ(5.99999999) = %fuzz(5.99999999) ;
```

SAS Log
```
1          %put FUZZ(5.9999999999999) = %fuzz(5.9999999999999) ;
FUZZ(5.9999999999999) = 6
2          %put FUZZ(5.99999999) = %fuzz(5.99999999) ;
FUZZ(5.99999999) = 5.99999999
```

SAS Listing
This sample program does not have any listing output.

%GAMINV

Purpose
GAMINV macro function similar to the GAMINV data step function. It returns a quantile from the gamma distribution.

Syntax
%gaminv(p,a)

    p is a numeric probability. Range: 0 <= p < 1

    a is a numeric shape parameter. Range: a > 0

See Also
%GAMMA, %LGAMMA, %GAMINV

Notes
GAMINV is the inverse of the PROBGAM function.

Example

Sample Program
```
%put GAMINV(0.5,9) = %gaminv(0.5,9) ;
%put GAMINV(0.1,2.1) = %gaminv(0.1,2.1) ;
```

SAS Log
```
1          %put GAMINV(0.5,9) = %gaminv(0.5,9) ;
GAMINV(0.5,9) = 8.66895118437037
2          %put GAMINV(0.1,2.1) = %gaminv(0.1,2.1) ;
GAMINV(0.1,2.1) = 0.5841932368992
```

SAS Listing
This sample program does not have any listing output.

%GAMMA

Purpose
GAMMA macro function similar to the GAMMA data step function. It returns the value of the gamma function.

Syntax
%gamma(argument)

> *argument* is a positive number (argument > 0)

See Also
%GAMMA, %LGAMMA, %GAMINV

Example

Sample Program
```
%put GAMMA(10) = %gamma(10) ;
%put GAMMA(25) = %gamma(25) ;
%put GAMMA(.5) = %gamma(.5) ;
```

SAS Log
```
1          %put GAMMA(10) = %gamma(10) ;
GAMMA(10) = 362880
2          %put GAMMA(25) = %gamma(25) ;
GAMMA(25) = 620448401733239141564416
3          %put GAMMA(.5) = %gamma(.5) ;
GAMMA(.5) = 1.77245385090551
```

SAS Listing
This sample program does not have any listing output.

%GETVAR

Purpose
Returns the value of a variable for a specific observation in a given data set.

Syntax
%getvar (data, var, obs)

> *DATA* is a valid SAS data set name. The data set must exist.
>
> *VAR* is the variable to retrieve from the data set DATA.
>
> *OBS* is the observation number to retrieve.

See Also
%GETVAR, %GETVARC, %GETVARN

Notes

If the given data set does not exist, the function returns a null string. If the data set does exist and the variable does not, the function returns a zero.

Example

Sample Program

```
%put The value of SALES in SASHELP.SHOES for obs number 4 is %getvar (sashelp.shoes, sales, 4) ;
%put The value of REGION in SASHELP.SHOES for obs number 4 is %getvar (sashelp.shoes, region, 4) ;
```

SAS Log

```
1    %put The value of SALES in SASHELP.SHOES for obs number 4 is %getvar (sashelp.shoes, sales, 4) ;
The value of SALES in SASHELP.SHOES for obs number 4 is 62819
2    %put The value of REGION in SASHELP.SHOES for obs number 4 is %getvar (sashelp.shoes, region, 4) ;
The value of REGION in SASHELP.SHOES for obs number 4 is Africa
```

SAS Listing

This sample program does not have any listing output.

%GETVARC

Purpose

Returns the value of a character variable for a specific observation in a given data set.

Syntax

%getvarc (data, var, obs)

> *DATA* is a valid SAS data set name. The data set must exist.
>
> *VAR* is the variable to retrieve from the data set DATA.
>
> *OBS* is the observation number to retrieve

See Also

%GETVAR, %GETVARC, %GETVARN

Notes

If the macro cannot find the value for the given data set, variable, or observation number, it returns a NULL STRING. The macro functions %GETVARN and %GETVARC have been created to match the naming of data step functions GETVARN and GETVARC, but it would be easier to only use the macro function %GETVAR because it will retrieve a value regardless of the type of variable in the data set.

If a NUMERIC value is entered in the macro function, it reads the value and returns it while giving a numeric-to-character conversion message (even though technically no such conversion takes place at the macro variable level.)

Example

Sample Program

```
%put The value of SALES in SASHELP.SHOES for obs number 4 is %getvarc (sashelp.shoes, sales, 4) ;
```

```
%put The value of SALES in SASHELP.SHOES for obs number 4 is %getvarc (sashelp.shoes, region, 4) ;
```

SAS Log

```
1    %put The value of SALES in SASHELP.SHOES for obs number 4 is %getvarc (sashelp.shoes, sales, 4) ;
NOTE: Character values have been converted to numeric values in macro function %getvarc.
The value of SALES in SASHELP.SHOES for obs number 4 is 62819
2    %put The value of SALES in SASHELP.SHOES for obs number 4 is %getvarc (sashelp.shoes, region, 4) ;
The value of SALES in SASHELP.SHOES for obs number 4 is Africa
```

SAS Listing

This sample program does not have any listing output.

%GETVARN

Purpose

Returns the value of a numeric variable for a specific observation in a given data set.

Syntax

%getvarn (data, var, obs)

> *DATA* is a valid SAS data set name. The data set must exist.
>
> *VAR* is the variable to retrieve from the data set DATA.
>
> *OBS* is the observation number to retrieve

See Also

%GETVAR, %GETVARC, %GETVARN

Notes

If the macro cannot find the value for the given data set, variable, or observation number, it returns a NULL STRING. The macro functions %GETVARN and %GETVARC have been created to match the naming of data step functions GETVARN and GETVARC, but it would be easier to only use the macro function %GETVAR because it will retrieve a value regardless of the type of variable in the data set. If a CHARACTER value is entered in the macro function, it reads the value and returns it while giving a character-to-numeric conversion message (even though technically no such conversion takes place at the macro variable level.)

Example

Sample Program

```
%put The value of SALES in SASHELP.SHOES for obs number 4 is %getvarn (sashelp.shoes, sales, 4) ;
%put The value of SALES in SASHELP.SHOES for obs number 4 is %getvarn (sashelp.shoes, region, 4) ;
```

SAS Log

```
1    %put The value of SALES in SASHELP.SHOES for obs number 4 is %getvarn (sashelp.shoes, sales, 4) ;
The value of SALES in SASHELP.SHOES for obs number 4 is 62819
2    %put The value of SALES in SASHELP.SHOES for obs number 4 is %getvarn (sashelp.shoes, region, 4) ;
NOTE: Numeric values have been converted to character values in macro function %GETVARN.
The value of SALES in SASHELP.SHOES for obs number 4 is Africa
```

SAS Listing

This sample program does not have any listing output.

%IBESSEL

Purpose

IBESSEL macro function similar to the IBESSEL data step function. It returns the value of the modified bessel function.

Syntax

%ibessel(nu,x,kode)

    nu is numeric. Range: nu >= 0

    x is numeric. Range: x >= 0

    kode is a non-negative integer.

See Also

%IBESSEL, %JBESSEL

Notes

The IBESSEL function returns the value of the modified bessel function of order nu evaluated at x (Abramowitz, Stegun 1964-Amos, Daniel, Weston 1977).

Example

Sample Program

```
%put IBESSEL(2,2,0) = %ibessel(2,2,0) ;
```

SAS Log

```
1          %put IBESSEL(2,2,0) = %ibessel(2,2,0) ;
IBESSEL(2,2,0) = 0.68894844769873
```

SAS Listing

This sample program does not have any listing output.

%IEFBR14

Purpose

This macro takes an infinite amount of input and has absolutely no output. WHY? Because there may be a condition sometime to always have a macro called, but the macro name could be conditional and the result should be nothing. If that case ever arises, use this one. It gets its name from the MVS JCL executable IEFBR14.

Syntax

%iefbr14 (argument-1, argument-2, argument3, ... argumentN)

ARGUMENTx can be anything or nothing. Any and all input strings are ignored. It does not matter as long as you avoid unbalanced quotation marks, parenthesis, and semicolons.

Notes
Standard macro and SAS protocol is broken here by placing everything on one line with no blanks to ensure that NOTHING happens.

Example

Sample Program
```
%put This macro goes nowhere and does nothing: %iefbr14(parm1, parm2, parm3, parm4) ;
```

SAS Log
```
1          %put This macro goes nowhere and does nothing: %iefbr14(parm1, parm2, parm3, parm4) ;
This macro goes nowhere and does nothing:
```

SAS Listing
This sample program does not have any listing output.

%INDEXC

Purpose
INDEXC macro function similar to INDEXC data step function. It searches a character expression for specific characters. The INDEXC macro function searches source, from left to right, for the first occurrence of any character present in the excerpts and returns the position in source of that character. If none of the characters in EXCERPT are found in SOURCE, INDEXC returns a value of 0.

Syntax
%indexc(source, excerpt)

>*source* specifies the character expression to search.

>*excerpt* specifies the characters to search for in the character expression. If you specify more than one excerpt, separate them with a comma.

See Also
%INDEXC, %INDEXW

Example

Sample Program
```
%put INDEXC=%indexc(abcdefg, zdef) ;
%put INDEXC=%indexc(abcdefg, hijklmno) ;
%put INDEXC=%indexc(abcdefg) ;
%put INDEXC=%indexc ;
```

SAS Log

```
1          %put INDEXC=%indexc(abcdefg, zdef) ;
INDEXC=4
2          %put INDEXC=%indexc(abcdefg, hijklmno) ;
INDEXC=0
3          %put INDEXC=%indexc(abcdefg) ;
NOTE:  Argument 2 to macro function %INDEXC is missing or out of range.
INDEXC=0
4          %put INDEXC=%indexc ;
NOTE:  Argument 1 to macro function %INDEXC is missing or out of range.
INDEXC=.
```

SAS Listing

This sample program does not have any listing output.

%INDEXW

Purpose

INDEXW macro function similar to INDEXW data step function. It searches a character expression for a specified string as a word. The INDEXW function searches source, from left to right, for the first occurrence of excerpt and returns the position in source of the substrings first character.

If the substring is not found in source, INDEXW returns a value of 0. If there are multiple occurrences of the string, INDEXW returns only the position of the first occurrence. The substring pattern must begin and end on a word boundary.

For INDEXW, word boundaries are blanks, the beginning of source, and the end of source. Punctuation marks are not word boundaries.

Syntax

%indexw(source, excerpt)

> *source* specifies the character expression to search.

> *excerpt* specifies the characters to search for in the character expression. If you specify more than one excerpt, separate them with a comma.

See Also

%INDEXC, %INDEXW

Example

Sample Program

```
%put INDEXW=%indexw (asdf adog dog, dog) ;
%put INDEXW=%indexw (abcdef x=y, def) ;
%put INDEXW=%indexw (abcdefg) ;
%put INDEXW=%indexw ;
%put INDEXW=%indexw (,4) ;
%put INDEXW=%indexw (4,4) ;
%put INDEXW=%indexw (4,4 5) ;
```

SAS Log

```
1          %put INDEXW=%indexw (asdf adog dog, dog) ;
INDEXW=11
2          %put INDEXW=%indexw (abcdef x=y, def) ;
INDEXW=0
3          %put INDEXW=%indexw (abcdefg) ;
NOTE:  Argument 2 to macro function %INDEXW is missing or out of range.
INDEXW=0
4          %put INDEXW=%indexw ;
NOTE:  Argument 1 to macro function %INDEXW is missing or out of range.
INDEXW=.
5          %put INDEXW=%indexw (,4) ;
NOTE:  Argument 1 to macro function %INDEXW is missing or out of range.
INDEXW=.
6          %put INDEXW=%indexw (4,4) ;
INDEXW=1
7          %put INDEXW=%indexw (4,4 5) ;
INDEXW=0
```

SAS Listing

This sample program does not have any listing output.

%INFO

Purpose

This macro creates an INFO note

Syntax

%info (_message_)   [required]

See Also

%DATANOTE, %FILENOTE, %TIMENOTE, %INFO

Notes

No COMMAS are allowed in the message.

Example

Sample Program

```
options msglevel=i mprint ;
%info (This INFO statement will appear) ;
%info (%str(This INFO statement will also appear and it is very long.  So long, in
            fact, that it will probably be put on another line. You will also notice
            that it has several line breaks in it when entered but will not necessarily
            have that same line break in it when it is written to the SAS log.  Also,
            notice that the COMMA is included, thus forcing the use of the STR() SAS
            Macro Function.)) ;

options msglevel=n nomprint ;
%info (This INFO statement will not appear) ;
```

SAS Log

```
1    options msglevel=i mprint ;
2    %info (This INFO statement will appear) ;
```

```
INFO: This INFO statement will appear
3          %info (%str(This INFO statement will also appear and it is very long.  So long, in

4                    fact, that it will probably be put on another line. You will also notice

5                    that it has several line breaks in it when entered but will not necessarily

6                    have that same line break in it when it is written to the SAS log.  Also,

7                    notice that the COMMA is included, thus forcing the use of the STR() SAS

8                    Macro Function.)) ;
INFO: This INFO statement will also appear and it is very long. So long in fact that it will
      probably be put on another line. You will also notice that it has several line breaks
      in it when entered but will not necessarily have that same line break in it when it is
      written to the SAS log. Also notice that the COMMA is included thus forcing the use of
      the STR() SAS Macro Function.
9
10    options msglevel=n nomprint ;
11    %info (This INFO statement will not appear) ;
```

SAS Listing

This sample program does not have any listing output.

%INT

Purpose

INT macro function similar to the INT data step function

Syntax

%int(argument)

   argument is numeric.

Example

Sample Program

```
%put INT(PI) = %int(%pi) ;
%put INT(-PI) = %int(-%pi) ;
%put INT(A) = %int(a) ;
```

SAS Log

```
1          %put INT(PI) = %int(%pi) ;
INT(PI) = 3
2          %put INT(-PI) = %int(-%pi) ;
INT(-PI) = -3
3          %put INT(A) = %int(a) ;
NOTE:  Invalid numeric data a in Argument 1 for macro function %INT.
INT(A) = .
```

SAS Listing

This sample program does not have any listing output.

%INTCK

Purpose
INTCK macro function similar to the INTCK data step function. It returns the integer number of time intervals in a given time span.

Syntax
%intck (interval, from, to)

> *interval* is the character constant or variable. Interval can appear in uppercase or lowercase. The value of the character constant or variable must be one of these: DAY, DTDAY, HOUR, WEEKDAY, MINUTE, DTWEEKDAY, WEEK, DTWEEK, SECOND, TENDAY, DTTENDAY, SEMIMONTH, DTSEMIMONTH, MONTH, DTMONTH, QTR, DTQTR, SEMIYEAR, DTSEMIYEAR, YEAR, DTYEAR.
>
> *from* is the SAS expression that represents a SAS date, time, or datetime value that identifies the beginning of the time span.
>
> *to* specifies a SAS expression that represents a SAS date, time, or datetime value that identifies the end of the time span.

See Also
%INTCK, %INTCX

Example

Sample Program
```
%put qtr  = %intck('qtr','10jan95'd,'01jul95'd) ;
%put year = %intck('year','31dec94'd,'01jan95'd) ;
%put year = %intck('year','01jan94'd, '31dec94'd) ;
%put year = %intck('year','01jan94'd, "&sysdate"d) ;
```

SAS Log
```
1          %put qtr  = %intck('qtr','10jan95'd,'01jul95'd) ;
qtr = 2
2          %put year = %intck('year','31dec94'd,'01jan95'd) ;
year = 1
3          %put year = %intck('year','01jan94'd, '31dec94'd) ;
year = 0
4          %put year = %intck('year','01jan94'd, "&sysdate"d) ;
year = 12
```

SAS Listing
This sample program does not have any listing output.

%INTNX

Purpose
INTNX macro function similar to the INTNX data step function. It advances a date, time, or datetime value by a given interval, and returns a date, time, or datetime value.

Syntax

%intnx ('interval', start-from, increment)

>*interval* is a character constant or variable. Interval can appear in uppercase or lowercase. The value of the character constant or variable must be one of these: DAY, DTDAY, HOUR, WEEKDAY, MINUTE, DTWEEKDAY, WEEK, DTWEEK, SECOND, TENDAY, DTTENDAY, SEMIMONTH, DTSEMIMONTH, MONTH, DTMONTH, QTR, DTQTR, SEMIYEAR, DTSEMIYEAR, YEAR, DTYEAR.
>
>*start-from* is the SAS expression that represents a SAS date, time, or datetime value that identifies the beginning of the time span.
>
>*increment* is the numeric integer increment value

See Also

%INTCK, %INTCX

Notes

The data step function INTNX also has an optional fourth argument ALIGNMENT that is not used in this macro function.

Example

Sample Program

```
%put new date = %intnx('qtr','10jan95'd, 1) ;
%put new date = %intnx('year','31dec94'd, 10) ;
%put new date = %intnx('year','01jan94'd, -15) ;
%put new date = %intnx('year','01jan94'd, 0) ;
```

SAS Log

```
1          %put new date = %intnx('qtr','10jan95'd, 1) ;
new date = 12874
2          %put new date = %intnx('year','31dec94'd, 10) ;
new date = 16071
3          %put new date = %intnx('year','01jan94'd, -15) ;
new date = 6940
4          %put new date = %intnx('year','01jan94'd, 0) ;
new date = 12419
```

SAS Listing

This sample program does not have any listing output.

%INTRR

Purpose

INTRR macro function similar to the INTRR data step function. It returns the internal rate of return as a fraction.

Syntax

%intrr (freq, c0, cl, . . . , cn)

freq is numeric, the number of payments over a specified base period of time associated with the desired internal rate of return. Range: freq > 0. Exception: The case freq = 0 is a flag to allow continuous compounding.

c0, c1, . . . , cn are numeric, the optional cash payments.

See Also
%IRR

Example

Sample Program

```
%*----------------------------------------------------------*
 | For an initial outlay of $400 and expected payments of    |
 | $100, $200, and $300 over the following three years,      |
 | the annual internal rate of return can be expressed as    |
 | follows:                                                  |
 *----------------------------------------------------------* ;

%put INTRR=%intrr(1, -400, 100, 200, 300) ;
```

SAS Log
```
9          %put INTRR=%intrr(1, -400, 100, 200, 300) ;
INTRR=0.19437709962746
```

SAS Listing
This sample program does not have any listing output.

%IRR

Purpose
IRR macro function similar to the IRR data step function. It returns the internal rate of return as a percentage.

Syntax
%irr (freq, c0, c1, . . . , cn)

freq is numeric, the number of payments over a specified base period of time associated with the desired internal rate of return. Range: freq > 0. Exception: The case freq = 0 is a flag to allow continuous compounding.

c0, c1, . . . , cn are numeric, the optional cash payments.

See Also
%INTIRR

Example

Sample Program
```
%*----------------------------------------------------------*
 | For an initial outlay of $400 and expected payments of    |
```

```
|  $100, $200, and $300 over the following three years,  |
|  the annual internal rate of return can be expressed as  |
|  follows:                                                |
*--------------------------------------------------------* ;

%put IRR=%irr(1, -400, 100, 200, 300) ;
```

SAS Log
```
9          %put IRR=%irr(1, -400, 100, 200, 300) ;
IRR=19.4377099627464
```

SAS Listing
This sample program does not have any listing output.

%JBESSEL

Purpose
JBESSEL macro function similar to the JBESSEL data step function. It returns the value of the bessel function.

Syntax
%jbessel(nu,x)

> *nu* is numeric nu >= 0
>
> *x* is numeric x >= 0

See Also
%IBESSEL, %JBESSEL

Notes
The JBESSEL function returns the value of the bessel function of order nu evaluated at x (For more information, see Abramowitz and Stegun 1964 Amos, Daniel, and Weston 1977).

Example

Sample Program
```
%put JBESSEL(2,2) = %jbessel(2,2) ;
%put JBESSEL(2,-2) = %jbessel(2,-2) ;
```

SAS Log
```
1          %put JBESSEL(2,2) = %jbessel(2,2) ;
JBESSEL(2,2) = 0.35283402861563
2          %put JBESSEL(2,-2) = %jbessel(2,-2) ;
NOTE:  Argument 2 to macro function %JBESSEL is missing or out of range.
JBESSEL(2,-2) = .
```

SAS Listing
This sample program does not have any listing output.

%KURTOSIS

Purpose
KURTOSIS macro function similar to the KURTOSIS data step function. It returns the kurtosis.

Syntax
%kurtosis(argument, argument, . . . argument)

> *argument* is numeric. At least four arguments are required.

See Also
%CSS, %VAR, %N, %NMISS, %SUM, %SKEWNESS, %KURTOSIS, %RANGE, %CV, %USS, %STD, %STDERR, %MIN, %MAX

Example

Sample Program
```
%put KURTOSIS=%kurtosis(1,2,3,4,5) ;
%put KURTOSIS=%kurtosis(1,2,A,4,5) ;
%put KURTOSIS=%kurtosis ;
%put KURTOSIS=%kurtosis(1) ;
%put KURTOSIS=%kurtosis(1,2,3,4,.) ;
```

SAS Log
```
1          %put KURTOSIS=%kurtosis(1,2,3,4,5) ;
KURTOSIS=-1.2
2          %put KURTOSIS=%kurtosis(1,2,A,4,5) ;
NOTE: Invalid numeric data A in argument 3 for macro function %KURTOSIS.
KURTOSIS=.
3          %put KURTOSIS=%kurtosis ;
NOTE: Argument 1 to macro function %KURTOSIS is missing or out of range.
KURTOSIS=.
4          %put KURTOSIS=%kurtosis(1) ;
NOTE: Argument 2 to macro function %KURTOSIS is missing or out of range.
KURTOSIS=.
5          %put KURTOSIS=%kurtosis(1,2,3,4,.) ;
KURTOSIS=-1.2
```

SAS Listing
This sample program does not have any listing output.

%LIBREF

Purpose
Verifies that a libref has been assigned and returns a value.

Syntax
%LIBREF (*libref*)

> *libref* specifies the libref to be verified.

See Also

%CEXIST, %EXIST, %FEXIST, %FILEEXIST, %LIBREF

Notes

%LIBREF returns 0 if the operation was successful, 0 if it was not successful. Yes, this seems backwards from all other verification methods--but it is done this way to most closely resemble the original data step function written by The SAS Institute.

Example

Sample Program

```
%put LIBREF=%libref(work) ;
%put LIBREF=%libref(nolib) ;
%put LIBREF=%libref ;
```

SAS Log

```
1    %put LIBREF=%libref(work) ;
LIBREF=0
2    %put LIBREF=%libref(nolib) ;
LIBREF=70006
3    %put LIBREF=%libref ;
LIBREF=1
```

SAS Listing

This sample program does not have any listing output.

%LGAMMA

Purpose

LGAMMA macro function similar to the LGAMMA data step function. It returns the natural logarithm of the Gamma function.

Syntax

%lgamma(argument)

    argument is a positive number

See Also

%GAMMA, %LGAMMA, %GAMINV

Example

Sample Program

```
%put LGAMMA(5) = %lgamma(5) ;
%put LGAMMA(X) = %lgamma(X) ;
```

SAS Log

```
1         %put LGAMMA(5) = %lgamma(5) ;
LGAMMA(5) = 3.17805383034794
```

```
2          %put LGAMMA(X) = %lgamma(X) ;
NOTE:  Invalid numeric data X in Argument 1 for macro function %LGAMMA.
LGAMMA(X) = .
```

SAS Listing

This sample program does not have any listing output.

%LOG

Purpose
LOG macro function similar to the LOG data step function. It returns the base 10 logarithm.

Syntax
%log(x)

    x is a positive number (x > 0)

See Also
%LOG, %LOG2, %LOG10

Example

Sample Program
```
%put LOG(3.4) = %log(3.4) ;
%put LOG(e) = %log(%e) ;
```

SAS Log
```
1          %put LOG(3.4) = %log(3.4) ;
LOG(3.4) = 1.22377543162211
2          %put LOG(e) = %log(%e) ;
LOG(e) = 0.99999999999999
```

SAS Listing
This sample program does not have any listing output.

%LOG10

Purpose
LOG10 macro function similar to the LOG10 data step function. It returns the base 10 logarithm.

Syntax
%log10(x)

    x is a positive number (x > 0)

See Also
%LOG, %LOG2, %LOG10

Example

Sample Program
```
%put LOG10(3.4) = %log10(3.4) ;
%put LOG10(10) = %log10(10) ;
```

SAS Log

```
1          %put LOG10(3.4) = %log10(3.4) ;
LOG10(3.4) = 0.53147891704225
2          %put LOG10(10) = %log10(10) ;
LOG10(10) = 1
```

SAS Listing

This sample program does not have any listing output.

%LOG2

Purpose

LOG2 macro function similar to the LOG2 data step function. It returns the base 2 logarithm.

Syntax

%log2 (x)

    x is a positive number (x > 0)

See Also

%LOG, %LOG2, %LOG10

Example

Sample Program

```
%put LOG2(3.4) = %log2 (3.4) ;
%put LOG2(10) = %log2 (2) ;
```

SAS Log

```
1          %put LOG2(3.4) = %log2 (3.4) ;
LOG2(3.4) = 1.765534746362970
2          %put LOG2(10) = %log2 (2) ;
LOG2(10) = 1
```

SAS Listing

This sample program does not have any listing output.

%LOGPDF

Purpose

LOGPDF macro function similar to the LOGPDF data step function. It computes the logarithm of a probability density (mass) function.

Syntax

%LOGPDF (dist,quantile,parm-1, . . . ,parm-k)

    dist is a character string that identifies the distribution. Valid distributions are as follows:

- Bernoulli - BERNOULLI

- Beta - BETA
- Binomial - BINOMIAL
- Cauchy - CAUCHY
- Chi squared - CHISQUARED
- Exponential - EXPONENTIAL
- F - F
- Gamma - GAMMA
- Geometric - GEOMETRIC
- Hypergeometric - HYPERGEOMETRIC
- Laplace - LAPLACE
- Logistic - LOGISTIC
- Lognormal - LOGNORMAL
- Negative binomial - NEGBINOMIAL
- Normal - NORMAL or GAUSS
- Pareto - PARETO
- Poisson - POISSON
- T - T
- Uniform - UNIFORM
- Wald (inverse Gaussian) - WALD or IGAUSS
- Weibull - WEIBULL

Note: Except for T and F, any distribution can be minimally identified by its first four characters. To keep with the spirit of the data step function LOGPDF, the DIST option can be quoted or unquoted (unquoted is preferred).

quantile is a numeric random variable.

parm-1, . . . ,parm-k are shape, location, or scale parameters appropriate for the specific distribution. See the description for each distribution in Details under the HELP library for the data step function LOGPDF for complete information about these parameters.

See Also
%CDF, %LOGCDF, %PDF, %SDF, %LOGSDF

Example

Sample Program
```
%put LOGPDF=%logpdf(POISSON, 2, 1) ;
%put LOGPDF=%logpdf('POISSON', 2, 1) ;
%put LOGPDF=%logpdf("POISSON", 2, 1) ;
%put LOGPDF=%logpdf(POISSON) ;
%put LOGPDF=%logpdf(POISSON, 2) ;
```

SAS Log
```
1          %put LOGPDF=%logpdf(POISSON, 2, 1) ;
LOGPDF=-1.69314718055994
2          %put LOGPDF=%logpdf('POISSON', 2, 1) ;
LOGPDF=-1.69314718055994
3          %put LOGPDF=%logpdf("POISSON", 2, 1) ;
LOGPDF=-1.69314718055994
4          %put LOGPDF=%logpdf(POISSON) ;
NOTE: Argument 2 to macro function %LOGPDF is missing or out of range.
LOGPDF=.
```

```
5          %put LOGPDF=%logpdf(POISSON, 2) ;
NOTE: Argument 3 to macro function %LOGPDF is missing or out of range.
LOGPDF=.
```

SAS Listing

This sample program does not have any listing output.

%LOGSDF

Purpose

LOGSDF macro function similar to the LOGSDF data step function. It computes the logarithm of a survival function.

Syntax

%LOGSDF (dist,quantile,parm-1, . . . ,parm-k)

> *dist* is a character string that identifies the distribution. Valid distributions are as follows:
>
> - Bernoulli - BERNOULLI
> - Beta - BETA
> - Binomial - BINOMIAL
> - Cauchy - CAUCHY
> - Chi squared - CHISQUARED
> - Exponential - EXPONENTIAL
> - F - F
> - Gamma - GAMMA
> - Geometric - GEOMETRIC
> - Hypergeometric - HYPERGEOMETRIC
> - Laplace - LAPLACE
> - Logistic - LOGISTIC
> - Lognormal - LOGNORMAL
> - Negative binomial - NEGBINOMIAL
> - Normal - NORMAL or GAUSS
> - Pareto - PARETO
> - Poisson - POISSON
> - T - T
> - Uniform - UNIFORM
> - Wald (inverse Gaussian) - WALD or IGAUSS
> - Weibull - WEIBULL
>
> Note: Except for T and F, any distribution can be minimally identified by its first four characters. To keep with the spirit of the data step function LOGPDF, the DIST option can be quoted or unquoted (unquoted is preferred).
>
> *quantile* is a numeric random variable.
>
> *parm-1, . . . ,parm-k* are shape, location, or scale parameters appropriate for the specific distribution. See the description for each distribution in Details under the HELP library for the data step function LOGPDF for complete information about these parameters.

See Also
%CDF, %LOGCDF, %PDF, %SDF, %LOGSDF

Example

Sample Program
```
%put LOGSDF=%logsdf(POISSON, 2, 1) ;
%put LOGSDF=%logsdf('POISSON', 2, 1) ;
%put LOGSDF=%logsdf("POISSON", 2, 1) ;
%put LOGSDF=%logsdf(POISSON) ;
%put LOGSDF=%logsdf(POISSON, 2) ;
```

SAS Log
```
1          %put LOGSDF=%logsdf(POISSON, 2, 1) ;
LOGSDF=-2.5219682600314
2          %put LOGSDF=%logsdf('POISSON', 2, 1) ;
LOGSDF=-2.5219682600314
3          %put LOGSDF=%logsdf("POISSON", 2, 1) ;
LOGSDF=-2.5219682600314
4          %put LOGSDF=%logsdf(POISSON) ;
NOTE:  Argument 2 to macro function %LOGSDF is missing or out of range.
LOGSDF=.
5          %put LOGSDF=%logsdf(POISSON, 2) ;
NOTE:  Argument 3 to macro function %LOGSDF is missing or out of range.
LOGSDF=.
```

SAS Listing
This sample program does not have any listing output.

%MACEPS

Purpose
Returns the machine precision constant

Syntax
%maceps

See Also
%CONSTANT

Example

Sample Program
```
%put MACEPS=%maceps ;
```

SAS Log
```
1          %put MACEPS=%maceps ;
MACEPS=2.2204460492503E-16
```

SAS Listing
This sample program does not have any listing output.

%MAX

Purpose
MAX macro function similar to the MAX data step function. It returns the largest value

Syntax
%max (argument, argument, . . .)

    argument is numeric. At least two arguments are required.

See Also
%CSS, %VAR, %N, %NMISS, %SUM, %SKEWNESS, %KURTOSIS, %RANGE, %CV, %USS, %STD, %STDERR, %MIN, %MAX

Example

Sample Program
```
%put MAX=%max(1,2,3,4,5) ;
%put MAX=%max(1,2,A,4,5) ;
%put MAX=%max ;
%put MAX=%max(1) ;
```

SAS Log
```
1          %put MAX=%max(1,2,3,4,5) ;
```

```
MAX=5
2          %put MAX=%max(1,2,A,4,5) ;
NOTE: Invalid numeric data A in Argument 3 for macro function %MAX.
MAX=.
3          %put MAX=%max ;
NOTE: Argument 1 to macro function %MAX is missing or out of range.
MAX=.
4          %put MAX=%max(1) ;
NOTE: Argument 2 to macro function %MAX is missing or out of range.
MAX=.
```

SAS Listing

This sample program does not have any listing output.

%MEAN

Purpose

MEAN macro function similar to the MEAN data step function. It returns the arithmetic mean.

Syntax

%mean (argument, argument, . . .)

argument is numeric. At least one argument id required.

See Also

%CSS, %VAR, %N, %NMISS, %SUM, %SKEWNESS, %KURTOSIS, %RANGE, %CV, %USS, %STD, %STDERR, %MIN, %MAX

Example

Sample Program

```
%put MEAN=%mean(1,2,3,4,5) ;
%put MEAN=%mean(1,2,A,4,5) ;
%put MEAN=%mean ;
%put MEAN=%mean(1) ;
%put MEAN=%mean(1,2,3,4,.) ;
```

SAS Log

```
1          %put MEAN=%mean(1,2,3,4,5) ;
MEAN=3
2          %put MEAN=%mean(1,2,A,4,5) ;
NOTE: Invalid numeric data A in argument 3 for macro function %MEAN.
MEAN=.
3          %put MEAN=%mean ;
NOTE: Argument 1 to macro function %MEAN is missing or out of range.
MEAN=.
4          %put MEAN=%mean(1) ;
MEAN=1
5          %put MEAN=%mean(1,2,3,4,.) ;
MEAN=2.5
```

SAS Listing

This sample program does not have any listing output.

%MEM

Purpose

This macro creates a SAS data set containing the OS memory for the Windows Operating System.

Syntax

%mem (out = _SAS_Output_data_set, [required]

<,DEBUG = YES | Y | NO | N>)

See Also

%COMMAND, %DOSPATH, %DIRECTORY, %CURRENTPATH, %FINDFILE, %SYSVARS, %DATAPATH, %DATAMEM, and %MEM

Example

Sample Program

```
%mem (out=memory)

proc print data=memory label ;
run ;
```

SAS Log

```
11   %mem (out=memory)
NOTE: The data set WORK.MEMORY has 7 observations and 2 variables.
NOTE: The MACRO %MEM used:
      real time          0.49 seconds
      cpu time           unknown

12
13   proc print data=memory label ;
14   run ;

NOTE: There were 7 observations read from the data set WORK.MEMORY.
NOTE: PROCEDURE PRINT used:
      real time          0.01 seconds
      cpu time           0.00 seconds
```

SAS Listing

Obs	Memory Descriptor	Memory
1	bytes total conventional memory	655,360
2	bytes available to MS-DOS	655,360
3	largest executable program size	628,592
4	bytes total contiguous extended memory	1,048,576
5	bytes available contiguous extended memory	0
6	bytes available XMS memory	941,056
7	MS-DOS resident in High Memory Area	.

%MIN

Purpose
MIN macro function similar to the MIN data step function. It returns the smallest value

Syntax
%min (argument, argument, . . .)

> *argument* is numeric. At least two arguments are required.

See Also
%CSS, %VAR, %N, %NMISS, %SUM, %SKEWNESS, %KURTOSIS, %RANGE, %CV, %USS, %STD, %STDERR, %MIN, %MAX

Example

Sample Program
```
%put MIN=%min(1,2,3,4,5) ;
%put MIN=%min(1,2,A,4,5) ;
%put MIN=%min ;
%put MIN=%min(1) ;
```

SAS Log
```
1          %put MIN=%min(1,2,3,4,5) ;
MIN=1
2          %put MIN=%min(1,2,A,4,5) ;
NOTE:   Invalid numeric data A in Argument 3 for macro function %MIN.
MIN=.
3          %put MIN=%min ;
NOTE:   Argument 1 to macro function %MIN is missing or out of range.
MIN=.
4          %put MIN=%min(1) ;
NOTE:   Argument 2 to macro function %MIN is missing or out of range.
MIN=.
```

SAS Listing
This sample program does not have any listing output.

%MORT

Purpose
Returns amortization parameters

Syntax
%MORT(a,p,r,n)

> *a* is numeric, the initial amount.
>
> *p* is numeric, the periodic payment.
>
> *r* is numeric, the periodic interest rate that is expressed as a fraction.

n is an integer, the number of compounding periods. Range: n>=0

See Also
%SAVING, %COMPOUND, %MORT

Notes
The MORT function returns the missing argument in the list of four arguments from an amortization calculation with a fixed interest rate that is compounded each period. One missing argument must be provided. It is then calculated from the remaining three. No adjustment is made to convert the results to round numbers.

Example

Sample Program
```
%put MORT=%mort(50000, . , .10/12,30*12) ;
```

SAS Log
```
1          %put MORT=%mort(50000, . , .10/12,30*12) ;
MORT=438.785785044251
```

SAS Listing
This sample program does not have any listing output.

%MPUT

Purpose
MPUT macro function similar to the PUT data step function. It returns a value using a specified format

Syntax
%mput(string, format)

> *string* is a character expression
>
> *format* is character or numeric format

Notes
The macro MPUT is the macro version of the PUT function. It has a different name because PUT is a reserved word in the SAS Macro language.

Example

Sample Program
```
%put MPUT("&sysdate"d, date9.) = %mput("&sysdate"d, date9.) ;

proc format ;
   value $xyz 'XYZ' = 'FORMAT VALUE' ;
run ;

%put MPUT(XYZ, $XYZ) = %mput(XYZ, $XYZ.) ;
```

SAS Log

```
1    %put MPUT("&sysdate"d, date9.) = %mput("&sysdate"d, date9.) ;
MPUT("06JUL06"d, date9.) =
2
3    proc format ;
4       value $xyz 'XYZ' = 'FORMAT VALUE' ;
NOTE: Format $XYZ has been output.
5    run ;

NOTE: PROCEDURE FORMAT used:
      real time           0.04 seconds
      cpu time            0.00 seconds

6
7    %put MPUT(XYZ, $XYZ) = %mput(XYZ, $XYZ.) ;
MPUT(XYZ, $XYZ) = FORMAT VALUE
```

SAS Listing

This sample program does not have any listing output.

%N

Purpose
N macro function similar to the N data step function. It returns the number of the non-missing numeric arguments.

Syntax
%n(argument, . . .)

> *argument* is numeric. At least one argument is required.

See Also
%CSS, %VAR, %N, %NMISS, %SUM, %SKEWNESS, %KURTOSIS, %RANGE, %CV, %USS, %STD, %STDERR, %MIN, %MAX

Example

Sample Program
```
%put N=%n(1,2,3,4,5) ;
%put N=%n(1,2,A,4,5) ;
%put N=%n(1,2,.,.) ;
%put N=%n ;
%put N=%n(1) ;
```

SAS Log
```
1          %put N=%n(1,2,3,4,5) ;
N=5
2          %put N=%n(1,2,A,4,5) ;
NOTE: Invalid numeric data A in argument 3 for macro function %N.
N=.
3          %put N=%n(1,2,.,.) ;
N=2
4          %put N=%n ;
NOTE: Argument 1 to macro function %N is missing or out of range.
N=.
5          %put N=%n(1) ;
N=1
```

SAS Listing
This sample program does not have any listing output.

%NAME

Purpose
NAME macro function takes a given input string and returns a valid SAS Name of 32 characters or less.

Syntax
%name(argument, <length>)

> *ARGUMENT* is any string
>
> *LENGTH* (optional) is the length of the result. The default is 32.

Notes

This macro takes a given input string and creates a valid SAS name from the information given. It removes special characters, ensures that the first character is A-Z or underscore, replaces side-by-side blanks with a single blank, and replaces blanks with an underscore. This macro could be used to generate a valid SAS variable from a given string. It does NOT verify that the result does not already exist in a given library, data set, etc. If the input string ARGUMENT contains a COMMA, it must be called inside the %STR() function.

Example

Sample Program

```
%put NAME=%name(make a     name) ;
%put NAME=%name("make a     name") ;
%put NAME=%name(%str("make,a,name")) ;
%put NAME=%name(make a na$me) ;
%put NAME=%name(1make a na$me) ;
%put NAME=%name(!make a na$me) ;
%put NAME=%name(1make a na$me from a very long phrase that is over 32 characters in length) ;
%put NAME=%name(1make a na$me from a very long phrase that is over 32 characters in length, 8) ;
%put NAME=%name(1) ;
%put NAME=%name(%str(1make, a na$me)) ;
%put NAME=%name ;
```

SAS Log

```
1          %put NAME=%name(make a     name) ;
NAME=MAKE_A_NAME
2          %put NAME=%name("make a     name") ;
NAME=MAKE_A_NAME
3          %put NAME=%name(%str("make,a,name")) ;
NAME=MAKEANAME
4          %put NAME=%name(make a na$me) ;
NAME=MAKE_A_NAME
5          %put NAME=%name(1make a na$me) ;
NAME=_1MAKE_A_NAME
6          %put NAME=%name(!make a na$me) ;
NAME=MAKE_A_NAME
7          %put NAME=%name(1make a na$me from a very long phrase that is over 32 characters in
7        ! length) ;
NAME=_1MAKE_A_NAME_FROM_A_VERY_LONG_P
8          %put NAME=%name(1make a na$me from a very long phrase that is over 32 characters in
8        ! length, 8) ;
NAME=_1MAKE_A
9          %put NAME=%name(1) ;
NAME=_1
10         %put NAME=%name(%str(1make, a na$me)) ;
NAME=_1MAKE_A_NAME
```

```
11          %put NAME=%name ;
NAME=_
```

SAS Listing

This sample program does not have any listing output.

%NETPV

Purpose

Returns the net present value as a fraction

Syntax

%NETPV(r,freq,c0,c1, . . . ,cn)

>*r* is numeric, the interest rate over a specified base period of time expressed as a fraction.
>
>*freq* is numeric, the number of payments during the base period of time that is specified with the rate r. Range: freq > 0 Exception: The case freq = 0 is a flag to allow continuous discounting.
>
>*c1-cn* are numeric cash flows that represent cash outlays (payments) or cash inflows (income) occurring at times 0, 1, ... n. These cash flows are assumed to be equally spaced, beginning of period values. Negative values represent payments, positive values represent income, and values of 0 represent no cash flow at a given time. The c0 argument and the c1 argument are required.

See Also

%NETPV, %NPV

Notes

The NETPV function returns the net present value at time 0 for the set of cash payments $c_0, c_1, \ldots, c_n$, with a rate r over a specified base period of time. The argument freq>0 describes the number of payments that occur over the specified base period of time. Missing values in the payments are treated as 0 values. When freq>0, the rate r is the effective rate over the specified base period. To compute with a quarterly rate (the base period is three months) of 4 percent with monthly cash payments, set freq to 3 and set r to .04. If freq is 0, continuous discounting is assumed.

The base period is the time interval between two consecutive payments, and the rate r is a nominal rate. To compute with a nominal annual interest rate of 11 pct discounted continuously with monthly pmts, set freq to 0 and set r to .11/12.

Example

Sample Program

```
%put NETPV=%netpv(.10,.5,-500,200,300,400) ;
```

SAS Log

```
1           %put NETPV=%netpv(.10,.5,-500,200,300,400) ;
NETPV=95.982864829379
```

SAS Listing

This sample program does not have any listing output.

%NEXTDATA

Purpose
The macro %NEXTDATA returns the next available new data set in the given libname (i.e. WORK.DATAn).

Syntax
%NEXTDATA (*libname*)

>*libname* is the SAS libname to create the new data set in. If the LIBNAME does not exist, the macro defaults to the WORK libname

See Also
%DATA, %NEXTDATA

Example

Sample Program
```
%put The next freely-available data set name is %nextdata(work) ;

data data1 ;
   i = 1 ;
run ;

%put The next freely-available data set name is %nextdata(work) ;
```

SAS Log
```
1    %put The next freely-available data set name is %nextdata(work) ;
The next freely-available data set name is WORK.DATA1
2
3    data data1 ;
4       i = 1 ;
5    run ;

NOTE: The data set WORK.DATA1 has 1 observations and 1 variables.
NOTE: DATA statement used:
      real time           0.01 seconds
      cpu time            0.01 seconds

6
7    %put The next freely-available data set name is %nextdata(work) ;
The next freely-available data set name is WORK.DATA2
```

SAS Listing
This sample program does not have any listing output.

%NMISS

Purpose
NMISS macro function similar to the NMISS data step function. It returns the number of the missing numeric arguments.

Syntax

%nmiss(argument, . . .)

> *argument* is numeric. At least one argument is required.

See Also

%CSS, %VAR, %N, %NMISS, %SUM, %SKEWNESS, %KURTOSIS, %RANGE, %CV, %USS, %STD, %STDERR, %MIN, %MAX

Example

Sample Program

```
%put NMISS=%nmiss(1,2,3,4,5) ;
%put NMISS=%nmiss(1,2,A,4,5) ;
%put NMISS=%nmiss(1,2,.,.) ;
%put NMISS=%nmiss ;
%put NMISS=%nmiss(1) ;
```

SAS Log

```
1          %put NMISS=%nmiss(1,2,3,4,5) ;
NMISS=0
2          %put NMISS=%nmiss(1,2,A,4,5) ;
NOTE:  Invalid numeric data A in argument 3 for macro function %NMISS.
NMISS=.
3          %put NMISS=%nmiss(1,2,.,.) ;
NMISS=2
4          %put NMISS=%nmiss ;
NOTE:  Argument 1 to macro function %NMISS is missing or out of range.
NMISS=.
5          %put NMISS=%nmiss(1) ;
NMISS=0
```

SAS Listing

This sample program does not have any listing output.

%NORMAL

Purpose
NORMAL macro function similar to the NORMAL data step function. It returns a random variate from a normal distribution.

Syntax
%normal(seed)

>*SEED* is a positive integer

See Also
%NORMAL, %UNIFORM, %RANBINARY, %RANBIN, %RANCAU, %RANEXP, %RANGAM, %RANNOR, %RANPOI, %RANTRI, %RANUNI

Example

Sample Program
```
%put NORMAL(4) = %normal(4) ;
```

SAS Log
```
1          %put NORMAL(4) = %normal(4) ;
NORMAL(4) = 0.56706919864237
```

SAS Listing
This sample program does not have any listing output.

%NPV

Purpose
Returns the net present value with the rate expressed as a percentage

Syntax
%NPV(r,freq,c0,c1, . . . ,cn)

>*r* is numeric, the interest rate over a specified base period of time expressed as a percentage.
>
>*freq* is numeric, the number of payments during the base period of time that is specified with the rate r. Range: freq > 0 Exception: The case freq = 0 is a flag to allow continuous discounting.
>
>*c1-cn* are numeric cash flows that represent cash outlays (payments) or cash inflows (income) occurring at times 0, 1, ... n. These cash flows are assumed to be equally spaced, beginning of period values. Negative values represent payments, positive values represent income, and values of 0 represent no cash flow at a given time. The c0 argument and the c1 argument are required.

See Also
%NETPV, %NPV

Notes
The NPV function is identical to NETPV, except that the r argument is provided as a percentage.

Example

Sample Program
```
%put NPV=%npv(10,.5,-500,200,300,400) ;
```

SAS Log
```
1          %put NPV=%npv(10,.5,-500,200,300,400) ;
NPV=95.982864829379
```

SAS Listing
This sample program does not have any listing output.

%NUMERIC

Purpose
Returns a list of all numeric variables in a given SAS data set

Syntax
%numeric (data)

data is a valid SAS data set name. The data set must exist.

See Also
%CHARACTER, %NUMERIC, *CHARACTER*, *NUMERIC*, *ALL*

Notes
If no NUMERIC variables are found in the data set, a NULL STRING is returned. This can be used to get a specific list of NUMERIC variables when the automatic variable *NUMERIC* cannot be used. To create a list of all variables, use both of the macros %CHARACTER and %NUMERIC to build a list.

Example

Sample Program
```
%put Numeric variables in SASHELP.SHOES: %numeric(sashelp.shoes) ;
```

SAS Log
```
1         %put Numeric variables in SASHELP.SHOES: %numeric(sashelp.shoes) ;
Numeric variables in SASHELP.SHOES: Stores Sales Inventory Returns
```

SAS Listing
This sample program does not have any listing output.

%OBSCNT

Purpose
This macro returns the number of observations in a dataset. It does not work on data views or tape datasets. If the macro cannot find a data set it will return the missing value.

Syntax
%obscnt (data)

>*data* is a valid SAS data set name. The data set must exist.

See Also
%OBSCNT, %RECCNT, %VARCNT, %WORDCNT

Example

Sample Program
```
%put NOTE: The number of observations in SASHELP.SHOES is %obscnt(sashelp.shoes) ;
```

SAS Log
```
1          %put NOTE: The number of observations in SASHELP.SHOES is %obscnt(sashelp.shoes) ;
NOTE: The number of observations in SASHELP.SHOES is 395
```

SAS Listing
This sample program does not have any listing output.

%ORDINAL

Purpose
Returns any specified order statistic

Syntax
ORDINAL(count,argument,argument, . . .)

>*count* is an integer that is less than the number of elements in the list of arguments.
>
>*argument* is numeric. At least two arguments are required.

Notes
The ORDINAL function sorts the list and returns the nth argument in the list.

Example

Sample Program
```
%put ORDINAL=%ordinal(3, 1, 2, 3, 4) ;
%put ORDINAL=%ordinal(3, 1, 2, A, 4) ;
%put ORDINAL=%ordinal(37, 1, 2, 3, 4) ;
%put ORDINAL=%ordinal ;
```

```
%put ORDINAL=%ordinal(37) ;
%put ORDINAL=%ordinal(1, 1) ;
```

SAS Log

```
1          %put ORDINAL=%ordinal(3, 1, 2, 3, 4) ;
ORDINAL=3
2          %put ORDINAL=%ordinal(3, 1, 2, A, 4) ;
NOTE:  Invalid numeric data A in argument 4 for macro function %ORDINAL.
ORDINAL=.
3          %put ORDINAL=%ordinal(37, 1, 2, 3, 4) ;
NOTE: Argument 1 to macro %ORDINAL is missing or out of range.
ORDINAL=.
4          %put ORDINAL=%ordinal ;
NOTE: Argument 1 to macro %ORDINAL is missing or out of range.
ORDINAL=.
5          %put ORDINAL=%ordinal(37) ;
NOTE:  Argument 2 to macro function %ORDINAL is missing or out of range.
ORDINAL=.
6          %put ORDINAL=%ordinal(1, 1) ;
NOTE:  Argument 3 to macro function %ORDINAL is missing or out of range.
ORDINAL=.
```

SAS Listing

This sample program does not have any listing output.

%PFD

Purpose

PDF macro function similar to the PDF data step function. It computes probability density (mass) functions.

Syntax

%PDF (dist,quantile,parm-1, . . . ,parm-k)

> *dist* is a character string that identifies the distribution. Valid distributions are as follows:
>
> - Bernoulli - BERNOULLI
> - Beta - BETA
> - Binomial - BINOMIAL
> - Cauchy - CAUCHY
> - Chi squared - CHISQUARED
> - Exponential - EXPONENTIAL
> - F - F
> - Gamma - GAMMA
> - Geometric - GEOMETRIC
> - Hypergeometric - HYPERGEOMETRIC
> - Laplace - LAPLACE
> - Logistic - LOGISTIC
> - Lognormal - LOGNORMAL
> - Negative binomial - NEGBINOMIAL
> - Normal - NORMAL or GAUSS
> - Pareto - PARETO
> - Poisson - POISSON
> - T - T

- Uniform - UNIFORM
- Wald (inverse Gaussian) - WALD or IGAUSS
- Weibull - WEIBULL

Note: Except for T and F, any distribution can be minimally identified by its first four characters. To keep with the spirit of the data step function PDF, the DIST option can be quoted or unquoted (unquoted is preferred).

quantile is a numeric random variable.

parm-1, . . . ,parm-k are shape, location, or scale parameters appropriate for the specific distribution. See the description for each distribution in Details under the HELP library for the data step function PDF for complete information about these parameters.

See Also
%CDF, %LOGCDF, %PDF, %SDF, %LOGSDF

Example

Sample Program
```
%put PDF=%pdf(POISSON, 2, 1) ;
%put PDF=%pdf('POISSON', 2, 1) ;
%put PDF=%pdf("POISSON", 2, 1) ;
%put PDF=%pdf(POISSON) ;
%put PDF=%pdf(POISSON, 2) ;
```

SAS Log
```
1          %put PDF=%pdf(POISSON, 2, 1) ;
PDF=0.18393972058572
2          %put PDF=%pdf('POISSON', 2, 1) ;
PDF=0.18393972058572
3          %put PDF=%pdf("POISSON", 2, 1) ;
PDF=0.18393972058572
4          %put PDF=%pdf(POISSON) ;
NOTE: Argument 2 to macro function %PDF is missing or out of range.
PDF=.
5          %put PDF=%pdf(POISSON, 2) ;
NOTE: Argument 3 to macro function %PDF is missing or out of range.
PDF=.
```

SAS Listing
This sample program does not have any listing output.

%PERM

Purpose
PERM macro function similar to the PERM data step function. It computes the number of permutations of n items taken r at a time and returns a value.

Syntax
%perm(PERM(n, r)

    n is an integer that represents the total number of elements from which the sample is chosen.

r is an integer value that represents the number of chosen elements.

Example

Sample Program
```
%put PERM(5,1) = %perm(5,1) ;
```

SAS Log
```
1          %put PERM(5,1) = %perm(5,1) ;
PERM(5,1) = 5
```

SAS Listing
This sample program does not have any listing output.

%PI

Purpose
Returns the approximate value of PI

Syntax
%pi

See Also
%CONSTANT

Example

Sample Program
```
%put PI=%pi ;
```

SAS Log
```
1          %put PI=%pi ;
PI=3.14159265358979
```

SAS Listing
This sample program does not have any listing output.

%POISSON

Purpose
POISSON macro function similar to the POISSON data step function. It returns the probability from a Poisson distribution.

Syntax
%poisson(m,n)

m is a numeric mean parameter. Range: m >= 0

n is an integer random variable. Range: n >= 0

Example

Sample Program
```
%put POISSON(5, 1) = %poisson(5, 1) ;
```

SAS Log
```
1          %put POISSON(5, 1) = %poisson(5, 1) ;
POISSON(5, 1) = 0.04042768199451
```

SAS Listing
This sample program does not have any listing output.

%PREFIX

Purpose
This macro adds the same prefix to a suffix list.

Syntax
%prefix(list, suffix, <dlm>)

    list is a list of space-delimited strings

    suffix is a string of characters

    dlm (optional) is the delimiter. Default is a blank space.

See Also
%PREFIX, %SUFFIX, %STRING, %REPEAT

Example

Sample Program
```
%put %prefix (Larry. Curly. Moe., My favorite stooge is) ;
%put %prefix (Larry. Curly. Moe., %str( My favorite stooge is )) ;
%put %prefix (a.b.c.d.e, N, .) ;
```

SAS Log
```
1          %put %prefix (Larry. Curly. Moe., My favorite stooge is) ;
My favorite stooge isLarry. My favorite stooge isCurly. My favorite stooge isMoe
2          %put %prefix (Larry. Curly. Moe., %str( My favorite stooge is )) ;
My favorite stooge is Larry.  My favorite stooge is Curly.  My favorite stooge is Moe.
3          %put %prefix (a.b.c.d.e, N, .) ;
.Na.Nb.Nc.Nd.Ne
```

SAS Listing
This sample program does not have any listing output.

%PROBBETA

Purpose
PROBBETA macro function similar to the PROBBETA data step function. It returns the probability from a beta distribution.

Syntax
%probbeta(x,a,b)

>*x* is a numeric random variable. Range: $0 <= x <= 1$
>
>*a* is a numeric shape parameter. Range: $a > 0$
>
>*b* is a numeric shape parameter. Range: $b > 0$

See Also
%PROBT, %PROBNORM, %PROBNEGB, %PROBIT, %PROBHYPR, %PROBGAM, %PROBF, %PROBCHI, %PROBBNRM, %PROBNML, %PROBBETA

Notes
The PROBBETA function returns the probability that an observation from a beta distribution, with shape parameters a and b, is less than or equal to x.

Example

Sample Program
```
%put PROBBETA = %probbeta(.2,3,4) ;
```

SAS Log
```
1          %put PROBBETA = %probbeta(.2,3,4) ;
PROBBETA = 0.09888
```

SAS Listing
This sample program does not have any listing output.

%PROBBNML

Purpose
PROBBNML macro function similar to the PROBBNML data step function. Returns the probability from a binomial distribution.

Syntax
%probbnml(p,n,m)

>*p* is a numeric probability of success parameter. RANGE: $0 <= p <= 1$
>
>*n* is the number of Bernoulli trials parameter (positive integer)
>
>*m* is an integer representing the number of successes random var. RANGE: $0 <= m <= n$

See Also

%PROBT, %PROBNORM, %PROBNEGB, %PROBIT, %PROBHYPR, %PROBGAM, %PROBF, %PROBCHI, %PROBBNRM, %PROBNML, %PROBBETA

Notes

The PROBBNML function returns the probability that an observation from a binomial distribution, with probability of success p, number of trials n, and number of successes m, is less than or equal to m. To compute the probability that an observation is equal to a given value m, compute the difference of two probabilities from the binomial distribution for m and m-1 successes.

Example

Sample Program

```
%put PROBBNML(0.5,10,4) = %probbnml(0.5,10,4) ;
```

SAS Log

```
1          %put PROBBNML(0.5,10,4) = %probbnml(0.5,10,4) ;
PROBBNML(0.5,10,4) = 0.376953125
```

SAS Listing

This sample program does not have any listing output.

%PROBBNRM

Purpose

PROBBNRM macro function similar to the PROBBNRM data step function. It computes a probability from the bivariate normal distribution and returns a value

Syntax

%probbnrm(x,y,r)

    x is a numeric variable.

    y is a numeric variable.

    r is a numeric correlation coefficient. Range: $-1 \le r \le 1$

See Also

%PROBT, %PROBNORM, %PROBNEGB, %PROBIT, %PROBHYPR, %PROBGAM, %PROBF, %PROBCHI, %PROBBNRM, %PROBNML, %PROBBETA

Notes

The PROBBNRM function returns the probability that an observation (X, Y) from a standardized bivariate normal distribution of mean 0, variance 1, and a correlation coefficient r, is less than or equal to (x, y). That is, it returns the probability that Xx and Yy.

Example

Sample Program
```
%put PROBBNRM(.4,-3,.2) = %probbnrm(.4, -3, .2) ;
```

SAS Log
```
1          %put PROBBNRM(.4,-3,.2) = %probbnrm(.4, -3, .2) ;
PROBBNRM(.4,-3,.2) = 0.00115986372159
```

SAS Listing
This sample program does not have any listing output.

%PROBCHI

Purpose
PROBCHI macro function similar to the PROBCHI data step function. It returns the probability from a chi-squared distribution.

Syntax
%probchi(x, df, nc)

    x is a numeric random variable. Range: x >= 0

    df is the numeric degrees of freedom parameter. Range: df > 0

    nc is the numeric non-centrality parameter. Range: nc >= 0

See Also
%PROBT, %PROBNORM, %PROBNEGB, %PROBIT, %PROBHYPR, %PROBGAM, %PROBF, %PROBCHI, %PROBBNRM, %PROBNML, %PROBBETA

Notes
The PROBCHI function returns the probability that an observation from a chi-square distribution, with degrees of freedom df and non-centrality parameter nc, is less than or equal to x. This function accepts a non-integer degrees of freedom parameter df. In DATA STEP function PROBCHI(), the value NC is optional, but in the macro function it is required.

Example

Sample Program
```
%put PROBCHI(11.264,11, 0) = %probchi(11.264,11, 0) ;
%put PROBCHI(11.264,11, 2) = %probchi(11.264,11, 2) ;
```

SAS Log
```
1          %put PROBCHI(11.264,11, 0) = %probchi(11.264,11, 0) ;
PROBCHI(11.264,11, 0) = 0.5785813293173
2          %put PROBCHI(11.264,11, 2) = %probchi(11.264,11, 2) ;
PROBCHI(11.264,11, 2) = 0.42424778162633
```

SAS Listing
This sample program does not have any listing output.

%PROBF

Purpose
PROBF macro function similar to the PROBF data step function. It returns the probability from an F distribution.

Syntax
%probf (x, ndf, ddf, nc)

>*x* is a numeric random variable. Range: x >= 0
>
>*ndf* is the numeric numerator degrees of freedom parameter. ndf > 0
>
>*ddf* is the numeric denominator degrees of freedom parameter. ddf >0
>
>*nc* is the numeric non-centrality parameter. nc >= 0

See Also
%PROBT, %PROBNORM, %PROBNEGB, %PROBIT, %PROBHYPR, %PROBGAM, %PROBF, %PROBCHI, %PROBBNRM, %PROBNML, %PROBBETA

Notes
The PROBF function returns the probability that an observation from an F distribution, with numerator degrees of freedom ndf, denominator degrees of freedom ddf, and non-centrality parameter nc, is less than or equal to x. The PROBF function accepts non-integer degrees of freedom parameters ndf and ddf. The significance level for an F test statistic is given by the equation p = 1-probf(x,ndf,ddf).

Example

Sample Program
```
%put PROBF(3.32,2,3, 0) = %probf(3.32,2,3, 0) ;
%put PROBF(3.32,2,3, 2) = %probf(3.32,2,3, 2) ;
```

SAS Log
```
1          %put PROBF(3.32,2,3, 0) = %probf(3.32,2,3, 0) ;
PROBF(3.32,2,3, 0) = 0.82639336022431
2          %put PROBF(3.32,2,3, 2) = %probf(3.32,2,3, 2) ;
PROBF(3.32,2,3, 2) = 0.66010728681924
```

SAS Listing
This sample program does not have any listing output.

%PROBGAM

Purpose
PROBGAM macro function similar to the PROBGAM data step function. It returns the probability from a gamma distribution.

Syntax
%probgam(x,a)

> *x* is a non-negative numeric random variable
>
> *a* is a positve numeric shape parameter

See Also
%PROBT, %PROBNORM, %PROBNEGB, %PROBIT, %PROBHYPR, %PROBGAM, %PROBF, %PROBCHI, %PROBBNRM, %PROBNML, %PROBBETA

Notes
The PROBGAM function returns the probability that an observation from a gamma distribution, with shape parameter a, is less than or equal to x.

Example

Sample Program
```
%put PROBGAM = %probgam(.2,3) ;
```

SAS Log
```
1          %put PROBGAM = %probgam(.2,3) ;
PROBGAM = 0.00114848124486
```

SAS Listing
This sample program does not have any listing output.

%PROBHYPR

Purpose
PROBHYPR macro function similar to the PROBHYPR data step function. It returns the probability from a hyper-geometric distribution.

Syntax
%probhypr(S,K,n,x,r)

> *S* is a positive integer population size parameter
>
> *K* is an integer representing the number of items in the category of interest parameter Range: 0 <= K <= S
>
> *n* is the integer sample size parameter. Range: 0 <= n <= S

x is the integer random variable. Range: max(0, K + n-S) <= x <= min(K,n)

r is the numeric odds ratio parameter. Range: r >= 0

See Also
%PROBT, %PROBNORM, %PROBNEGB, %PROBIT, %PROBHYPR, %PROBGAM, %PROBF, %PROBCHI, %PROBBNRM, %PROBNML, %PROBBETA

Notes
The PROBHYPR function returns the probability that an observation from an extended hyper-geometric distribution, with population size S, number of items K, sample size n, and odds ratio r, is less than or equal to x.

Example

Sample Program
```
%put PROBHYPR(200,50,10,2,1) = %probhypr(200,50,10,2,1) ;
```

SAS Log
```
1          %put PROBHYPR(200,50,10,2,1) = %probhypr(200,50,10,2,1) ;
PROBHYPR(200,50,10,2,1) = 0.52367340812159
```

SAS Listing
This sample program does not have any listing output.

%PROBIT

Purpose
PROBIT macro function similar to the PROBIT data step function. It returns a quantile from the standard normal distribution.

Syntax
%probit (p)

p is the numeric probability. Range: 0 <= p < 1

See Also
%PROBT, %PROBNORM, %PROBNEGB, %PROBIT, %PROBHYPR, %PROBGAM, %PROBF, %PROBCHI, %PROBBNRM, %PROBNML, %PROBBETA

Example

Sample Program
```
%put PROBIT(.5) = %probit(.5) ;
```

SAS Log
```
1          %put PROBIT(.5) = %probit(.5) ;
PROBIT(.5) = -4.0637937369081E-17
```

SAS Listing
This sample program does not have any listing output.

%PROBNEGB

Purpose
PROBNEGB macro function similar to the PROBNEGB data step function. It returns the probability from a negative binomial distribution.

Syntax
%probnegb (p, n, m)

  p is the numeric probability of success parameter. Range: $0 <= p <= 1$

  n is the positive integer number of successes parameter

  m is the positive integer random variable, the number of failures

See Also
%PROBT, %PROBNORM, %PROBNEGB, %PROBIT, %PROBHYPR, %PROBGAM, %PROBF, %PROBCHI, %PROBBNRM, %PROBNML, %PROBBETA

Notes
The PROBNEGB function returns the probability that an observation from a negative binomial distribution, with probability of success p and number of successes n, is less than or equal to m. To compute the probability that an observation is equal to a given value m, compute the difference of two probabilities from the negative binomial distribution for m and m-1.

Example

Sample Program
```
%put PROBNEGB(0.5,2,1) = %probnegb(0.5,2,1) ;
```

SAS Log
```
1          %put PROBNEGB(0.5,2,1) = %probnegb(0.5,2,1) ;
PROBNEGB(0.5,2,1) = 0.5
```

SAS Listing
This sample program does not have any listing output.

%PROBNORM

Purpose
PROBNORM macro function similar to the PROBNORM data step function. It returns the probability from the standard normal distribution.

Syntax

%probnorm (x)

>*x* is a numeric random variable

See Also

%PROBT, %PROBNORM, %PROBNEGB, %PROBIT, %PROBHYPR, %PROBGAM, %PROBF, %PROBCHI, %PROBBNRM, %PROBNML, %PROBBETA

Notes

The PROBNORM function returns the probability that an observation from the standard normal distribution is less than or equal to x.

Example

Sample Program

```
%put PROBNORM(.5) = %probnorm(.5) ;
```

SAS Log

```
1          %put PROBNORM(.5) = %probnorm(.5) ;
PROBNORM(.5) = 0.69146246127401
```

SAS Listing

This sample program does not have any listing output.

%PROBT

Purpose

PROBT macro function similar to the PROBT data step function. It returns the probability from a *t* distribution.

Syntax

%probt(x,df,nc)

>*x* is a numeric random variable.
>
>*df* is the numeric degrees of freedom parameter. Range: df > 0
>
>*nc* is the numeric non-centrality parameter

See Also

%PROBT, %PROBNORM, %PROBNEGB, %PROBIT, %PROBHYPR, %PROBGAM, %PROBF, %PROBCHI, %PROBBNRM, %PROBNML, %PROBBETA

Notes

The PROBT function returns the probability that an observation from a Students T distribution, with degrees of freedom df and non-centrality parameter nc, is less than or equal to x. This function accepts a non-integer degree of freedom parameter df. The significance level of a two-tailed t test is given by the equation p = (1-probt(abs(x),df))*2

Example

Sample Program
```
%put PROBT(0.9,5,0) = %probt(0.9,5, 0) ;
```

SAS Log
```
1          %put PROBT(0.9,5,0) = %probt(0.9,5, 0) ;
PROBT(0.9,5,0) = 0.79531439982768
```

SAS Listing
This sample program does not have any listing output.

%RANBIN

Purpose
RANBIN macro function similar to the RANBIN data step function. It returns a random variate from a binomial distribution.

Syntax
%ranbin(seed, n, p)

>*seed* is an integer. If seed <= 0, the time of day is used to initialize the seed stream.
>
>*n* is a positive integer representing the number of Bernoulli trials parameter
>
>*p* is the numeric probability of success parameter. Range: $0 < p < 1$

See Also
%NORMAL, %UNIFORM, %RANBINARY, %RANBIN, %RANCAU, %RANEXP, %RANGAM, %RANNOR, %RANPOI, %RANTRI, %RANUNI

Notes
The RANBIN function returns a variate that is generated from a binomial distribution with mean np and variance np(1-p). If n <= 50, np <= 5, or n(1-p) <= 5, an inverse transform method applied to a RANUNI uniform variate is used. If n > 50, np > 5, and n(1-p) > 5, the normal approximation to the binomial distribution is used. In that case, the Box-Muller transformation of RANUNI uniform variates is used.

Example

Sample Program
```
%put RANBIN(5, 5, .5) = %ranbin(5, 5, .5) ;
```

SAS Log
```
1          %put RANBIN(5, 5, .5) = %ranbin(5, 5, .5) ;
RANBIN(5, 5, .5) = 4
```

SAS Listing
This sample program does not have any listing output.

%RANBINARY

Purpose
RANBINARY macro function. It returns a random 1 or 0.

Syntax
%ranbinary(seed)

>*seed* is an integer. If seed <= 0 or missing, the time of day is used to initialize the seed stream.

See Also
%NORMAL, %UNIFORM, %RANBINARY, %RANBIN, %RANCAU, %RANEXP, %RANGAM, %RANNOR, %RANPOI, %RANTRI, %RANUNI

Notes
The ranbinary function randomly returns a 0 or 1 based on a uniform distribution. It simulates a coin toss.

Example

Sample Program
```
%put ranbinary(0) = %ranbinary(0) ;
```

SAS Log
```
1          %put ranbinary(0) = %ranbinary(0) ;
ranbinary(0) = 0
```

SAS Listing
This sample program does not have any listing output.

%RANCAU

Purpose
RANCAU macro function similar to the RANCAU data step function. It returns a random variate from a Cauchy distribution

Syntax
%rancau(seed)

>*seed* is an integer. If seed <= 0, the time of day is used to initialize the seed stream.

See Also
%NORMAL, %UNIFORM, %RANBINARY, %RANBIN, %RANCAU, %RANEXP, %RANGAM, %RANNOR, %RANPOI, %RANTRI, %RANUNI

Notes

The RANCAU function returns a variate that is generated from a Cauchy distribution with location parameter 0 and scale parameter 1. An acceptance-rejection procedure applied to RANUNI uniform variates is used. If u and v are independent uniform (-1/2, ½) variables and $U^2 + V^2 <= ¼$, then u/v is a Cauchy variate. A Cauchy variate X with location parameter ALPHA and scale parameter BETA can be generated with the equation x = alpha+beta*rancau(seed)

Example

Sample Program
```
%put RANCAU(5) = %rancau(5) ;
```

SAS Log
```
1          %put RANCAU(5) = %rancau(5) ;
RANCAU(5) = 0.31182742906868
```

SAS Listing
This sample program does not have any listing output.

%RANEXP

Purpose
RANEXP macro function similar to the RANEXP data step function. It returns a random variate from an exponential distribution.

Syntax
%ranexp(seed)

seed is an integer. If seed <= 0, the time of day is used to initialize the seed stream.

See Also
%NORMAL, %UNIFORM, %RANBINARY, %RANBIN, %RANCAU, %RANEXP, %RANGAM, %RANNOR, %RANPOI, %RANTRI, %RANUNI

Notes
The RANEXP function returns a variate that is generated from an exponential distribution with parameter 1. An inverse transform method applied to a RANUNI uniform variate is used. An exponential variate X with parameter LAMBDA can be generated using the equation x = ranexp(seed)/lambda. An extreme value variate X with location parameter ALPHA and scale parameter BETA can be generated using the equation x = alpha-beta*log(ranexp(seed)). A geometric variate X with parameter P can be generated with the equation x = floor(-ranexp(seed)/log(1-p))

Example

Sample Program
```
%put RANEXP(5) = %ranexp(5) ;
```

SAS Log
```
1          %put RANEXP(5) = %ranexp(5) ;
RANEXP(5) = 0.07816388722631
```

SAS Listing
This sample program does not have any listing output.

%RANGAM

Purpose
RANGAM macro function similar to the RANGAM data step function. It returns a random variate from a gamma distribution

Syntax
%rangam(seed, a)

> *seed* is an integer. If seed <= 0, the time of day is used to initialize the seed stream.
>
> *a* is the positive numeric shape parameter

See Also
%NORMAL, %UNIFORM, %RANBINARY, %RANBIN, %RANCAU, %RANEXP, %RANGAM, %RANNOR, %RANPOI, %RANTRI, %RANUNI

Notes
The RANGAM function returns a variate that is generated from an exponential distribution with parameter 1. An inverse transform method applied to a RANUNI uniform variate is used. An exponential variate X with parameter LAMBDA can be generated using the equation x = rangam(seed)/lambda. An extreme value variate X with location parameter ALPHA and scale parameter BETA can be generated using the equation x = alpha-beta*log(rangam(seed)). A geometric variate X with parameter P can be generated with the equation x = floor(-rangam(seed)/log(1-p))

Example

Sample Program
```
%put RANGAM(5, 1) = %rangam(5, 1) ;
```

SAS Log
```
1          %put RANGAM(5, 1) = %rangam(5, 1) ;
RANGAM(5, 1) = 0.07816388722631
```

SAS Listing
This sample program does not have any listing output.

%RANGE

Purpose
RANGE macro function similar to the RANGE data step function. It returns the range of the values. The RANGE function returns the difference between the largest and the smallest of the non-missing arguments.

Syntax
%range (argument, argument, . . .)

    argument is numeric. At least two arguments are required.

See Also
%CSS, %VAR, %N, %NMISS, %SUM, %SKEWNESS, %KURTOSIS, %RANGE, %CV, %USS, %STD, %STDERR, %MIN, %MAX

Example

Sample Program
```
%put RANGE=%range(1,2,3,4,5) ;
%put RANGE=%range(1,2,A,4,5) ;
%put RANGE=%range ;
%put RANGE=%range(1) ;
```

SAS Log
```
1          %put RANGE=%range(1,2,3,4,5) ;
RANGE=4
2          %put RANGE=%range(1,2,A,4,5) ;
NOTE:  Invalid numeric data A in argument 3 for macro function %RANGE.
RANGE=.
3          %put RANGE=%range ;
NOTE:  Argument 1 to macro function %RANGE is missing or out of range.
RANGE=.
4          %put RANGE=%range(1) ;
NOTE:  Argument 2 to macro function %RANGE is missing or out of range.
RANGE=.
```

SAS Listing
This sample program does not have any listing output.

%RANK

Purpose
RANK macro function similar to the RANK data step function. It returns the position of a character in the ASCII or EBCDIC collating sequence.

Syntax
%rank(c)

    c is a character expression

See Also
%BYTE, %COLLATE, %RANK

Notes
The RANK function returns an integer that represents the position of the first character in the character expression. The result depends on your operating environment.

Example

Sample Program
```
%put RANK(a) = %rank(a) ;
%put RANK(A) = %rank(A) ;
```

SAS Log
```
1          %put RANK(a) = %rank(a) ;
RANK(a) = 97
2          %put RANK(A) = %rank(A) ;
RANK(A) = 65
```

SAS Listing
This sample program does not have any listing output.

%RANNOR

Purpose
RANNOR macro function similar to the RANNOR data step function. It Returns a random variate from a normal distribution

Syntax
%rannor(seed)

    seed is an integer. If seed <= 0, the time of day is used to initialize the seed stream.

See Also
%NORMAL, %UNIFORM, %RANBINARY, %RANBIN, %RANCAU, %RANEXP, %RANGAM, %RANNOR, %RANPOI, %RANTRI, %RANUNI

Notes
The RANNOR function returns a variate that is generated from an exponential distribution with parameter 1. An inverse transform method applied to a RANUNI uniform variate is used. An exponential variate X with parameter LAMBDA can be generated using the equation x = rannor(seed)/lambda. An extreme value variate X with location parameter ALPHA and scale parameter BETA can be generated using the equation x = alpha-beta*log(rannor(seed)). A geometric variate X with parameter P can be generated with the equation x = floor(-rannor(seed)/log(1-p))

Example

Sample Program
```
%put RANNOR(5) = %rannor(5) ;
```

SAS Log
```
1          %put RANNOR(5) = %rannor(5) ;
RANNOR(5) = 0.23329094477573
```

SAS Listing
This sample program does not have any listing output.

%RANPOI

Purpose
RANPOI macro function similar to the RANPOI data step function. It Returns a random variate from a poisson distribution

Syntax
%ranpoi(seed, m)

    seed is an integer. If seed <= 0, the time of day is used to initialize the seed stream.

    m is a positive numeric mean parameter

See Also

%NORMAL, %UNIFORM, %RANBINARY, %RANBIN, %RANCAU, %RANEXP, %RANGAM, %RANNOR, %RANPOI, %RANTRI, %RANUNI

Notes
The RANPOI function returns a variate that is generated from a Poisson distribution with mean m. For m < 85, an inverse transform method applied to a RANUNI uniform variate is used (Fishman 1976). For m >= 85, the normal approximation of a Poisson random variable is used. To expedite execution, internal variables are calculated only on initial calls (that is, with each new m).

Example

Sample Program
```
%put RANPOI(5, 1) = %ranpoi(5, 1) ;
```

SAS Log
```
1          %put RANPOI(5, 1) = %ranpoi(5, 1) ;
RANPOI(5, 1) = 3
```

SAS Listing
This sample program does not have any listing output.

%RANTRI

Purpose
RANTRI macro function similar to the RANTRI data step function. It Returns a random variate from a triangular distribution

Syntax
%rantri(seed, h)

    seed is an integer. If seed <= 0, the time of day is used to initialize the seed stream.

    h is numeric between 0 and 1

See Also
%NORMAL, %UNIFORM, %RANBINARY, %RANBIN, %RANCAU, %RANEXP, %RANGAM, %RANNOR, %RANPOI, %RANTRI, %RANUNI

Notes
The RANTRI function returns a variate that is generated from the triangular distribution on the interval (0,1) with parameter h, which is the modal value of the distribution. An inverse transform method applied to a RANUNI uniform variate is used. A triangular distribution X on the interval [A,B] with mode C, where A C B, can be generated using the equation: x = (b-a)*rantri(seed,(c-a)/(b-a))+a

Example

Sample Program
```
%put RANTRI(5, .) = %rantri(5, .5) ;
```

SAS Log
```
1          %put RANTRI(5, .) = %rantri(5, .5) ;
RANTRI(5, .) = 0.80610937246784
```

SAS Listing
This sample program does not have any listing output.

%RANUNI

Purpose
RANUNI macro function similar to the RANUNI data step function. It returns a random variate from a uniform distribution

Syntax
%ranuni(seed)

    seed is an integer. If seed <= 0, the time of day is used to initialize the seed stream.

See Also
%NORMAL, %UNIFORM, %RANBINARY, %RANBIN, %RANCAU, %RANEXP, %RANGAM, %RANNOR, %RANPOI, %RANTRI, %RANUNI

Notes
The RANUNI function returns a number that is generated from the uniform distribution on the interval (0,1) using a prime modulus multiplicative generator with modulus 231- and multiplier 397204094 (Fishman and Moore 1982). You can use a multiplier to change the length of the interval and an added constant to move the interval. For example, random_variate=a*ranuni(seed)+b returns a number that is generated from the uniform distribution on the interval (b,a+b).

Example

Sample Program
```
%put RANUNI(5) = %ranuni(5) ;
```

SAS Log
```
1          %put RANUNI(5) = %ranuni(5) ;
RANUNI(5) = 0.92481284911037
```

SAS Listing
This sample program does not have any listing output.

%RECCNT

Purpose
This macro returns the number of records in a given file

Syntax
%reccnt (filename)

filename is the file name or file reference to calculate the count.

See Also
%OBSCNT, %RECCNT, %VARCNT, %WORDCNT

Notes
This is not a very efficient macro, but it does work in open code. Present benchmarks show that files of record counts greater than 10,000 will become cumbersome to the system and an alternate method should be used. This macro currently does not work on files of a LRECL greater than 256.

Example

Sample Program
```
filename autoexec '!sasroot\autoexec.sas' ;
%put NOTE: The file AUTOEXEC.SAS has %reccnt(autoexec) records. ;
```

SAS Log

```
1       filename autoexec '!sasroot\autoexec.sas' ;
2       %put NOTE: The file AUTOEXEC.SAS has %reccnt(autoexec) records. ;
NOTE: The file AUTOEXEC.SAS has 168 records.
```

SAS Listing

This sample program does not have any listing output.

%REPEAT

Purpose

REPEAT macro function similar to the REPEAT data step function. It repeats a character expression. The REPEAT function returns a string value consisting of the first argument repeated n times. Thus the first argument appears n+1 times in the result.

Syntax

%REPEAT (argument, n)

> *argument* specifies any SAS character expression. N specifies the number of times to repeat argument. n>0 OPTION:

> *n* may be specified as LS or LINESIZE. This repeats the argument enough times to fill one line of the given output listing. In the event of a rounding issue, it rounds down.

See Also

%PREFIX, %SUFFIX, %STRING, %REPEAT

Example

Sample Program

```
%put REPEAT=%repeat(string, 1) ;
%put REPEAT=%repeat(a, 4) ;
%put %repeat(_, LS) ;
%put %repeat(-:, LINESIZE) ;
%put REPEAT=%repeat ;
%put REPEAT=%repeat(1) ;
%put REPEAT=%repeat(1, 1.4) ;
%put REPEAT=%repeat(1, 0) ;
```

SAS Log

```
1         %put REPEAT=%repeat(string, 1) ;
REPEAT=stringstring
2         %put REPEAT=%repeat(a, 4) ;
REPEAT=aaaaa
3         %put %repeat(_, LS) ;
_____
4         %put %repeat(-:, LINESIZE) ;
-:-:-:-:-:-:-:-:-:-:-:-:-:-:-:-:-:-:-:-:-:-:-:-:-:-:-:-:-:-:-:-:
5         %put REPEAT=%repeat ;
NOTE: Argument 1 to macro function %REPEAT is missing or out of range.
REPEAT=.
6         %put REPEAT=%repeat(1) ;
NOTE: Argument 2 to macro function %REPEAT is missing or out of range.
REPEAT=.
```

```
7          %put REPEAT=%repeat(1, 1.4) ;
NOTE: Argument 2 to macro function %REPEAT is missing or out of range.
REPEAT=.
8          %put REPEAT=%repeat(1, 0) ;
NOTE: Argument 2 to macro function %REPEAT is missing or out of range.
REPEAT=.
```

SAS Listing

This sample program does not have any listing output.

%REVERSE

Purpose

REVERSE macro function similar to the REVERSE data step function. It reverses a character expression.

Syntax

%reverse (argument)

> *argument* is any string of characters

Notes

Probably one of the shortest macros ever written, but it is in line with the spirit of having a macro function for each possible data step function.

Example

Sample Program

```
%put REVERSE(10) = %reverse(10) ;
%put REVERSE(%str(1,0)) = %reverse(%str(1,0)) ;
%put REVERSE(All work and no play makes Jack a dull boy.)  = %reverse(All work and no play makes Jack a dull boy.) ;
%put REVERSE(170) = %reverse(170) ;
%put REVERSE = %reverse ;
```

SAS Log

```
1          %put REVERSE(10) = %reverse(10) ;
REVERSE(10) = 01
2          %put REVERSE(%str(1,0)) = %reverse(%str(1,0)) ;

REVERSE(1,0) = 0,1
3          %put REVERSE(All work and no play makes Jack a dull boy.)  = %reverse(All work and no
3        ! play makes Jack a dull boy.) ;
REVERSE(All work and no play makes Jack a dull boy.)  = .yob llud a kcaJ sekam yalp on dna krow
llA
4          %put REVERSE(170) = %reverse(170) ;
REVERSE(170) = 071
5          %put REVERSE = %reverse ;
REVERSE =
```

SAS Listing

This sample program does not have any listing output.

%ROUND

Purpose
ROUND macro function similar to the ROUND data step function. It rounds to the nearest round-off unit.

Syntax
%round(x, r)

> *x* is a numeric argument
>
> *r* is the numeric non-negative round-off unit

Notes
The ROUND function returns a value rounded to the nearest round-off unit.

Example

Sample Program
```
%put PI=%round(3.141592653589, .00001) ;
```

SAS Log
```
1          %put PI=%round(3.141592653589, .00001) ;
PI=3.14159
```

SAS Listing
This sample program does not have any listing output.

%SAVING

Purpose
SAVING macro function similar to the SAVING data step function. It returns values of saving rate interest calculations.

Syntax
%saving(f,p,r,n)

> *f* is non-negative numeric, the future amount.
>
> *p* is non-negative numeric, the payment
>
> *r* is non-negative numeric, the periodic interest rate expressed as a fraction. Range: r >= 0
>
> *n* is non-negative integer, the number of saving periods.

See Also
%SAVING, %COMPOUND, %MORT

Notes

The SAVING function returns the missing argument in the list of four arguments from a periodic saving. One missing argument must be provided. It is then calculated from the remaining three. No adjustment is made to convert the results to round numbers.

Example

Sample Program

```
%put number = %saving(12000,100,.05/12,.) ;
```

SAS Log

```
1    %put number = %saving(12000,100,.05/12,.) ;
number = 97.1813464602066
```

SAS Listing

This sample program does not have any listing output.

%SDF

Purpose

SDF macro function similar to the SDF data step function. It computes a survival function.

Syntax

%SDF (dist,quantile,parm-1, . . . ,parm-k)

dist is a character string that identifies the distribution. Valid distributions are as follows:

- Bernoulli - BERNOULLI
- Beta - BETA
- Binomial - BINOMIAL
- Cauchy - CAUCHY
- Chi squared - CHISQUARED
- Exponential - EXPONENTIAL
- F - F
- Gamma - GAMMA
- Geometric - GEOMETRIC
- Hyper-geometric - HYPERGEOMETRIC
- Laplace - LAPLACE
- Logistic - LOGISTIC
- Lognormal – LOG or NORMAL
- Negative binomial - NEGBINOMIAL
- Normal - NORMAL or GAUSS
- Pareto - PARETO
- Poisson - POISSON
- T - T
- Uniform - UNIFORM
- Wald (inverse Gaussian) - WALD or IGAUSS

- Weibull - WEIBULL

Note: Except for T and F, any distribution can be minimally identified by its first four characters. To keep with the spirit of the data step function SDF, the DIST option can be quoted or unquoted (unquoted is preferred).

quantile is a numeric random variable. parm-1, . . . ,parm-k are shape, location, or scale parameters appropriate for the specific distribution. See the description for each distribution in Details under the HELP library for the data step function SDF for complete information about these parameters.

See Also
%CDF, %LOGCDF, %PDF, %SDF, %LOGSDF

Example

Sample Program
```
%put SDF=%sdf(POISSON, 2, 1) ;
%put SDF=%sdf('POISSON', 2, 1) ;
%put SDF=%sdf("POISSON", 2, 1) ;
%put SDF=%sdf(POISSON) ;
%put SDF=%sdf(POISSON, 2) ;
```

SAS Log
```
1    %put SDF=%sdf(POISSON, 2, 1) ;
SDF=0.08030139707139
2    %put SDF=%sdf('POISSON', 2, 1) ;
SDF=0.08030139707139
3    %put SDF=%sdf("POISSON", 2, 1) ;
SDF=0.08030139707139
4    %put SDF=%sdf(POISSON) ;
NOTE:  Argument 2 to macro function %SDF is missing or out of range.
SDF=.
5    %put SDF=%sdf(POISSON, 2) ;
NOTE:  Argument 3 to macro function %SDF is missing or out of range.
SDF=.
```

SAS Listing
This sample program does not have any listing output.

%SIGN

Purpose
SIGN macro function similar to the SIGN data step function

Syntax
%sign(argument)

> *argument* is numeric

Example

Sample Program
```
%put %sign(-1) ;
```

```
%put %sign(%pi) ;
%put %sign(0) ;
%put %sign(A) ;
```

SAS Log

```
1    %put %sign(-1) ;
1
2    %put %sign(%pi) ;
1
3    %put %sign(0) ;
0
4    %put %sign(A) ;
NOTE:  Invalid numeric data A in Argument 1 for macro function %SIGN.
.
```

SAS Listing

This sample program does not have any listing output.

%SIN

Purpose

SIN macro function similar to the SIN data step function. It returns the value of the triginometric SINE function.

Syntax

%sin(x)

> *x* is numeric, specified in radians

See Also

%ARCOS, %ARSIN, %ATAN, %COS, %COSH, %SIN, %SINH, %TAN, %TANH

Example

Sample Program

```
%put %sin(-1) ;
%put %sin(%pi) ;
%put %sin(0) ;
%put %sin(A) ;
```

SAS Log

```
1    %put %sin(-1) ;
0.84147098480789
2    %put %sin(%pi) ;
3.2310851043326E-15
3    %put %sin(0) ;
0
4    %put %sin(A) ;
NOTE:  Invalid numeric data A in Argument 1 for macro function %SIN.
.
```

SAS Listing

This sample program does not have any listing output.

%SINH

Purpose
SINH macro function similar to the SINH data step function. It returns the value of the Hyperbolic Sine function.

Syntax
%sinh(x)

> *x* is numeric, specified in radians

See Also
%ARCOS, %ARSIN, %ATAN, %COS, %COSH, %SIN, %SINH, %TAN, %TANH

Example

Sample Program
```
%put %sinh(-1) ;
%put %sinh(%pi) ;
%put %sinh(0) ;
%put %sinh(A) ;
```

SAS Log
```
1    %put %sinh(-1) ;
1.1752011936438
2    %put %sinh(%pi) ;
11.5487393572577
3        %put %sinh(0) ;
0
4        %put %sinh(A) ;
NOTE:  Invalid numeric data A in Argument 1 for macro function %SINH.
.
```

SAS Listing
This sample program does not have any listing output.

%SKEWNESS

Purpose
SKEWNESS macro function similar to the SKEWNESS data step function. It returns the skewness.

Syntax
%skewness (argument, argument, . . .)

> *argument* is numeric. At least three arguments are required.

See Also
%CSS, %VAR, %N, %NMISS, %SUM, %SKEWNESS, %KURTOSIS, %RANGE, %CV, %USS, %STD, %STDERR, %MIN, %MAX

Example

Sample Program
```
%put SKEWNESS=%skewness(1,2,3,4,5) ;
%put SKEWNESS=%skewness(1,2,A,4,5) ;
%put SKEWNESS=%skewness ;
%put SKEWNESS=%skewness(1) ;
%put SKEWNESS=%skewness(1,2,3,4,.) ;
```

SAS Log
```
1          %put SKEWNESS=%skewness(1,2,3,4,5) ;
SKEWNESS=0
2          %put SKEWNESS=%skewness(1,2,A,4,5) ;
NOTE:  Invalid numeric data A in argument 3 for macro function %SKEWNESS.
SKEWNESS=.
3          %put SKEWNESS=%skewness ;
NOTE:  Argument 1 to macro function %SKEWNESS is missing or out of range.
SKEWNESS=.
4          %put SKEWNESS=%skewness(1) ;
NOTE:  Argument 2 to macro function %SKEWNESS is missing or out of range.
SKEWNESS=.
5          %put SKEWNESS=%skewness(1,2,3,4,.) ;
SKEWNESS=0
```

SAS Listing
This sample program does not have any listing output.

%SLEEP

Purpose
SLEEP macro function Suspends execution of a SAS DATA step for a specified number of seconds and returns that number.

Syntax
SLEEP(seconds, option)

> *seconds* specifies the number of seconds you want to suspend execution of the SAS System. The num-seconds argument is a numeric constant that must be greater than or equal to 0. Negative or missing values for SECONDS are invalid.
>
> *option* (undocumented in SAS System) This option must be numeric and is probably the result of some crazy undocumented feature from SAS. If OPTION is not used, a POPUP window will be put to the screen displaying when SAS will no longer sleep. If, however, a numeric value is entered, two things happen: 1) The POPUP will NOT occur, and 2) The SLEEP time is multiplied by the value of OPTION. It is recommended that users submit either NO OPTION or the OPTION 1.

See Also
%SLEEP, %WAKEUP

Notes
The SLEEP function suspends execution of the SAS System for a specified number of seconds. The return value of the num-seconds argument is the number of seconds slept. The maximum sleep period for the SLEEP

function is approximately 46 days. When you submit a program that calls the SLEEP function, a pop-up window appears telling you how long the SAS System is going to sleep. Your SAS session remains inactive until the sleep period is over. If you want to cancel the call to the SLEEP function, use the CTRL+BREAK attention sequence. You can suppress the pop-up window by submitting the option 1.

Example

Sample Program

```
%let rc = %sleep(1) ;
%put rc=&rc ;
%let rc = %sleep(2, 2) ;
%put rc=&rc ;
```

SAS Log

```
1    %let rc = %sleep(1) ;
2    %put rc=&rc ;
rc=1
3    %let rc = %sleep(2, 2) ;
4    %put rc=&rc ;
rc=2
```

SAS Listing

This sample program does not have any listing output.

%SMALL

Purpose

Returns the smallest double-precision number

Syntax

%small

See Also

%CONSTANT

Example

Sample Program

```
%put SMALL=%small ;
```

SAS Log

```
1          %put SMALL=%small ;
SMALL=2.2250738585072E-308
```

SAS Listing

This sample program does not have any listing output.

%SORTLIST

Purpose
This macro returns a string of words in sorted order

Syntax
%sortlist (list, dlm, options)

> *list* is any string of characters or numbers that does not contain a comma, quote, ampersand, percent sign, or semicolon.
>
> *dlm* (optional) is any character delimiter other than a comma, quote, or semicolon. The delimiter may be more than one character but excludes special characters.
>
> *Options* (optional) are the sorting options. Valid values are NODUP removes duplicates DESC, DESCENDING, or REVERSE sorts in descending order

Notes
This macro function is not very efficient for large sorts. It can be modified to add various sort methods based on the size of the input string. For a reference on adding more sort logic, visit
http://linux.wku.edu/~lamonml/algor/sort/sort.html

A COMMA (,) semicolon, ampersand, percent sign, and single or double-quotes cannot be used as a delimiter.

Current options allowed are: NODUP: Removes duplicate tokens from the input string. DESC: Sorts the tokens in descending order. Also DESCENDING and REVERSE are accepted.

Example

Sample Program
```
%put NOTE: SORTLIST=%sortlist (7 5 6 15 21 0 5 5 5 -1) ;
%put NOTE: SORTLIST=%sortlist (lib.data5 lib.data2 lib.data4) ;
%put NOTE: SORTLIST=%sortlist (a) ;
%put NOTE: SORTLIST=%sortlist(1.2...1.6..6, .) ;
%put NOTE: SORTLIST=%sortlist(1.2.5.32.5.1.6.34.546.6, .) ;
%put NOTE: SORTLIST=%sortlist(1.2.5.32.5.1.6.34.546.6, ., desc) ;
%put NOTE: SORTLIST=%sortlist (7 5 6 15 21 0 5 5 5 -1, %str( ), nodup) ;
%put NOTE: SORTLIST=%sortlist(1.2.5.32.5.1.6.34.546.6, ., nodup) ;
%put NOTE: SORTLIST=%sortlist(1 2 3 3 3, %str( ), desc nodup) ;
%put NOTE: SORTLIST=%sortlist(a ab abc cde, %str( ), nodup reverse) ;
%put NOTE: SORTLIST=%sortlist (7.23 5.444 6.74 27.15 21 0 5.2 5.3 6.5 3.14159 5 -1) ;
%put NOTE: %sortlist(a||c||b, ||) ;
```

SAS Log
```
1          %put NOTE: SORTLIST=%sortlist (7 5 6 15 21 0 5 5 5 -1) ;
NOTE: SORTLIST=-1 0 5 5 5 5 6 7 15 21
2          %put NOTE: SORTLIST=%sortlist (lib.data5 lib.data2 lib.data4) ;
NOTE: SORTLIST=lib.data2 lib.data4 lib.data5
3          %put NOTE: SORTLIST=%sortlist (a) ;
NOTE: SORTLIST=a
4          %put NOTE: SORTLIST=%sortlist(1.2...1.6..6, .) ;
NOTE: SORTLIST=...1.1.2.6.6
5          %put NOTE: SORTLIST=%sortlist(1.2.5.32.5.1.6.34.546.6, .) ;
NOTE: SORTLIST=1.1.2.5.5.6.6.32.34.546
6          %put NOTE: SORTLIST=%sortlist(1.2.5.32.5.1.6.34.546.6, ., desc) ;
NOTE: SORTLIST=546.34.32.6.6.5.5.2.1.1
```

```
7          %put NOTE: SORTLIST=%sortlist (7 5 6 15 21 0 5 5 5 -1, %str( ), nodup) ;
NOTE: SORTLIST=-1 0 5 6 7 15 21
8          %put NOTE: SORTLIST=%sortlist(1.2.5.32.5.1.6.34.546.6, ., nodup) ;
NOTE: SORTLIST=1.2.5.6.32.34.546
9          %put NOTE: SORTLIST=%sortlist(1 2 3 3 3, %str( ), desc nodup) ;
NOTE: SORTLIST=3 2 1
10         %put NOTE: SORTLIST=%sortlist(a ab abc cde, %str( ), nodup reverse) ;
NOTE: SORTLIST=cde abc ab a
11         %put NOTE: SORTLIST=%sortlist (7.23 5.444 6.74 27.15 21 0 5.2 5.3 6.5 3.14159 5 -1) ;
NOTE: SORTLIST=-1 0 3.14159 5 5.2 5.3 5.444 6.5 6.74 7.23 21 27.15
12         %put NOTE: %sortlist(a||c||b, ||) ;
NOTE: a||b||c
```

SAS Listing

This sample program does not have any listing output.

%SQRT

Purpose

SQRT macro function similar to the SQRT data step function

Syntax

%sqrt(x)

> x is non-negative numeric

Example

Sample Program

```
%put %sqrt(%pi) ;
%put %sqrt(0) ;
```

SAS Log

```
1          %put %sqrt(%pi) ;
1.77245385090551
2    %put %sqrt(0) ;
0
```

SAS Listing

This sample program does not have any listing output.

%SQRTBIG

Purpose

Returns the square root of the largest double-precision number

Syntax

%sqrtbig

See Also

%CONSTANT

Example

Sample Program
```
%put SQRTBIG=%sqrtbig ;
```

SAS Log
```
1    %put SQRTBIG=%sqrtbig ;
SQRTBIG=1.3407807929942E154
```

SAS Listing
This sample program does not have any listing output.

%SQRTMACEPS

Purpose
Returns the square root of the machine precision constant

Syntax
%sqrtmaceps

See Also
%CONSTANT

Example

Sample Program
```
%put SQRTMACEPS=%sqrtmaceps ;
```

SAS Log
```
1    %put SQRTMACEPS=%sqrtmaceps ;
SQRTMACEPS=1.4901161193847E-8
```

SAS Listing
This sample program does not have any listing output.

%SQRTSMALL

Purpose
Returns the square root of the smallest double-precision number

Syntax
%sqrtsmall

See Also
%CONSTANT

Example

Sample Program
```
%put SQRTSMALL=%sqrtsmall ;
```

SAS Log
```
1    %put SQRTSMALL=%sqrtsmall ;
SQRTSMALL=1.49166814624E-154
```

SAS Listing
This sample program does not have any listing output.

%STD

Purpose
STD macro function similar to the STD data step function. It returns the standard deviation

Syntax
%std (argument, argument, . . .)

> *argument* is numeric. At least two arguments are required.

See Also
%CSS, %VAR, %N, %NMISS, %SUM, %SKEWNESS, %KURTOSIS, %RANGE, %CV, %USS, %STD, %STDERR, %MIN, %MAX

Example

Sample Program
```
%put STD=%std(1,2,3,4,5) ;
%put STD=%std(1,2,A,4,5) ;
%put STD=%std ;
%put STD=%std(1) ;
```

SAS Log
```
1    %put STD=%std(1,2,3,4,5) ;
STD=1.581138830084190
2    %put STD=%std(1,2,A,4,5) ;
NOTE:  Invalid numeric data A in argument 3 for macro function %STD.
STD=.
3    %put STD=%std ;
NOTE:  Argument 1 to macro function %STD is missing or out of range.
STD=.
4    %put STD=%std(1) ;
NOTE:  Argument 2 to macro function %STD is missing or out of range.
STD=.
```

SAS Listing
This sample program does not have any listing output.

%STDERR

Purpose
STDERR macro function similar to the STDERR data step function. It returns the standard error of the mean.

Syntax
%stderr (argument, argument, . . .)

    argument is numeric. At least two arguments are required.

See Also
%CSS, %VAR, %N, %NMISS, %SUM, %SKEWNESS, %KURTOSIS, %RANGE, %CV, %USS, %STD, %STDERR, %MIN, %MAX

Example

Sample Program
```
%put STDERR=%stderr(1,2,3,4,5) ;
%put STDERR=%stderr(1,2,A,4,5) ;
%put STDERR=%stderr ;
%put STDERR=%stderr(1) ;
```

SAS Log
```
1    %put STDERR=%stderr(1,2,3,4,5) ;
STDERR=0.70710678118654
2    %put STDERR=%stderr(1,2,A,4,5) ;
NOTE:  Invalid numeric data A in argument 3 for macro function %STDERR.
STDERR=.
3    %put STDERR=%stderr ;
NOTE:  Argument 1 to macro function %STDERR is missing or out of range.
STDERR=.
4    %put STDERR=%stderr(1) ;
NOTE:  Argument 2 to macro function %STDERR is missing or out of range.
STDERR=.
```

SAS Listing
This sample program does not have any listing output.

%STFIPS

Purpose
Converts state postal codes to FIPS state codes

Syntax
STFIPS(postal-code)

postal-code specifies a character expression that contains the two-character standard state postal code. Characters can be mixed case. The function ignores leading and trailingblanks. Can be quoted or unquoted.

See Also

%FIPNAME, %FIPNAMEL, %FIPSTATE, %STFIPS, %STNAME, %STNAMEL, %ZIPFIPS, %ZIPNAME, %ZIPNAMEL, %ZIPSTATE

Notes

The STFIPS function converts a two-character state postal code (or world-wide GSA geographic code for U.S. territories) to the corresponding numeric U.S. Federal Information Processing Standards (FIPS) code. If an invalid STATE-CODE is entered, the %SYSFUNC will return the error. This is a deviation of standard RDS macros to have the macro do the error check. This decision was made due to the large amount of possible inputs.

Example

Sample Program

```
%put STFIPS=%stfips(NC) ;
%put STFIPS=%stfips('NC') ;
```

SAS Log

```
1    %put STFIPS=%stfips(NC) ;
STFIPS=37
2    %put STFIPS=%stfips('NC') ;
STFIPS=37
```

SAS Listing

This sample program does not have any listing output.

%STNAME

Purpose

Converts state postal codes to uppercase state names

Syntax

STNAME(postal-code)

postal-code specifies a character expression that contains the two-character standard state postal code. Characters can be mixed case. The function ignores leading and trailingblanks. Can be quoted or unquoted.

See Also

%FIPNAME, %FIPNAMEL, %FIPSTATE, %STFIPS, %STNAME, %STNAMEL, %ZIPFIPS, %ZIPNAME, %ZIPNAMEL, %ZIPSTATE

Notes

The STNAME function converts a two-character state postal code (or world-wide GSA geographic code for U.S. territories) to the corresponding numeric U.S. Federal Information Processing Standards (FIPS) code. If an invalid STATE-CODE is entered, the %SYSFUNC will return the error. This is a deviation of standard RDS macros to have the macro do the error check. This decision was made due to the large amount of possible inputs.

Example

Sample Program

```
%put STNAME=%stname(NC) ;
%put STNAME=%stname('NC') ;
```

SAS Log

```
1    %put STNAME=%stname(NC) ;
STNAME=NORTH CAROLINA
2    %put STNAME=%stname('NC') ;
STNAME=NORTH CAROLINA
```

SAS Listing

This sample program does not have any listing output.

%STNAMEL

Purpose

Converts state postal codes to mixed case state names

Syntax

stnamel(postal-code)

> *postal*-code specifies a character expression that contains the two-character standard state postal code. Characters can be mixed case. The function ignores leading and trailingblanks. Can be quoted or unquoted.

See Also

%FIPNAME, %FIPNAMEL, %FIPSTATE, %STFIPS, %STNAME, %STNAMEL, %ZIPFIPS, %ZIPNAME, %ZIPNAMEL, %ZIPSTATE

Notes

The stnamel function converts a two-character state postal code (or world-wide GSA geographic code for U.S. territories) to the corresponding numeric U.S. Federal Information Processing Standards (FIPS) code. If an invalid STATE-CODE is entered, the %SYSFUNC will return the error. This is a deviation of standard RDS macros to have the macro do the error check. This decision was made due to the large amount of possible inputs.

Example

Sample Program
```
%put STNAMEL=%stnamel(NC) ;
%put STNAMEL=%stnamel('NC') ;
```

SAS Log
```
1    %put STNAMEL=%stnamel(NC) ;
STNAMEL=North Carolina
2    %put STNAMEL=%stnamel('NC') ;
STNAMEL=North Carolina
```

SAS Listing
This sample program does not have any listing output.

%STRING

Purpose
This macro returns a string of words in the form pre1 pre2 pre3 ...

Syntax
%string(prefix = *prefix*,   [required]
    from = _from_value_,   [optional]
to = _to_value_,   [required]
by = _increment_value_)   [optional]

See Also
%PREFIX, %SUFFIX, %STRING, %REPEAT

Notes
The format of this macro does not follow a standard macro function because it was written before those standards were created and it exists in many other macros.

Example

Sample Program
```
%put %string(prefix=var, from=1, to=10, by=2) ;
%put %string(prefix=prefix, from=2, to=10) ;
```

SAS Log
```
1    %put %string(prefix=var, from=1, to=10, by=2) ;
var1 var3 var5 var7 var9
2    %put %string(prefix=prefix, from=2, to=10) ;
prefix2 prefix3 prefix4 prefix5 prefix6 prefix7 prefix8 prefix9 prefix10
```

SAS Listing
This sample program does not have any listing output.

%SUFFIX

Purpose
This macro adds the same suffix to a prefix list.

Syntax
%suffix(list, suffix, <dlm>)

> *list* is a list of space-delimited strings
>
> *suffix* is a string of characters
>
> *dlm* (optional) is the delimiter. Default is a blank space.

See Also
%PREFIX, %SUFFIX, %STRING, %REPEAT

Example

Sample Program
```
%put %suffix (Larry Curly Moe, is a stooge.) ;
%put %suffix (Larry Curly Moe, %str( is a stooge.  )) ;
%put %suffix (a.b.c.d.e, N, .) ;
```

SAS Log
```
1    %put %suffix (Larry Curly Moe, is a stooge.) ;
Larryis a stooge. Curlyis a stooge. Moeis a stooge
2    %put %suffix (Larry Curly Moe, %str( is a stooge.  )) ;
Larry is a stooge.   Curly is a stooge.   Moe is a stooge
3    %put %suffix (a.b.c.d.e, N, .) ;
.aN.bN.cN.dN.eN
```

SAS Listing
This sample program does not have any listing output.

%SUM

Purpose
SUM macro function similar to the SUM data step function. It returns the sum of the non-missing arguments.

Syntax
%sum(argument, . . .)

> *argument* is numeric. At least one argument is required.

See Also
%CSS, %VAR, %N, %NMISS, %SUM, %SKEWNESS, %KURTOSIS, %RANGE, %CV, %USS, %STD, %STDERR, %MIN, %MAX

Example

Sample Program
```
%put SUM=%sum(1,2,3,4,5) ;
```

SAS Log
```
1    %put SUM=%sum(1,2,3,4,5) ;
SUM=15
```

SAS Listing
This sample program does not have any listing output.

%SYSMSG

Purpose
Returns the text of error messages or warning messages from the last data set or external file function execution.

Syntax
%SYSMSG

Notes
SYSMSG returns the text of error messages or warning messages that are produced when a data set or external file access function encounters an error condition. If no error message is available, the returned value is blank. The internally stored error message is reset to blank after a call to SYSMSG, so subsequent calls to SYSMSG before another error condition occurs return blank values.

Example

Sample Program
```
%put obscnt = %obscnt(nodata) ;
%put SYSMSG=%sysmsg ;
```

SAS Log
```
1    %put obscnt = %obscnt(nodata) ;
WARNING: Open for dataset WORK.NODATA failed
WARNING: Macro %OBSCNT will return the number of observations as missing.
ERROR: File WORK.NODATA.DATA does not exist.
     ERROR: File WORK.NODATA.DATA does not exist.
     ERROR:
File WORK.NODATA.DATA does not exist.
obscnt = .
2    %put SYSMSG=%sysmsg ;
SYSMSG=
```

SAS Listing
This sample program does not have any listing output.

%TAN

Purpose

TAN macro function similar to the TAN data step function. It returns the value of the triginometric tangent function.

Syntax

%tan(x)

> x is numeric, cannot be an odd multiple of PI/2

See Also

%ARCOS, %ARSIN, %ATAN, %COS, %COSH, %SIN, %SINH, %TAN, %TANH

Notes

Although the value of X must not be an odd multiple of PI/2, we do not check for that condition because the number of significant digits available in processing help to ensure that we do not find such a number in real-world data processing.

Example

Sample Program

```
%put %tan(-1) ;
%put %tan(%pi) ;
%put %tan(0) ;
%put %tan(A) ;
```

SAS Log

```
1    %put %tan(-1) ;
1.5574077246549
2    %put %tan(%pi) ;
3.2310851043326E-15
3    %put %tan(0) ;
0
4    %put %tan(A) ;
NOTE:  Invalid numeric data A in Argument 1 for macro function %TAN.
```

SAS Listing

This sample program does not have any listing output.

%TANH

Purpose

TANH macro function similar to the TANH data step function. It returns the value of the Hyperbolic Tangent function.

Syntax

%tanh(x)

x is numeric, cannot be an odd multiple of PI/2

See Also
%ARCOS, %ARSIN, %ATAN, %COS, %COSH, %SIN, %SINH, %TAN, %TANH

Notes
Although the value of X must not be an odd multiple of PI/2, we do not check for that condition because the number of significant digits available in processing help to ensure that we do not find such a number in real-world data processing.

Example

Sample Program
```
%put %tanh(-1) ;
%put %tanh(%pi) ;
%put %tanh(0) ;
%put %tanh(A) ;
```

SAS Log
```
1    %put %tanh(-1) ;
0.76159415595576
2    %put %tanh(%pi) ;
0.99627207622075
3         %put %tanh(0) ;
0
4         %put %tanh(A) ;
NOTE:  Invalid numeric data A in Argument 1 for macro function %TANH.
```

SAS Listing
This sample program does not have any listing output.

%TIME

Purpose
Returns the current time of day in format TIME.

Syntax
%time

See Also
%DATETIME, %FILEDT, %TODAY, %DATE, %TIME

Notes
This macro differs from the automatic macro variable &SYSTIME by returning the CURRENT time, not the SAS SESSION STARTUP TIME.

Example

Sample Program
```
%put TIME=%time ;
```

SAS Log
```
1          %put TIME=%time ;
TIME=15:59:55
```

SAS Listing
This sample program does not have any listing output.

%TODAY

Purpose
Returns the current date as DATE9. format.

Syntax
%TODAY

See Also
%DATETIME, %FILEDT, %TODAY, %DATE, %TIME

Notes
This macro function is the same as %DATE. It differes from the &SYSDATE automatic macro variable because it evaluates the CURRENT DATE and not the DATE AT STARTUP.

Example

Sample Program
```
%put TODAY=%today ;
```

SAS Log
```
1          %put TODAY=%today ;
TODAY=30JUN2006
```

SAS Listing
This sample program does not have any listing output.

%TRANSLATE

Purpose
TRANSLATE macro function similar to TRANSLATE data step function

Syntax
%translate(source, to, from)

source specifies the SAS expression that contains the original character value.
to specifies the characters that you want TRANSLATE to use as substitutes.
from specifies the characters that you want TRANSLATE to replace.

See Also
%TRANSLATE, %TRANWRD

Example

Sample Program
```
%let string = hello there ;
%let trans = %translate(&string, _, %str( )) ;
%put NOTE: string=&string trans=&trans ;

%let root = c:\myroot ;
%let string = "&root\subdir\myfile.txt" ;
%let trans = %translate(&string, %bquote('), %bquote(")) ;
%put NOTE: string=&string trans=&trans ;

%let string = 'c:\&root\subdir\myfile.txt' ;
%let trans = %translate(&string, %bquote('), %bquote(")) ;
%put NOTE: string=&string trans=&trans ;
```

SAS Log
```
1          %let string = hello there ;
2          %let trans = %translate(&string, _, %str( )) ;
3          %put NOTE: string=&string trans=&trans ;
NOTE: string=hello there trans=hello_there
5          %let root = c:\myroot ;
6          %let string = "&root\subdir\myfile.txt" ;
7          %let trans = %translate(&string, %bquote('), %bquote(")) ;
8          %put NOTE: string=&string trans=&trans ;
NOTE: string="c:\myroot\subdir\myfile.txt" trans='c:\myroot\subdir\myfile.txt'
10         %let string = 'c:\&root\subdir\myfile.txt' ;
11         %let trans = %translate(&string, %bquote('), %bquote(")) ;
12         %put NOTE: string=&string trans=&trans ;
NOTE: string='c:\&root\subdir\myfile.txt' trans='c:\&root\subdir\myfile.txt'
```

SAS Listing
This sample program does not have any listing output.

%TRANWRD

Purpose
Tranwrd macro function similar to tranwrd data step function. It replaces or removes all occurrences of a word in a character string.

Syntax
%TRANWRD(source, target, replacement)

source specifies the source string that you want to translate.

target specifies the string searched for in source.

replacement specifies the string that replaces target.

See Also
%TRANSLATE, %TRANWRD

Notes
The TRANWRD function replaces or removes all occurrences of a given word (or a pattern of characters) within a character string. The TRANWRD function does not remove trailing blanks in the target string and the replacement string.

Example

Sample Program
```
%put TRANWRD (Shemp Howard, Shemp, Jerome)=%tranwrd (Shemp Howard, Shemp, Jerome) ;
%put TRANWRD (football, foot, base)=%tranwrd (football, foot, base) ;
```

SAS Log
```
1          %put TRANWRD (Shemp Howard, Shemp, Jerome)=%tranwrd (Shemp Howard, Shemp, Jerome) ;
TRANWRD (Shemp Howard, Shemp, Jerome)=Jerome Howard
2          %put TRANWRD (football, foot, base)=%tranwrd (football, foot, base) ;
TRANWRD (football, foot, base)=baseball
```

SAS Listing
This sample program does not have any listing output.

%TRIGAMMA

Purpose
TRIGAMMA macro function similar to the TRIGAMMA data step function. It returns the value of the trigamma function.

Syntax
%trigamma(argument)

> *argument* is a positive number.

Notes
The TRIGAMMA function returns the first derivative of the DIGAMMA function. For X > 0, the TRIGAMMA function is the second derivative of the LGAMMA function.

Example

Sample Program
```
%put TRIGAMMA(10) = %trigamma(10) ;
%put TRIGAMMA(25) = %trigamma(25) ;
%put TRIGAMMA(.5) = %trigamma(.5) ;
```

SAS Log
```
1          %put TRIGAMMA(10) = %trigamma(10) ;
TRIGAMMA(10) = 0.10516633568168
2          %put TRIGAMMA(25) = %trigamma(25) ;
```

```
TRIGAMMA(25) = 0.04081066325722
3          %put TRIGAMMA(.5) = %trigamma(.5) ;
TRIGAMMA(.5) = 4.93480220054467
```

SAS Listing

This sample program does not have any listing output.

%UNIQUE

Purpose

This macro returns a list of unique tokens from a given list of tokens. All values are returned and all comparisons are made in UPPERCASE.

Syntax

%unique (list, prefix)

> *list* is a list of space-delimited tokens
>
> *prefix* (optional) is the prefix string to use to replace any duplicate tokens in the LIST

See Also

%SORTLIST

Notes

This macro can be used to generate a unique list of variable names when reading in a list of variables that may have duplicate names. If the given list contains values similar to the replacement token list the numerical order may not occur in incremental order but the results will still be unique. See last demo.

Example

Sample Program

```
%put UNIQUE=%unique(a b c d e b g b a u b q) ;
%put UNIQUE=%unique(a b b a, v) ;
%put UNIQUE=%unique(v1 v1 v1 v2 v3, v) ;
```

SAS Log

```
1          %put UNIQUE=%unique(a b c d e b g b a u b q) ;
UNIQUE=A B C D E VAR1 G VAR2 VAR3 U VAR4 Q
2          %put UNIQUE=%unique(a b b a, v) ;
UNIQUE=A B V1 V2
3          %put UNIQUE=%unique(v1 v1 v1 v2 v3, v) ;
UNIQUE=V1 V5 V2 V3 V4
```

SAS Listing

This sample program does not have any listing output.

%USS

Purpose
USS macro function similar to the USS data step function. It returns the uncorrected sum of squares.

Syntax
%uss (argument, argument, . . .)

>*argument* is numeric. At least two arguments are required.

See Also
%CSS, %VAR, %N, %NMISS, %SUM, %SKEWNESS, %KURTOSIS, %RANGE, %CV, %USS, %STD, %STDERR, %MIN, %MAX

Example

Sample Program
```
%put USS=%uss(1,2,3,4,5) ;
%put USS=%uss(1,2,A,4,5) ;
%put USS=%uss ;
%put USS=%uss(1) ;
```

SAS Log
```
1          %put USS=%uss(1,2,3,4,5) ;
USS=55
2          %put USS=%uss(1,2,A,4,5) ;
NOTE:  Invalid numeric data A in Argument 3 for macro function %USS.
USS=.
3          %put USS=%uss ;
NOTE:  Argument 1 to macro function %USS is missing or out of range.
USS=.
4          %put USS=%uss(1) ;
NOTE:  Argument 2 to macro function %USS is missing or out of range.
USS=.
```

SAS Listing
This sample program does not have any listing output.

%VAR

Purpose
VAR macro function similar to the VAR data step function. It returns the variance.

Syntax
%var (argument, argument, . . .)

>*argument* is numeric. At least two arguments are required.

See Also
%CSS, %VAR, %N, %NMISS, %SUM, %SKEWNESS, %KURTOSIS, %RANGE, %CV, %USS, %STD, %STDERR, %MIN, %MAX

Example

Sample Program
```
%put VAR=%var(1,2,3,4,5) ;
%put VAR=%var(1,2,A,4,5) ;
%put VAR=%var ;
%put VAR=%var(1) ;
```

SAS Log
```
1          %put VAR=%var(1,2,3,4,5) ;
VAR=2.5
2          %put VAR=%var(1,2,A,4,5) ;
NOTE:  Invalid numeric data A in Argument 3 for macro function %VAR.
VAR=.
3          %put VAR=%var ;
NOTE:  Argument 1 to macro function %VAR is missing or out of range.
VAR=.
4          %put VAR=%var(1) ;
NOTE:  Argument 2 to macro function %VAR is missing or out of range.
VAR=.
```

SAS Listing
This sample program does not have any listing output.

%VARCNT

Purpose
This macro returns the number of variables in a SAS dataset.

Syntax
%varcnt (data)

>*data* is a valid SAS data set name. The data set must exist.

See Also
%OBSCNT, %RECCNT, %VARCNT, %WORDCNT

Example

Sample Program
```
%put NOTE:  SASHELP.SHOES contains %trim(%left(%varcnt(sashelp.shoes))) variables. ;
```

SAS Log
```
1          %put NOTE:  SASHELP.SHOES contains %trim(%left(%varcnt(sashelp.shoes))) variables. ;
NOTE:  SASHELP.SHOES contains 7 variables.
```

SAS Listing
This sample program does not have any listing output.

%VARFMT

Purpose
Returns the format assigned to a SAS data set variable.

Syntax
%varfmt (data, var)

    data is a valid SAS data set name. The data set must exist.

    var is a valid SAS variable that exists in the data set DATA.

See Also
%VARLEN, %VARLABEL, %VARINFMT, %VARFMT, %VARNUM, %VARTYPE

Notes
If the given data set does not exist, the function returns a null string. If the data set does exist and the variable does not, the function returns a zero.

Example

Sample Program
```
%put The format for SALES in SASHELP.SHOES is %varfmt(sashelp.shoes, sales) ;
%put The format for SALES in SASHELP.SHOES is %varfmt(sashelp.shoes, novar) ;
%put The format for SALES in SASHELP.SHOES is %varfmt(nodata, novar) ;
```

SAS Log
```
1          %put The format for SALES in SASHELP.SHOES is %varfmt(sashelp.shoes, sales) ;
The format for SALES in SASHELP.SHOES is DOLLAR12.
2          %put The format for SALES in SASHELP.SHOES is %varfmt(sashelp.shoes, novar) ;
WARNING: Variable NOVAR not found in data set SASHELP.SHOES.
The format for SALES in SASHELP.SHOES is 0
3          %put The format for SALES in SASHELP.SHOES is %varfmt(nodata, novar) ;
WARNING: Data set WORK.NODATA does not exist.
The format for SALES in SASHELP.SHOES is
```

SAS Listing
This sample program does not have any listing output.

%VARINFMT

Purpose
Returns the informat assigned to a SAS data set variable.

Syntax
%varinfmt (data, var)

data is a valid SAS data set name. The data set must exist.

var is a valid SAS variable that exists in the data set DATA.

See Also
%VARLEN, %VARLABEL, %VARINFMT, %VARFMT, %VARNUM, %VARTYPE

Notes
If the given data set does not exist, the function returns a null string. If the data set does exist and the variable does not, the function returns a zero.

Example

Sample Program
```
%put The informat for SALES in SASHELP.SHOES is %varinfmt(sashelp.shoes, sales) ;
%put The informat for SALES in SASHELP.SHOES is %varinfmt(sashelp.shoes, novar) ;
%put The informat for SALES in SASHELP.SHOES is %varinfmt(nodata, novar) ;
```

SAS Log
```
1          %put The informat for SALES in SASHELP.SHOES is %varinfmt(sashelp.shoes, sales) ;
The informat for SALES in SASHELP.SHOES is DOLLAR12.
2          %put The informat for SALES in SASHELP.SHOES is %varinfmt(sashelp.shoes, novar) ;
WARNING: Variable NOVAR not found in data set SASHELP.SHOES.
The informat for SALES in SASHELP.SHOES is 0
3          %put The informat for SALES in SASHELP.SHOES is %varinfmt(nodata, novar) ;
WARNING: Data set WORK.NODATA does not exist.
The informat for SALES in SASHELP.SHOES is
```

SAS Listing
This sample program does not have any listing output.

%VARLABEL

Purpose
Returns the label assigned to a SAS data set variable.

Syntax
%varlabel (data, var)

data is a valid SAS data set name. The data set must exist.

var is a valid SAS variable that exists in the data set DATA.

See Also
%VARLEN, %VARLABEL, %VARINFMT, %VARFMT, %VARNUM, %VARTYPE

Notes
If the given data set does not exist, the function returns a null string. If the data set does exist and the variable does not, the function returns a zero. The result returned is unquoted.

Example

Sample Program

```
%put The label for SALES in SASHELP.SHOES is %varlabel(sashelp.shoes, sales) ;
%put The label for SALES in SASHELP.SHOES is %varlabel(sashelp.shoes, novar) ;
%put The label for SALES in SASHELP.SHOES is %varlabel(nodata, novar) ;
```

SAS Log

```
1          %put The label for SALES in SASHELP.SHOES is %varlabel(sashelp.shoes, sales) ;
The label for SALES in SASHELP.SHOES is Total Sales
2          %put The label for SALES in SASHELP.SHOES is %varlabel(sashelp.shoes, novar) ;
NOTE: Variable NOVAR not found in data set SASHELP.SHOES.
The label for SALES in SASHELP.SHOES is 0
3          %put The label for SALES in SASHELP.SHOES is %varlabel(nodata, novar) ;
NOTE: Data set WORK.NODATA does not exist.
The label for SALES in SASHELP.SHOES is
```

SAS Listing

This sample program does not have any listing output.

%VARLEN

Purpose

Returns the length assigned to a SAS data set variable.

Syntax

%varlen (data, var)

> *data* is a valid SAS data set name. The data set must exist.
>
> *var* is a valid SAS variable that exists in the data set DATA.

See Also

%VARLEN, %VARLABEL, %VARINFMT, %VARFMT, %VARNUM, %VARTYPE

Notes

If the given data set does not exist, the function returns a null string. If the data set does exist and the variable does not, the function returns a zero.

Example

Sample Program

```
%put The length for SALES in SASHELP.SHOES is %varlen(sashelp.shoes, sales) ;
%put The length for SALES in SASHELP.SHOES is %varlen(sashelp.shoes, novar) ;
%put The length for SALES in SASHELP.SHOES is %varlen(nodata, novar) ;
```

SAS Log

```
1          %put The length for SALES in SASHELP.SHOES is %varlen(sashelp.shoes, sales) ;
The length for SALES in SASHELP.SHOES is 8
2          %put The length for SALES in SASHELP.SHOES is %varlen(sashelp.shoes, novar) ;
WARNING: Variable NOVAR not found in data set SASHELP.SHOES.
The length for SALES in SASHELP.SHOES is 0
3          %put The length for SALES in SASHELP.SHOES is %varlen(nodata, novar) ;
```

```
WARNING: Data set WORK.NODATA does not exist.
The length for SALES in SASHELP.SHOES is
```

SAS Listing

This sample program does not have any listing output.

%VARLIST

Purpose

Returns a list of all variables in a given SAS data set

Syntax

%varlist (data)

>   *data* is a valid SAS data set name. The data set must exist.

See Also

%CHARACTER, %NUMERIC, %VARLIST, *CHARACTER, NUMERIC, ALL*

Example

Sample Program

```
%put Variables in SASHELP.SHOES: %varlist(sashelp.shoes) ;
```

SAS Log

```
1          %put Variables in SASHELP.SHOES: %varlist(sashelp.shoes) ;
Variables in SASHELP.SHOES: Region Product Subsidiary Stores Sales Inventory Returns
```

SAS Listing

This sample program does not have any listing output.

%VARNUM

Purpose

Returns the position assigned to a SAS data set variable or 0 if the variable does not exist.

Syntax

%varnum (data, var)

>   *data* is a valid SAS data set name. The data set must exist.
>
>   *var* is a valid SAS variable that exists in the data set DATA.

See Also

%VARLEN, %VARLABEL, %VARINFMT, %VARFMT, %VARNUM, %VARTYPE

Notes
The macro function returns a NULL STRING if the named data set does not exist.

Example

Sample Program
```
%put The position for SALES in SASHELP.SHOES is %varnum(sashelp.shoes, sales) ;
%put The position for SALES in SASHELP.SHOES is %varnum(sashelp.shoes, novar) ;
%put The position for SALES in SASHELP.SHOES is %varnum(nodata, novar) ;
```

SAS Log
```
1          %put The position for SALES in SASHELP.SHOES is %varnum(sashelp.shoes, sales) ;
The position for SALES in SASHELP.SHOES is 5
2          %put The position for SALES in SASHELP.SHOES is %varnum(sashelp.shoes, novar) ;
The position for SALES in SASHELP.SHOES is 0
3          %put The position for SALES in SASHELP.SHOES is %varnum(nodata, novar) ;
WARNING: Data set WORK.NODATA does not exist.
The position for SALES in SASHELP.SHOES is
```

SAS Listing
This sample program does not have any listing output.

%VARTYPE

Purpose
Returns the type assigned to a SAS data set variable.

Syntax
%vartype (data, var)

> *data* is a valid SAS data set name. The data set must exist.
>
> *var* is a valid SAS variable that exists in the data set DATA.

See Also
%VARLEN, %VARLABEL, %VARINFMT, %VARFMT, %VARNUM, %VARTYPE

Notes
Return value/meaning:

- C / Character variable
- N / Numeric variable
- 0 / Variable does not exist in given existing data set
- null string / given data set does not exist

Example

Sample Program
```
%put The type for SALES in SASHELP.SHOES is %vartype(sashelp.shoes, sales) ;
%put The type for SALES in SASHELP.SHOES is %vartype(sashelp.shoes, region) ;
```

```
%put The type for SALES in SASHELP.SHOES is %vartype(sashelp.shoes, novar) ;
%put The type for SALES in SASHELP.SHOES is %vartype(nodata, novar) ;
```

SAS Log

```
1          %put The type for SALES in SASHELP.SHOES is %vartype(sashelp.shoes, sales) ;
The type for SALES in SASHELP.SHOES is N
2          %put The type for SALES in SASHELP.SHOES is %vartype(sashelp.shoes, region) ;
The type for SALES in SASHELP.SHOES is C
3          %put The type for SALES in SASHELP.SHOES is %vartype(sashelp.shoes, novar) ;
NOTE: Variable NOVAR not found.
The type for SALES in SASHELP.SHOES is 0
4          %put The type for SALES in SASHELP.SHOES is %vartype(nodata, novar) ;
NOTE: Data set WORK.NODATA does not exist.
The type for SALES in SASHELP.SHOES is
```

SAS Listing

This sample program does not have any listing output.

%WAKEUP

Purpose

WAKEUP macro function specifies the time the SAS System begins execution.

Syntax

WAKEUP(*until-when*)

> *until-when* specifies the time when the WAKEUP function will be executed.

See Also

%SLEEP, %WAKEUP

Notes

Use the WAKEUP function to specify the time the SAS System begins to execute. The return value is the number of seconds slept. The UNTIL-WHEN argument can be a SAS datetime value, SAS time value, or a numeric constant, as explained in the following list:

- DATETIME: the WAKEUP function sleeps until the specified date and time. If the specified date and time have already passed, the WAKEUP function does not sleep, and the return value is 0.
- TIME VALUE: the WAKEUP function sleeps until the specified time. If the specified time has already passed in that 24-hour period, the WAKEUP function sleeps until the specified time occurs again.
- NUMERIC: the WAKEUP function sleeps for that many seconds before or after the next occurring midnight. If the value is a positive numeric constant, the WAKEUP function sleeps for until-when seconds past midnight. If the value is a negative numeric constant, the WAKEUP function sleeps until until-when seconds before midnight.

Negative values for the *until-when* argument are allowed, but missing values are not. The maximum sleep period for the WAKEUP function is approximately 46 days. When you submit a program that calls the WAKEUP function, a pop-up window appears telling you when the SAS System is going to wake up. Your SAS session remains inactive until the waiting period is over.

If you want to cancel the call to the WAKEUP function, use the CTRL BREAK attention sequence.

Example

Sample Program

```
%*-------------------------------------*
 | NOTE:  1230814800 = '01JAN1999:13:00:00'dt |
 *-------------------------------------* ;

%let rc = %wakeup(1230814800) ;
%put rc=&rc ;

%let rc = %wakeup ('01JAN1999:13:00:00'dt) ;
%put rc=&rc ;
```

SAS Log

```
1          %*-------------------------------------*
2           | NOTE:  1230814800 = '01JAN1999:13:00:00'dt |
3           *-------------------------------------* ;
4          %let rc = %wakeup(1230814800) ;
5          %put rc=&rc ;
rc=0
6          %let rc = %wakeup ('01JAN1999:13:00:00'dt) ;
7          %put rc=&rc ;
rc=0
```

SAS Listing

This sample program does not have any listing output.

%WORDCNT

Purpose

This macro returns the number of words in the input string.

Syntax

%wordcnt (list, dlm)

> *list* is any string of characters or numbers that does not contain a comma, quote, ampersand, percent sign, or semicolon.
>
> *dlm* (optional) is any character delimiter other than a comma, quote, ampersand, percent sign, or semicolon. The delimiter may be more than one character.

See Also

%OBSCNT, %RECCNT, %VARCNT, %WORDCNT

Notes

A COMMA (,) semicolon, ampersand, percent sign, and single or double-quotes cannot be used as a delimiter.

Example

Sample Program

```
%put NOTE:  The number of words in the string is %wordcnt() ;
%let string = The quick brown fox jumped over the lazy dogs. ;
%put NOTE:  The number of words in the string is %wordcnt(&string) ;
```

```
%let string = This    sentence    has multiple blanks ;
%put NOTE:  The number of words in the string is %wordcnt(&string) ;
```

SAS Log

```
1          %put NOTE:  The number of words in the string is %wordcnt() ;
NOTE:  The number of words in the string is 0
2          %let string = The quick brown fox jumped over the lazy dogs. ;
3          %put NOTE:  The number of words in the string is %wordcnt(&string) ;
NOTE:  The number of words in the string is 9
4          %let string = This    sentence    has multiple blanks ;
5          %put NOTE:  The number of words in the string is %wordcnt(&string) ;
NOTE:  The number of words in the string is 5
```

SAS Listing

This sample program does not have any listing output.

%ZIPFIPS

Purpose

Converts ZIP codes to FIPS state codes

Syntax

%ZIPFIPS(zip)

> *zip* specifies any SAS character expression containing a five-digit ZIP code. Requirement: The character expressions you use must have a length of five.

See Also

%FIPNAME, %FIPNAMEL, %FIPSTATE, %STFIPS, %STNAME, %STNAMEL, %ZIPFIPS, %ZIPNAME, %ZIPNAMEL, %ZIPSTATE

Notes

The ZIPFIPS function returns the two-digit numeric U.S. Federal Information Processing Standards (FIPS) code corresponding to its five-character ZIP code argument.

Example

Sample Program

```
%put ZIPFIPS=%zipfips(60601) ;
%put ZIPFIPS=%zipfips(6A601) ;
%put ZIPFIPS=%zipfips(10000-0000) ;
%put ZIPFIPS=%zipfips(1000) ;
```

SAS Log

```
1          %put ZIPFIPS=%zipfips(60601) ;
ZIPFIPS=17
2          %put ZIPFIPS=%zipfips(6A601) ;
NOTE: Argument 1 (6A601) in macro %ZIPFIPS is not a valid ZIP code.
ZIPFIPS=.
3          %put ZIPFIPS=%zipfips(10000-0000) ;
NOTE: Argument 1 (10000-0000) in macro %ZIPFIPS is not a valid ZIP code.
ZIPFIPS=.
4          %put ZIPFIPS=%zipfips(1000) ;
```

```
NOTE: Argument 1 in macro %ZIPFIPS is missing or out of range.
ZIPFIPS=.
```

SAS Listing

This sample program does not have any listing output.

%ZIPNAME

Purpose

Converts ZIP codes to uppercase state names

Syntax

%zipname(zip)

> *zip* specifies any SAS character expression containing a five-digit ZIP code. Requirement: The character expressions you use must have a length of five.

See Also

%FIPNAME, %FIPNAMEL, %FIPSTATE, %STFIPS, %STNAME, %STNAMEL, %ZIPFIPS, %ZIPNAME, %ZIPNAMEL, %ZIPSTATE

Notes

ZIPNAME returns the name of the state or U.S. territory that corresponds to its five-character ZIP code argument. ZIPNAME returns character values up to 20 characters long, all in uppercase.

Example

Sample Program

```
%put ZIPNAME=%zipname(60601) ;
%put ZIPNAME=%zipname(01000) ;
```

SAS Log

```
1          %put ZIPNAME=%zipname(60601) ;
ZIPNAME=ILLINOIS
2          %put ZIPNAME=%zipname(01000) ;
ZIPNAME=MASSACHUSETTS
```

SAS Listing

This sample program does not have any listing output.

%ZIPNAMEL

Purpose

Converts ZIP codes to mixed case state names

Syntax

%zipnamel(zip)

zip specifies any SAS character expression containing a five-digit ZIP code. Requirement: The character expressions you use must have a length of five.

See Also
%FIPNAME, %FIPNAMEL, %FIPSTATE, %STFIPS, %STNAME, %STNAMEL, %ZIPFIPS, %ZIPNAME, %ZIPNAMEL, %ZIPSTATE

Notes
ZIPNAMEL returns the name of the state or U.S. territory that corresponds to its five-character ZIP code argument. ZIPNAMEL returns mixed case character values up to 20 characters long.

Example

Sample Program
```
%put ZIPNAMEL=%zipnamel(60601) ;
%put ZIPNAMEL=%zipnamel(01000) ;
```

SAS Log
```
1          %put ZIPNAMEL=%zipnamel(60601) ;
ZIPNAMEL=Illinois
2          %put ZIPNAMEL=%zipnamel(01000) ;
ZIPNAMEL=Massachusetts
```

SAS Listing
This sample program does not have any listing output.

%ZIPSTATE

Purpose
Converts ZIP codes to state postal codes

Syntax
%zipstate(zip)

> *zip* specifies any SAS character expression containing a five-digit ZIP code. Requirement: The character expressions you use must have a length of five.

See Also
%FIPNAME, %FIPNAMEL, %FIPSTATE, %STFIPS, %STNAME, %STNAMEL, %ZIPFIPS, %ZIPNAME, %ZIPNAMEL, %ZIPSTATE

Notes
ZIPSTATE returns the two-character state postal code (or world-wide GSA geographic code for U.S. territories) that corresponds to its five-character ZIP code argument. ZIPSTATE returns character values in uppercase.

Example

Sample Program

```
%put zipstate=%zipstate(60601) ;
%put zipstate=%zipstate(01000) ;
```

SAS Log

```
1          %put zipstate=%zipstate(60601) ;
zipstate=IL
2          %put zipstate=%zipstate(01000) ;
zipstate=MA
```

SAS Listing

This sample program does not have any listing output.

Macros

%BIGSORT

PURPOSE:
This macro breaks a data set into smaller data sets, sorts those smaller data sets, and then combines them back together in order. It is designed for sorting a very large dataset more efficiently by using less sort space.

SYNTAX:
%BIGSORT (DATA= *SAS-data-set*, OUT = *SAS-data-set*, BY = <DESCENDING> variable-1 <...<DESCENDING> variable-n> <,PARTS=parts> <,DEBUG = YES | Y | NO | N>)

Required Parameter(s)
DATA= SAS-data-set

    identifies the input SAS data set.

OUT = SAS-data-set

    identifies the output SAS data set.

BY = <DESCENDING> *variable-1* <...<DESCENDING> *variable-n*>

    specifies the variable by which PROC SORT sorts the observations. PROC SORT first arranges the data set by the values in ascending order, by default, of the first BY variable. PROC SORT then arranges any observations that have the same value of the first BY variable by the values in ascending order of the second BY variable. This sorting continues for every specified BY variable. DESCENDING reverses the sort order for the variable that immediately follows in the statement so that observations are sorted from the largest value to the smallest value.

Optional Parameter(s)
PARTS = *parts*

    States the positive integer value to "break into parts" for the completion of the sub-sorting routines. The default value is 10.

DEBUG = Y | YES | NO | N

    debugging flag, set to YES or NO. Alternatively, you can submit Y or N. Default is NO.

Notes
Because the data is broken into several pieces, PROC SORT options cannot be used.

EXAMPLE:

Sample Program
```
data bigdata ;
   do i = 1 to 1000000 ;
      ranuni1 = ranuni(0) ;
      ranuni2 = ranuni(0) ;
      ranuni3 = ranuni(0) ;
      ranuni4 = ranuni(0) ;
```

```
        ranuni5 = ranuni(0) ;
        ranuni6 = ranuni(0) ;
        output ;
    end ;
run ;

%bigsort (data=bigdata, out=sorted, by=ranuni1 ranuni2 ranuni3 ranuni4 ranuni5 ranuni6)
```

SAS Log

```
1    data bigdata ;
2        do i = 1 to 1000000 ;
3            ranuni1 = ranuni(0) ;
4            ranuni2 = ranuni(0) ;
5            ranuni3 = ranuni(0) ;
6            ranuni4 = ranuni(0) ;
7            ranuni5 = ranuni(0) ;
8            ranuni6 = ranuni(0) ;
9            output ;
10       end ;
11   run ;

NOTE: The data set WORK.BIGDATA has 1000000 observations and 7 variables.
NOTE: DATA statement used:
      real time          3.46 seconds
      cpu time           2.03 seconds


12
13   %bigsort (data=bigdata, out=sorted, by=ranuni1 ranuni2 ranuni3 ranuni4 ranuni5 ranuni6)

NOTE: The data set WORK.SORTED has 1000000 observations and 7 variables.
NOTE: The MACRO %BIGSORT used:
      real time          14.32 seconds
      cpu time           unknown
```

SAS Listing

This sample program does not have any listing output.

%BREAKOUT

Purpose

This macro is designed to create multiple SAS data sets from one given data set or view. Each data set contains the unique records that apply to a specific variable. For example, if the value of VAR is COLOR, then each output data set would contain all of the records for each one unique value of color. All of the records for BLUE would be in one data set, RED in another data set, GREEN in a third data set, etc.

Syntax

%BREAKOUT (DATA = *SAS-data-set*, VAR = *variable-name*, OUTLIB = *SAS-data-library*<, PATH = *OS-path-name*> <,DEBUG = YES | Y | NO | N>)

Required Parameter(s)

DATA = *SAS-data-set*

    identifies the input SAS data set.

VAR = *variable-name*

identifies the key variable for breaking out the SAS data set into various parts.

OUTLIB = *SAS-data-library*

identifies the output SAS data library.

Optional Parameter(s)

PATH = *OS-path-name*

represents the operating system path (for example, a Windows folder) where multiple output comma-separated value files can be written by the macro.

DEBUG = Y | YES | NO | N

debugging flag, set to YES or NO. Alternatively, you can submit Y or N. Default is NO.

Notes

There are three known issues with this macro:

1. Only one value for VAR can be used. Currently the macro does not support multiple key variables. If you need to use multiple key variables, precede the macro with a data step that combines the multiple variables into one variable using concatenation.

2. Large numbers of variable frequencies may result in a SAS Warning for unbalanced quotation marks. This can be ignored.

3. Key Variable Values cannot contain semicolons, concatenation characters, or double-quotes.

Example

Sample Program

```
%breakout (data   = sashelp.shoes,
           var    = region,
           path   = 'c:\temp',
           outlib = work)
```

SAS Log

```
1    %breakout (data   = sashelp.shoes,
2               var    = region,
3               path   = 'c:\temp',
4               outlib = work)
NOTE: There is a possibility of a WARNING (32-169) for unbalanced quotation marks
      in the following steps.  This is expected and can be ignored.  There is no
      fix for this at this time.
56 records created in c:\temp\region_Africa.csv from WORK.REGION1
14 records created in c:\temp\region_Asia.csv from WORK.REGION2
37 records created in c:\temp\region_Canada.csv from WORK.REGION3
32 records created in c:\temp\region_CentralAmerica-Caribbean.csv from WORK.REGION4
31 records created in c:\temp\region_EasternEurope.csv from WORK.REGION5
24 records created in c:\temp\region_MiddleEast.csv from WORK.REGION6
45 records created in c:\temp\region_Pacific.csv from WORK.REGION7
54 records created in c:\temp\region_SouthAmerica.csv from WORK.REGION8
40 records created in c:\temp\region_UnitedStates.csv from WORK.REGION9
62 records created in c:\temp\region_WesternEurope.csv from WORK.REGION10
NOTE: The data set WORK.REGION1 has 56 observations and 7 variables.
NOTE: The data set WORK.REGION2 has 14 observations and 7 variables.
NOTE: The data set WORK.REGION3 has 37 observations and 7 variables.
NOTE: The data set WORK.REGION4 has 32 observations and 7 variables.
NOTE: The data set WORK.REGION5 has 31 observations and 7 variables.
NOTE: The data set WORK.REGION6 has 24 observations and 7 variables.
```

```
NOTE: The data set WORK.REGION7 has 45 observations and 7 variables.
NOTE: The data set WORK.REGION8 has 54 observations and 7 variables.
NOTE: The data set WORK.REGION9 has 40 observations and 7 variables.
NOTE: The data set WORK.REGION10 has 62 observations and 7 variables.
NOTE: The MACRO %BREAKOUT used:
      real time           4.82 seconds
      cpu time            unknown
```

SAS Listing

This sample program does not have any listing output.

%CHECKALL

Purpose

This macro prints a check-all-that-apply report on a special kind of check-all-that-apply variable

Syntax

%CHECKALL (DATA = *SAS-data-set*, VAR = *variable-name*, LENGTH = *check-all-variable-length* <, FORMAT = *SAS-format*> <,DEBUG = YES | Y | NO | N>)

Required Parameter(s)

DATA = *SAS-data-set*

    identifies the input SAS data set.

VAR = *variable-name*

    identifies the large "checkall" variable.

LENGTH = *check-all-variable-length*

    identifies the numeric length of the substring "checkall" variable. Range: Positive Integer less than the length of the variable VAR.

Optional Parameter(s)

FORMAT = *SAS-format*

    The FORMAT statement associates a format with the substring of the check-all-that-apply variable. SAS uses the format to write the values of the variable that you specify

DEBUG = Y | YES | NO | N

    debugging flag, set to YES or NO. Alternatively, you can submit Y or N. Default is NO.

Example

Sample Program

```
*-------------------------------------------------------------------------*
| This macro is for reporting on a CHECK-ALL-THAT-APPLY variable where a survey |
| participant may check more than one response.  Consider the following sample  |
| survey:                                                                       |
|                                                                               |
| 1)  What is your name?                                                        |
| 2)  Of these selections, what foods would you like for dinner?                |
|     A)   Steak        F)  French Fries                                        |
|     B)   Broccoli     G)  Salad                                               |
```

```
    |          C)  Potatoes      H)  Garlic Bread                              |
    |          D)  Ice Cream     I)  Peas and Carrots                          |
    |          E)  Chicken       J)  Other                                     |
    |                                                                          |
    |  Our data is stored in the CARDS statement, read in, and processed.  A report  |
    |  is generated that is similar to PROC FREQ.                              |
    *--------------------------------------------------------------------------* ;

data survey ;
   input @1  name  $10.
         @11 foods $10. ;
cards ;
Will      ACDGH
Jill      ECI
Hester    AFG
Chester   EFG
Peter     ABH
Polly     BCGH
Tim       AGH
Tom       ABJ
Mary      ACDF
Larry     AGH
Clarinda  EFI
;
run ;

proc format ;
   value $foods 'A' = 'Steak'
                'B' = 'Broccoli'
                'C' = 'Potatoes'
                'D' = 'Ice Cream'
                'E' = 'Chicken'
                'F' = 'French Fries'
                'G' = 'Salad'
                'H' = 'Garlic Bread'
                'I' = 'Peas and Carrots'
                'J' = 'Other' ;
run ;

title1 'SPIKEware Rapid Decision Support SAS Macro Package v3.0 demo' ;
title2 '%CHECKALL macro for CHECK-ALL-THAT-APPLY variables' ;
%checkall (data=survey, var=foods, length=1, format=$foods.)
```

SAS Log

```
1       *--------------------------------------------------------------------------*
2       | This macro is for reporting on a CHECK-ALL-THAT-APPLY variable where a survey |
3       | participant may check more than one response.  Consider the following sample |
4       | survey:                                                                  |
5       |                                                                          |
6       | 1)  What is your name?                                                   |
7       | 2)  Of these selections, what foods would you like for dinner?           |
8       |          A)  Steak         F)  French Fries                              |
9       |          B)  Broccoli      G)  Salad                                     |
10      |          C)  Potatoes      H)  Garlic Bread                              |
11      |          D)  Ice Cream     I)  Peas and Carrots                          |
12      |          E)  Chicken       J)  Other                                     |
13      |                                                                          |
14      | Our data is stored in the CARDS statement, read in, and processed.  A report |
15      | is generated that is similar to PROC FREQ.                               |
16      *--------------------------------------------------------------------------* ;
17
18      data survey ;
19         input @1  name  $10.
20               @11 foods $10. ;
21      cards ;

NOTE: The data set WORK.SURVEY has 11 observations and 2 variables.
```

```
NOTE: DATA statement used:
      real time           0.01 seconds
      cpu time            0.01 seconds


33    ;
34    run ;
35
36    proc format ;
37       value $foods 'A' = 'Steak'
38                    'B' = 'Broccoli'
39                    'C' = 'Potatoes'
40                    'D' = 'Ice Cream'
41                    'E' = 'Chicken'
42                    'F' = 'French Fries'
43                    'G' = 'Salad'
44                    'H' = 'Garlic Bread'
45                    'I' = 'Peas and Carrots'
46                    'J' = 'Other' ;
NOTE: Format $FOODS has been output.
47    run ;

NOTE: PROCEDURE FORMAT used:
      real time           0.06 seconds
      cpu time            0.00 seconds

48
49    title1 'SPIKEware Rapid Decision Support SAS Macro Package v3.0 demo' ;
50    title2 '%CHECKALL macro for CHECK-ALL-THAT-APPLY variables' ;
51    %checkall (data=survey, var=foods, length=1, format=$foods.)
NOTE: The MACRO %CHECKALL used:
      real time           0.43 seconds
      cpu time            unknown
```

SAS Listing

```
          SPIKEware Rapid Decision Support SAS Macro Package v3.0 demo
                 %CHECKALL macro for CHECK-ALL-THAT-APPLY variables

                              The FREQ Procedure

                          Check-all-that-apply variable

                                              Cumulative   Cumulative
          foods            Frequency  Percent  Frequency     Percent
          ƒƒƒƒƒƒƒƒƒƒƒƒƒƒƒƒƒƒƒƒƒƒƒƒƒƒƒƒƒƒƒƒƒƒƒƒƒƒƒƒƒƒƒƒƒƒƒƒƒƒƒƒƒƒƒƒƒƒƒƒ
          Steak                    7    18.92          7       18.92
          Broccoli                 3     8.11         10       27.03
          Potatoes                 4    10.81         14       37.84
          Ice Cream                2     5.41         16       43.24
          Chicken                  3     8.11         19       51.35
          French Fries             4    10.81         23       62.16
          Salad                    6    16.22         29       78.38
          Garlic Bread             5    13.51         34       91.89
          Peas and Carrots         2     5.41         36       97.30
          Other                    1     2.70         37      100.00
```

%CHECKREC

Purpose

This macro prints a sample of the first records of an input file

Syntax

%CHECKREC (INFILE = *filename* | *"file-specification"*<, FILE = *filename* | *"file-specification"*> <,OBS = *n-observations*> <,DEBUG = YES | Y | NO | N>)

Required Parameter(s)

INFILE = *filename* | *"file-specification"*

> declares the input file.
>
>> *filename* specifies the fileref of an external file.
>>
>> *"file-specification"* specifies the physical name of an external file, which is enclosed in quotation marks. The physical name is the name by which the operating environment recognizes the file.
>
> Either the *filename* or *"file-specification"* must be declared, but not both.

Optional Parameter(s)

FILE = *filename* | *"file-specification"*

> declares the output file. Default is GARBAGE (temporary file location)
>
>> *filename* specifies the fileref of an external file.
>>
>> *"file-specification"* specifies the physical name of an external file, which is enclosed in quotation marks. The physical name is the name by which the operating environment recognizes the file.
>
> Either the *filename* or *"file-specification"* must be declared, but not both.

OBS = *n-observations*

> declares the number of observations to read (and consequently write) in the input data file. Default is 45. Range: Positive Integer.

DEBUG = Y | YES | NO | N

> debugging flag, set to YES or NO. Alternatively, you can submit Y or N. Default is NO.

Example

Sample Program

```
filename govt   '!sasroot\fedgovt.txt' ;
%checkrec (infile = govt, file='C:\temp\checkrec.txt')
```

SAS Log

```
1     filename govt   '!sasroot\fedgovt.txt' ;
2     %checkrec (infile = govt, file='C:\temp\checkrec.txt')
NOTE: The file 'C:\TEMP\CHECKREC.TXT' is:
      File Name=C:\TEMP\CHECKREC.TXT,
      RECFM=V,LRECL=256

NOTE: 30 records were written to the file 'C:\TEMP\CHECKREC.TXT'.
      The minimum record length was 0.
      The maximum record length was 78.
NOTE: The MACRO %CHECKREC used:
      real time             0.62 seconds
      cpu time              unknown
```

SAS Listing

```
Report of the first 45 records of SAS filename
GOVT=c:\sasv8\fedgovt.txt


LINE #          1         2         3         4         5         6
------ ----|----0----|----0----|----0----|----0----|----0----|----0----|----0
000001 The following is applicable to Federal Government or Federal Government
000002 Prime Contractor installations:
000003
000004                   Copyright, SAS Institute Inc.
000005                   Unpublished - All Rights Reserved
000006
000007
000008
000009        This software is a licensed product of SAS Institute Inc.
000010
000011
000012
000013                   U.S. Government Restricted Rights
000014
000015
000016
000017 Use, duplication, or disclosure of this software and related
000018 documentation by the U.S. government is subject to the Agreement with
000019 SAS Institute and the restrictions set forth in FAR 52.227-19,
000020 Commercial Computer Software - Restricted Rights (June 1987).  The
000021 Contractor/Licensor is SAS Institute Inc., located at SAS Campus Drive,
000022 Cary, North Carolina, USA 27513
```

%COMPARE

Purpose

This macro is used to compare multiple datasets and check for any similar variable names. It also does a comparison of the number of observations and prints a list of discrepencies of variable names and variable types.

Syntax

%COMPARE (DATALIST = SAS-data-set-1 SAS-data-set-2 <... SAS-data-set-n> <,DEBUG = YES | Y | NO | N>)

Required Parameter(s)

DATALIST = *SAS-data-set-1 SAS-data-set-2 <...SAS-data-set-n>*

    identifies the input SAS data sets for comparison. At least two data sets must be declared, and no more than 9,999,999 data sets may be declared.

Optional Parameter(s)

DEBUG = Y | YES | NO | N

    debugging flag, set to YES or NO. Alternatively, you can submit Y or N. Default is NO.

See Also

PROC COMPARE

Example

Sample Program

```
data jan feb mar apr may jun jul aug sep oct nov ;
    do day = '01jan2000'd to '30nov2000'd ;
        value1 = ranuni(0) ;
        value2 = ranuni(0) ;
        VALUE3 = ranuni(0) ;
        value4 = ranuni(0) ;
        Value5 = ranuni(0) ;
        value6 = ranuni(0) ;
        month = month(day) ;
        select (month) ;
            when (1) output jan ;
            when (2) output feb ;
            when (3) output mar ;
            when (4) output apr ;
            when (5) output may ;
            when (6) output jun ;
            when (7) output jul ;
            when (8) output aug ;
            when (9) output sep ;
            when (10) output oct ;
            when (11) output nov ;
            otherwise ;
        end ;
    end ;
run ;

data dec ;
    do day = '01dec2000'd to '31dec2000'd ;
        value1 = ranuni(0) ;
        value2 = ranuni(0) ;
        value3 = ranuni(0) ;
        value4 = 'character' ;
        value7 = ranuni(0) ;
        output ;
    end ;
run ;

title1 'SPIKEware Rapid Decision Support SAS Macro Package v3.1 demo' ;
title2 '%COMPARE runs a comparison of many SAS datasets' ;
%compare (datalist = jan feb mar apr may jun jul aug sep oct nov dec)
%compare (datalist = _all_)
```

SAS Log

```
1     data jan feb mar apr may jun jul aug sep oct nov ;
2         do day = '01jan2000'd to '30nov2000'd ;
3             value1 = ranuni(0) ;
4             value2 = ranuni(0) ;
5             VALUE3 = ranuni(0) ;
6             value4 = ranuni(0) ;
7             Value5 = ranuni(0) ;
8             value6 = ranuni(0) ;
9             month = month(day) ;
10            select (month) ;
11                when (1) output jan ;
12                when (2) output feb ;
13                when (3) output mar ;
14                when (4) output apr ;
15                when (5) output may ;
16                when (6) output jun ;
17                when (7) output jul ;
18                when (8) output aug ;
19                when (9) output sep ;
```

```
20              when (10) output oct ;
21              when (11) output nov ;
22              otherwise ;
23           end ;
24        end ;
25     run ;

NOTE: The data set WORK.JAN has 31 observations and 8 variables.
NOTE: The data set WORK.FEB has 29 observations and 8 variables.
NOTE: The data set WORK.MAR has 31 observations and 8 variables.
NOTE: The data set WORK.APR has 30 observations and 8 variables.
NOTE: The data set WORK.MAY has 31 observations and 8 variables.
NOTE: The data set WORK.JUN has 30 observations and 8 variables.
NOTE: The data set WORK.JUL has 31 observations and 8 variables.
NOTE: The data set WORK.AUG has 31 observations and 8 variables.
NOTE: The data set WORK.SEP has 30 observations and 8 variables.
NOTE: The data set WORK.OCT has 31 observations and 8 variables.
NOTE: The data set WORK.NOV has 30 observations and 8 variables.
NOTE: DATA statement used:
      real time            0.14 seconds
      cpu time             0.02 seconds


26
27     data dec ;
28        do day = '01dec2000'd to '31dec2000'd ;
29           value1 = ranuni(0) ;
30           value2 = ranuni(0) ;
31           value3 = ranuni(0) ;
32           value4 = 'character' ;
33           value7 = ranuni(0) ;
34           output ;
35        end ;
36     run ;

NOTE: The data set WORK.DEC has 31 observations and 6 variables.
NOTE: DATA statement used:
      real time            0.00 seconds
      cpu time             0.00 seconds


37
38     title1 'SPIKEware Rapid Decision Support SAS Macro Package v3.1 demo' ;
39     title2 '%COMPARE runs a comparison of many SAS datasets' ;
40     %compare (datalist = jan feb mar apr may jun jul aug sep oct nov dec)

NOTE: The MACRO %COMPARE used:
      real time            2.59 seconds
      cpu time             unknown

41     %compare (datalist = _all_)

NOTE: The MACRO %COMPARE used:
      real time            1.69 seconds
      cpu time             unknown
```

SAS Listing

```
                    SPIKEware Rapid Decision Support SAS Macro Package v3.1 demo
                                    comparison of sas datasets
WORK.APR WORK.AUG WORK.DEC WORK.FEB WORK.JAN WORK.JUL WORK.JUN WORK.MAR WORK.MAY WORK.NOV WORK.OCT

                    min obs = 29      mean obs = 30.5      max obs = 31

                    1 = yes
                    0 = no                                                        variable
Obs      name       <-- scroll check -->    description    length    format    type    match
```

```
    1    DAY       111111111111                      8         8       num      good
    2    MONTH     111111111110                      8         8       num      error = m
    3    VALUE1    111111111111                      8         8       num      good
    4    VALUE2    111111111111                      8         8       num      good
    5    VALUE3    111111111111                      8         8       num      good
    6    VALUE4    111111111111                      8         8       num      error = lt
    7    VALUE5    111111111110                      8         8       num      error = m
    8    VALUE6    111111111110                      8         8       num      error = m
    9    VALUE7    000000000001                      .         .       other    error = lt
```

SPIKEware Rapid Decision Support SAS Macro Package v3.1 demo
comparison of sas datasets

WORK.APR WORK.AUG WORK.DEC WORK.FEB WORK.JAN WORK.JUL WORK.JUN WORK.MAR WORK.MAY WORK.NOV WORK.OCT

correct match of data?

The FREQ Procedure

variable match

```
                                    Cumulative    Cumulative
    match        Frequency   Percent   Frequency     Percent
    ƒƒƒƒƒƒƒƒƒƒƒƒƒƒƒƒƒƒƒƒƒƒƒƒƒƒƒƒƒƒƒƒƒƒƒƒƒƒƒƒƒƒƒƒƒƒƒƒƒƒƒƒƒƒ
    error = lt       2        22.22          2         22.22
    error = m        3        33.33          5         55.56
    good             4        44.44          9        100.00
```

SPIKEware Rapid Decision Support SAS Macro Package v3.1 demo
comparison of sas datasets

WORK.APR WORK.AUG WORK.DEC WORK.FEB WORK.JAN WORK.JUL WORK.JUN WORK.MAR WORK.MAY WORK.NOV WORK.OCT

```
                      min obs = 29     mean obs = 30.5     max obs = 31

                          1 = yes
                          0 = no                                                  variable
    Obs    name       <-- scroll check -->   description   length   format   type    match

     1    DAY         111111111111                            8         8     num    good
     2    MONTH       110111111111                            8         8     num    error = m
     3    VALUE1      111111111111                            8         8     num    good
     4    VALUE2      111111111111                            8         8     num    good
     5    VALUE3      111111111111                            8         8     num    good
     6    VALUE4      111111111111                            8         8     num    good
     7    VALUE5      110111111111                            8         8     num    error = m
     8    VALUE6      110111111111                            8         8     num    error = m
     9    VALUE7      001000000000                            .         .     other  error = m
```

```
                   SPIKEware Rapid Decision Support SAS Macro Package v3.1 demo
                                    comparison of sas datasets
WORK.APR WORK.AUG WORK.DEC WORK.FEB WORK.JAN WORK.JUL WORK.JUN WORK.MAR WORK.MAY WORK.NOV WORK.OCT

                                       correct match of data?

                                        The FREQ Procedure

                                          variable match

                                                          Cumulative    Cumulative
                   match       Frequency     Percent      Frequency     Percent
                   ƒƒƒƒƒƒƒƒƒƒƒƒƒƒƒƒƒƒƒƒƒƒƒƒƒƒƒƒƒƒƒƒƒƒƒƒƒƒƒƒƒƒƒƒƒƒƒƒƒƒƒƒƒƒƒƒƒƒ
                   error = m        4         44.44           4          44.44
                   good             5         55.56           9         100.00
```

%CONTENTS

Purpose

This macro runs a proc contents and prints the first 20 records of the input dataset or datasets. The number of observations can be overridden to a specific value. The macro can also add a title to your output.

Syntax

%CONTENTS (<DATA|DATALIST = SAS-data-set-1< ... SAS-data-set-n>> <,OBS = observations> <,TITLE = Y | YES | NO | N > <, DEBUG = Y | YES | NO | N>)

Required Parameter(s)

This macro does not have any required parameters.

Optional Parameter(s)

DATA|DATALIST = SAS-data-set-1< ... SAS-data-set-n>

    identifies the input SAS data set or data sets. If DATA or DATALIST is not declared, the most recently created data set is used.

OBS = observations

    declares the number of observations to print for each given data set. Default is 20. Range: positive integer.

TITLE = Y | YES | NO | N

    declares if the %CONTENTS macro should automatically generate a TITLE for the SAS Output. Default is NO.

DEBUG = Y | YES | NO | N

    debugging flag, set to YES or NO. Alternatively, you can submit Y or N. Default is NO.

See Also

PROC CONTENTS, PROC PRINT

Notes

If no SAS dataset is specified, the last SAS dataset created is assumed. There is no difference between the DATA = and DATALIST = input parameters. If both DATA and DATALIST are declared, the macro will process all data sets declared on both declarations.

Example

Sample Program

```
%contents (data=sashelp.shoes sashelp.deskact sashelp.class, title=y)
```

SAS Log

```
1    %contents (data=sashelp.shoes sashelp.deskact sashelp.class, title=y)

NOTE: The MACRO %CONTENTS used:
      real time           1.46 seconds
      cpu time                 unknown
```

SAS Listing

```
                Sample of dataset SASHELP.CLASS:   20 of 19
                          The CONTENTS Procedure

     Data Set Name: SASHELP.CLASS                Observations:           19
     Member Type:   DATA                         Variables:              5
     Engine:        V8                           Indexes:                0
     Created:       15:34 Tuesday, August 10, 1999   Observation Length: 40
     Last Modified: 15:34 Tuesday, August 10, 1999   Deleted Observations: 0
     Protection:                                 Compressed:             NO
     Data Set Type:                              Sorted:                 NO
     Label:


                -----Engine/Host Dependent Information-----

     Data Set Page Size:         4096
     Number of Data Set Pages:   1
     First Data Page:            1
     Max Obs per Page:           101
     Obs in First Data Page:     19
     Number of Data Set Repairs: 0
     File Name:                  c:\sasv8\core\sashelp\class.sas7bdat
     Release Created:            8.0000M0
     Host Created:               WIN_NT


              -----Alphabetic List of Variables and Attributes-----

               #    Variable    Type    Len    Pos
               ƒƒƒƒƒƒƒƒƒƒƒƒƒƒƒƒƒƒƒƒƒƒƒƒƒƒƒƒƒƒƒƒƒƒƒƒƒƒ
               3    Age         Num     8      0
               4    Height      Num     8      8
               1    Name        Char    8      24
               2    Sex         Char    1      32
               5    Weight      Num     8      16

           Sample of dataset SASHELP.CLASS:   20 of 19

         Obs    Name      Sex    Age    Height    Weight

          1     Alfred     M      14     69.0     112.5
          2     Alice      F      13     56.5      84.0
          3     Barbara    F      13     65.3      98.0
```

```
         4    Carol      F    14    62.8    102.5
         5    Henry      M    14    63.5    102.5
         6    James      M    12    57.3     83.0
         7    Jane       F    12    59.8     84.5
         8    Janet      F    15    62.5    112.5
         9    Jeffrey    M    13    62.5     84.0
        10    John       M    12    59.0     99.5
        11    Joyce      F    11    51.3     50.5
        12    Judy       F    14    64.3     90.0
        13    Louise     F    12    56.3     77.0
        14    Mary       F    15    66.5    112.0
        15    Philip     M    16    72.0    150.0
        16    Robert     M    12    64.8    128.0
        17    Ronald     M    15    67.0    133.0
        18    Thomas     M    11    57.5     85.0
        19    William    M    15    66.5    112.0

            Sample of dataset SASHELP.DESKACT:  20 of 166
                         The CONTENTS Procedure
```

```
Data Set Name: SASHELP.DESKACT                 Observations:          166
Member Type:   DATA                            Variables:               7
Engine:        V8                              Indexes:                 1
Created:       17:46 Wednesday, June 21, 2006  Observation Length:    120
Last Modified: 17:46 Wednesday, June 21, 2006  Deleted Observations:    0
Protection:                                    Compressed:             NO
Data Set Type:                                 Sorted:                 NO
Label:         Version 1.13


            -----Engine/Host Dependent Information-----

        Data Set Page Size:          12288
        Number of Data Set Pages:    3
        First Data Page:             1
        Max Obs per Page:            102
        Obs in First Data Page:      88
        Index File Page Size:        4096
        Number of Index File Pages:  2
        Number of Data Set Repairs:  0
        File Name:                   c:\sasv8\SASCFG\deskact.sas7bdat
        Release Created:             8.0202M0
        Host Created:                WIN_PRO


            -----Alphabetic List of Variables and Attributes-----

              #    Variable    Type    Len    Pos
              ƒƒƒƒƒƒƒƒƒƒƒƒƒƒƒƒƒƒƒƒƒƒƒƒƒƒƒƒƒƒƒƒƒƒƒ
              5    action      Char     32     43
              6    desc        Char     40     75
              2    objtype     Char      8     27
              4    pos         Num       8      0
              1    product     Char     11     16
              3    subtype     Char      8     35
              7    where       Num       8      8


            -----Alphabetic List of Indexes and Attributes-----

                             # of
                            Unique
              #    Index    Values    Variables
              ƒƒƒƒƒƒƒƒƒƒƒƒƒƒƒƒƒƒƒƒƒƒƒƒƒƒƒƒƒƒƒƒƒƒƒƒƒƒ
              1    objsub     83      objtype subtype

            Sample of dataset SASHELP.DESKACT:  20 of 166
```

```
Obs    product    objtype    subtype    pos    action         desc            where

 1     foldptr                            2    _open_         Open              1
 2     foldptr                            4    _explore_      Explore           1
 3     folder                            20    _rename_       Rename            1
 4     folder                            30    _copy_         Copy              1
 5     adoappl                           10    _run_          Run               1
 6     sascmd                            10    _run_          Run               1
 7     hcmd                              10    _run_          Run               1
 8     file                              10    _edit_         Open              3
 9     file                              20    _import_       Import            1
10     file                              30    _print_        Print             3
11     file                              90    _redefine_     Redefine          1
12     file                             100    _remove_       Deassign          1
13     file                             110    _properties_   Properties        1
14     file       sas                    15                   SASView           2
15     file       sas                    18                   Batch Submit      2
16     file       sas                    25    _submit_       Submit            3
17     file       ss2                    25    _submit_       Submit            3
18     fileptr                           10    _edit_         Open              1
19     fileptr                           20    _import_       Import            1
20     fileptr                           30    _print_        Print             3
```

Sample of dataset SASHELP.SHOES: 20 of 395

The CONTENTS Procedure

```
Data Set Name: SASHELP.SHOES                    Observations:         395
Member Type:   DATA                             Variables:            7
Engine:        V8                               Indexes:              0
Created:       15:34 Tuesday, August 10, 1999   Observation Length:   88
Last Modified: 15:34 Tuesday, August 10, 1999   Deleted Observations: 0
Protection:                                     Compressed:           NO
Data Set Type:                                  Sorted:               NO
Label:         Fictitious Shoe Company Data
```

-----Engine/Host Dependent Information-----

```
Data Set Page Size:         8192
Number of Data Set Pages:   5
First Data Page:            1
Max Obs per Page:           92
Obs in First Data Page:     71
Number of Data Set Repairs: 0
File Name:                  c:\sasv8\core\sashelp\shoes.sas7bdat
Release Created:            8.0000M0
Host Created:               WIN_NT
```

-----Alphabetic List of Variables and Attributes-----

```
#   Variable    Type    Len    Pos    Format      Informat    Label
ƒƒƒƒƒƒƒƒƒƒƒƒƒƒƒƒƒƒƒƒƒƒƒƒƒƒƒƒƒƒƒƒƒƒƒƒƒƒƒƒƒƒƒƒƒƒƒƒƒƒƒƒƒƒƒƒƒƒƒƒƒƒƒƒƒƒƒƒ
6   Inventory   Num      8     16    DOLLAR12.   DOLLAR12.   Total Inventory
2   Product     Char    14     57
1   Region      Char    25     32
7   Returns     Num      8     24    DOLLAR12.   DOLLAR12.   Total Returns
5   Sales       Num      8      8    DOLLAR12.   DOLLAR12.   Total Sales
4   Stores      Num      8      0                            Number of Stores
3   Subsidiary  Char    12     71
```

Obs   Region   Product   Subsidiary   Stores   Sales   Inventory   Returns

1	Africa	Boot	Addis Ababa	12	$29,761	$191,821	$769
2	Africa	Men's Casual	Addis Ababa	4	$67,242	$118,036	$2,284
3	Africa	Men's Dress	Addis Ababa	7	$76,793	$136,273	$2,433
4	Africa	Sandal	Addis Ababa	10	$62,819	$204,284	$1,861
5	Africa	Slipper	Addis Ababa	14	$68,641	$279,795	$1,771
6	Africa	Sport Shoe	Addis Ababa	4	$1,690	$16,634	$79
7	Africa	Women's Casual	Addis Ababa	2	$51,541	$98,641	$940
8	Africa	Women's Dress	Addis Ababa	12	$108,942	$311,017	$3,233
9	Africa	Boot	Algiers	21	$21,297	$73,737	$710
10	Africa	Men's Casual	Algiers	4	$63,206	$100,982	$2,221
11	Africa	Men's Dress	Algiers	13	$123,743	$428,575	$3,621
12	Africa	Sandal	Algiers	25	$29,198	$84,447	$1,530
13	Africa	Slipper	Algiers	17	$64,891	$248,198	$1,823
14	Africa	Sport Shoe	Algiers	9	$2,617	$9,372	$168
15	Africa	Women's Dress	Algiers	12	$90,648	$266,805	$2,690
16	Africa	Boot	Cairo	20	$4,846	$18,965	$229
17	Africa	Men's Casual	Cairo	25	$360,209	$1,063,251	$9,424
18	Africa	Men's Dress	Cairo	5	$4,051	$45,962	$97
19	Africa	Sandal	Cairo	9	$10,532	$50,430	$598
20	Africa	Slipper	Cairo	9	$13,732	$54,117	$1,216

%DATANOTE

Purpose

This macro prints a standard SAS note about the contents of a SAS dataset into the log.

Syntax

%datanote (data)

Required Parameter(s)

data is a valid SAS data set name. The data set must exist.

Optional Parameter(s)

There are no optional parameters.

See Also

%DATANOTE, %FILENOTE, %TIMENOTE, %INFO

Notes

Technically, this macro works as a function in that it can be used anywhere in open code without concern—except that it does not return a value back to the SAS Supervisor and only puts notes in the SAS log. Therefore, it is listed as a MACRO UTILITY instead of a MACRO FUNCTION. If the requested data set (or data view) does not exist, the macro ends without any further action.

Example

Sample Program

```
data temp ;
   do i = 1 to 10 ;
      var1 = 'EENIE' ;
      var2 = 'MEENIE' ;
```

```
         var3 = 'MINEY' ;
         var4 = 'MOE' ;
         output ;
      end ;
run ;

%datanote (temp)
```

SAS Log

```
1    data temp ;
2       do i = 1 to 10 ;
3          var1 = 'EENIE' ;
4          var2 = 'MEENIE' ;
5          var3 = 'MINEY' ;
6          var4 = 'MOE' ;
7          output ;
8       end ;
9    run ;

NOTE: The data set WORK.TEMP has 10 observations and 5 variables.
NOTE: DATA statement used:
      real time           0.00 seconds
      cpu time            0.00 seconds


10
11   %datanote (temp)
NOTE: The data set WORK.TEMP has 10 observations and 5 variables.
```

SAS Listing

This sample program does not have any listing output.

%DECRYPT

Purpose

This macro decrypts a given encrypted file.

Syntax

%DECRYPT (INFILE = *filename* | *"file-specification"*, FILE = *filename* | *"file-specification"*, KEY = *encryption-key*> <, DEBUG = Y | YES | NO | N>)

Required Parameter(s)

INFILE = *filename* | *"file-specification"*

    declares the input file.

        filename specifies the fileref of an external file.

        "file-specification" specifies the physical name of an external file, which is enclosed in quotation marks. The physical name is the name by which the operating environment recognizes the file.

    Either the *filename* or *"file-specification"* must be declared, but not both.

FILE = *filename* | *"file-specification"*

    declares the output file.

filename specifies the fileref of an external file.

"file-specification" specifies the physical name of an external file, which is enclosed in quotation marks. The physical name is the name by which the operating environment recognizes the file.

Either the *filename* or *"file-specification"* must be declared, but not both.

Optional Parameter(s)

KEY = *encryption*-key

Declares the numeric encryption key. Default is 5. Range: non-negative integer less than 51.

DEBUG = Y | YES | NO | N

debugging flag, set to YES or NO. Alternatively, you can submit Y or N. Default is NO.

See Also
%DECRYPT, %ENCRYPT

Example

Sample Program
```
%decrypt (infile = 'C:\temp\license.enc',
          file   = 'C:\temp\license.txt',
          key    = 5)
```

SAS Log
```
1    %decrypt (infile = 'C:\temp\license.enc',
2              file   = 'C:\temp\license.txt',
3              key    = 5)
NOTE: The file 'C:\temp\license.txt' is:
      File Name=C:\temp\license.txt,
      RECFM=V,LRECL=256

NOTE: 68 records were written to the file 'C:\temp\license.txt'.
      The minimum record length was 0.
      The maximum record length was 94.
NOTE: The MACRO %DECRYPT used:
      real time            0.32 seconds
      cpu time             unknown
```

SAS Listing
This sample program does not have any listing output.

%DIRECTORY

Purpose
This macro reads the files in a drive including sub-directories and writes the results out to a standard SAS dataset. This macro only functions on the Microsoft Windows operating system.

Syntax
%DIRECTORY (DRIVE = *drive-letter*, OUT = *SAS-data-set*<, DEBUG = Y | YES | NO | N>)

Required Parameter(s)

DRIVE = *drive-letter*

> declares the MS-Windows-drive-letter and/or folder. The drive or folder must exist.

OUT = *SAS-data-set*

> identifies the input SAS data set or data sets. If DATA or DATALIST is not declared, the most recently

Optional Parameter(s)

DEBUG = Y | YES | NO | N

> debugging flag, set to YES or NO. Alternatively, you can submit Y or N. Default is NO.

See Also

%COMMAND, %DOSPATH, %DIRECTORY, %CURRENTPATH, %FINDFILE, %SYSVARS, %DATAPATH, %DATAMEM, %MEM

Example

Sample Program

```
%directory (drive=C:\windows, out=c_windows)

proc sql flow ;
select * from c_windows
quit ;
```

SAS Log

```
1    %directory (drive=C:\windows, out=c_windows)
NOTE: The data set WORK.C_WINDOWS has 166 observations and 5 variables.
NOTE: The MACRO %DIRECTORY used:
      real time              0.70 seconds
      cpu time               unknown

2
3    proc sql flow ;
4    select * from c_windows
5    quit ;
NOTE: PROCEDURE SQL used:
      real time              0.01 seconds
      cpu time               0.01 seconds
```

SAS Listing

```
                           The SAS System
                       Most
                       Recent
                       Write        File Size
Directory Name         Date         (in bytes)  File Owner        File Name
ffffffffffffffffffffffffffffffffffffffffffffffffffffffffffffffffffffffffffff
C:\WINDOWS             26JUN2006             0  BUILTIN\          0.log
                                                Administrators
C:\WINDOWS             23AUG2001         1,272  BUILTIN\          Blue Lace 16.bmp
                                                Administrators
C:\WINDOWS             24NOV2003         1,438  BUILTIN\          COM+.log
                                                Administrators
C:\WINDOWS             23AUG2001        17,062  BUILTIN\          Coffee Bean.bmp
                                                Administrators
C:\WINDOWS             21JUN2006           616  BUILTIN\          DtcInstall.log
```

%DOCUMENT

Purpose

This macro is designed to read all SAS programs in a directory and to create HTML documentation based on the comments in the file. Comments and program structure must be as declared in the SPIKEware SAS Programming Standards style manual.

Syntax

%DOCUMENT (PROGRAM_PATH = *program-folder*, DOCUMENT_PATH = *program-folder*<, TITLE = *title*> <, COPYRIGHT = *copyright-statement*> <, KEYWORDS = *HTML-keywords*> <, STYLESHEET = *cascading-style-sheet*> <, SCRIPTS = *file-folder*> <, HOME = *home-page*> <, HEADER = *header-script*> <, FOOTER = *footer-script*> <, DEBUG = Y | YES | NO | N>)

Required Parameter(s)

PROGRAM_PATH = *program-folder*

> The physical file folder holding all of the programs to be documented

DOCUMENT_PATH = *program-folder*

> The physical file folder to hold the output *.html documentation

Optional Parameter(s)

TITLE = *title*

> The TITLE to show in the HTML <TITLE> tag.

COPYRIGHT = *copyright-statement*

> The copyright statement (unquoted).

KEYWORDS = *HTML-keywords*

> Declares HTML keywords for the META tags.

STYLESHEET = *cascading-style-sheet*

> Physical address of the HTML stylesheet, if one is used. May be an internet address.

SCRIPTS = *file-folder*

> Physical address of any scripts used in the programming. May be an internet address.

HOME = *home-page*

> Documentation home page.

HEADER = *header-script*

> Script to define the top of the HTML documentation page—often used for navigation.

DEBUG = Y | YES | NO | N

> debugging flag, set to YES or NO. Alternatively, you can submit Y or N. Default is NO.

Notes

This macro is used to create documentation pages of a macro library. All macros in the library must use a SPIKEware standard header and conform to standard SPIKEware programming and documentation style. Each of the SAS programs in the library is documented in an easy-to-read *.html file and a standard index (or table of contents) is also created automatically. For different sites, there is also the ability to customize and to add various scripts to the *.html pages.

DEMO programs can be created at the end of each macro and the sample DEMO program will be added to the documentation file.

Example

Sample Program

```
%document (program_path  = C:\spikeware\rds,
           document_path = C:\spikeware\documents,
           title         = Rapid Decision Support)
```

SAS Log

```
1     %document (program_path  = C:\spikeware\rds,
2                document_path = C:\spikeware\documents,
3                title         = Rapid Decision Support)
NOTE: Created Rapid Decision Support documentation library in folder
      C:\spikeware\documents.
NOTE: The MACRO %DOCUMENT used:
      real time            11:29.47
      cpu time                      unknown
```

SAS Listing

This sample program does not have any listing output.

%DOCUMENT_RTF

Purpose

This macro is designed to read all SAS programs in a directory and to create *.rtf documentation based on the comments in the file.

Syntax

%DOCUMENT_RTF (PROGRAM_PATH = p*rogram-folder*, DOCUMENT_PATH = *document*-folder <,DEBUG = YES | Y | NO | N>)

Required Parameter(s)

PROGRAM_PATH = *program-folder*
    The physical file folder holding all of the programs to be documented

DOCUMENT_PATH = *program-folder*
    The physical file folder to hold the output *.rtf documentation

Optional Parameter(s)

DEBUG = Y | YES | NO | N

debugging flag, set to YES or NO. Alternatively, you can submit Y or N. Default is NO.

Notes

This macro is used to create documentation pages of a macro library. DEMO programs can be created at the end of each macro and the sample DEMO program will be added to the documentation file.

Example

Sample Program

```
title1 ;
footnote1 ;
options nodate nonumber ;
%document_rtf (program_path  = C:\spikeware\rds,
               document_path = C:\spikeware\documents);
```

SAS Log

```
1    title1 ;
2    footnote1 ;
3    options nodate nonumber ;
4    %document_rtf (program_path  = C:\spikeware\rds,
5                   document_path = C:\spikeware\documents);
NOTE: The MACRO %DOCUMENT_RTF used:
      real time            11:29.47
      cpu time             unknown
```

SAS Listing

This sample program does not have any listing output.

%DOUBLES

Purpose

This macro is designed to check for exact duplicate and/or near duplicate observations in a SAS dataset. It generates a printout of near duplicates for further manual examination and notes in the log changes made to the output dataset.

Syntax

%DOUBLES (OUT = *SAS-data-set*, VAR = *variable-list* <DATA = *SAS-data-set*> <, DOUBLES = *SAS-data-set*> <,NODUP = YES | Y | NO | N> <,DEBUG = YES | Y | NO | N>)

Required Parameter(s)

OUT = *SAS-data-set*

> identifies the output SAS data set.

VAR = *variable-list*

> Identifies the variables that are declared to be the unique record identifiers.

Optional Parameter(s)

DATA = *SAS-data-set*

Identifies the input data set. If DATA is not declared, the most recently created data set is used.

DOUBLES = *SAS-data-set*

Identifies a special output data set that contains all records that were removed because they were considered to be duplicates.

NODUP = Y | YES | NO | N

Complete the initial sort with the NODUP option.

DEBUG = Y | YES | NO | N

debugging flag, set to YES or NO. Alternatively, you can submit Y or N. Default is NO.

Example

Sample Program

```
data dupdata ;
   do id_num = 1 to 100 ;

      %*-------------------------------------*
       | the first part simulates input data |
       *-------------------------------------* ;

      var1 = ranuni(0) ;
      var2 = ranuni(0) ;
      var3 = ranuni(0) ;
      var4 = ranuni(0) ;
      output ;

      %*---------------------------------------------------------------*
       | the next part simulates extra records with a mis-matched keypunch |
       | error for var4--meaning the the first ten records were entered   |
       | twice but with different values for var4.                        |
       *---------------------------------------------------------------* ;

      if id_num < 10 then do ;
         var4 = var4 + 1 ;
         output ;
      end ;

      %*---------------------------------------------------------------*
       | the last part simulates exact duplicate records--meaning that |
       | the second ten records were entered twice without any further |
       | errors.                                                       |
       *---------------------------------------------------------------* ;

      if 10 < id_num < 20 then output ;
   end ;
run ;

title1 'SPIKEware Rapid Decision Support SAS Macro Package v3.0 demo' ;
title2 '%DOUBLES scrubs data for exact duplicate records and reports on near duplicate records' ;
%doubles (data=dupdata, out=cleaned, var=id_num, nodup=yes, doubles=doubles)
%doubles (data=dupdata, out=cleaned2, var=id_num, nodup=no, doubles=doubles2)
```

SAS Log

```
1    data dupdata ;
2       do id_num = 1 to 100 ;
3
4          %*-------------------------------------*
5           | the first part simulates input data |
6           *-------------------------------------* ;
```

```
7
8              var1 = ranuni(0) ;
9              var2 = ranuni(0) ;
10             var3 = ranuni(0) ;
11             var4 = ranuni(0) ;
12             output ;
13
14         %*------------------------------------------------------------------*
15          | the next part simulates extra records with a mis-matched keypunch |
16          | error for var4--meaning the the first ten records were entered   |
17          | twice but with different values for var4.                        |
18          *------------------------------------------------------------------* ;
19
20         if id_num < 10 then do ;
21            var4 = var4 + 1 ;
22            output ;
23         end ;
24
25         %*------------------------------------------------------------------*
26          | the last part simulates exact duplicate records--meaning that    |
27          | the second ten records were entered twice without any further    |
28          | errors.                                                          |
29          *------------------------------------------------------------------* ;
30
31         if 10 < id_num < 20 then output ;
32      end ;
33   run ;

NOTE: The data set WORK.DUPDATA has 118 observations and 5 variables.
NOTE: DATA statement used:
      real time            0.03 seconds
      cpu time             0.02 seconds


34
35    title1 'SPIKEware Rapid Decision Support SAS Macro Package v3.2 demo' ;
36    title2 '%DOUBLES scrubs data for exact duplicate records and reports on near duplicate
36 ! records' ;
37    %doubles (data=dupdata, out=cleaned, var=id_num, nodup=yes, doubles=doubles)

NOTE: Macro DOUBLES identified and removed 9 exact duplicate records and 18 near duplicate
records.
NOTE: The data set WORK.DOUBLES has 18 observations and 5 variables.
NOTE: The data set WORK.CLEANED has 91 observations and 5 variables.
NOTE: The MACRO %DOUBLES used:
      real time            0.34 seconds
      cpu time             unknown

38    %doubles (data=dupdata, out=cleaned2, var=id_num, nodup=no, doubles=doubles2)

NOTE: Macro DOUBLES identified and removed 36 duplicate records.
NOTE: The data set WORK.DOUBLES2 has 36 observations and 5 variables.
NOTE: The data set WORK.CLEANED2 has 82 observations and 5 variables.
NOTE: The MACRO %DOUBLES used:
      real time            0.20 seconds
      cpu time             unknown
```

SAS Listing

```
              SPIKEware Rapid Decision Support SAS Macro Package v3.2 demo                    1
       %DOUBLES scrubs data for exact duplicate records and reports on near duplicate records

                    id_num       var1        var2        var3        var4

                         1      0.59686     0.18013     0.02191     0.14754
                         1      0.59686     0.18013     0.02191     1.14754
                         2      0.26856     0.78119     0.24361     1.52383
```

	id_num	var1	var2	var3	var4
	2	0.26856	0.78119	0.24361	0.52383
	3	0.94393	0.54032	0.75454	1.46799
	3	0.94393	0.54032	0.75454	0.46799
	4	0.37682	0.11703	0.00441	0.16525
	4	0.37682	0.11703	0.00441	1.16525
	5	0.45837	0.08128	0.52928	1.46929
	5	0.45837	0.08128	0.52928	0.46929
	6	0.52633	0.94376	0.83437	1.39508
	6	0.52633	0.94376	0.83437	0.39508
	7	0.69357	0.35425	0.91576	1.08307
	7	0.69357	0.35425	0.91576	0.08307
	8	0.14179	0.26608	0.19662	0.40644
	8	0.14179	0.26608	0.19662	1.40644
	9	0.79568	0.46839	0.44342	1.52885
	9	0.79568	0.46839	0.44342	0.52885

SPIKEware Rapid Decision Support SAS Macro Package v3.2 demo   2
%DOUBLES scrubs data for exact duplicate records and reports on near duplicate records

id_num	var1	var2	var3	var4
1	0.59686	0.18013	0.02191	0.14754
1	0.59686	0.18013	0.02191	1.14754
2	0.26856	0.78119	0.24361	0.52383
2	0.26856	0.78119	0.24361	1.52383
3	0.94393	0.54032	0.75454	0.46799
3	0.94393	0.54032	0.75454	1.46799
4	0.37682	0.11703	0.00441	0.16525
4	0.37682	0.11703	0.00441	1.16525
5	0.45837	0.08128	0.52928	0.46929
5	0.45837	0.08128	0.52928	1.46929
6	0.52633	0.94376	0.83437	0.39508
6	0.52633	0.94376	0.83437	1.39508
7	0.69357	0.35425	0.91576	0.08307
7	0.69357	0.35425	0.91576	1.08307
8	0.14179	0.26608	0.19662	0.40644
8	0.14179	0.26608	0.19662	1.40644
9	0.79568	0.46839	0.44342	0.52885
9	0.79568	0.46839	0.44342	1.52885
11	0.83017	0.73951	0.74026	0.34336
11	0.83017	0.73951	0.74026	0.34336
12	0.93092	0.96388	0.61846	0.00096
12	0.93092	0.96388	0.61846	0.00096
13	0.21027	0.72866	0.79259	0.88538
13	0.21027	0.72866	0.79259	0.88538
14	0.74008	0.57296	0.54199	0.63085
14	0.74008	0.57296	0.54199	0.63085
15	0.37494	0.75503	0.47153	0.00173
15	0.37494	0.75503	0.47153	0.00173
16	0.66701	0.64354	0.68547	0.89223
16	0.66701	0.64354	0.68547	0.89223
17	0.61881	0.28901	0.55458	0.77675
17	0.61881	0.28901	0.55458	0.77675
18	0.42817	0.37985	0.18019	0.39806
18	0.42817	0.37985	0.18019	0.39806
19	0.02612	0.68093	0.70143	0.98489
19	0.02612	0.68093	0.70143	0.98489

%ENCRYPT

Purpose

This macro creates an encrypted file from a given input file.

Syntax

%ENCRYPT (INFILE = *filename* | *"file-specification"*, FILE = *filename* | *"file-specification"*, KEY = *encryption-key*> <, DEBUG = Y | YES | NO | N>)

Required Parameter(s)

INFILE = *filename* | *"file-specification"*

> declares the input file.
>
> > *filename* specifies the fileref of an external file.
> >
> > *"file-specification"* specifies the physical name of an external file, which is enclosed in quotation marks. The physical name is the name by which the operating environment recognizes the file.
>
> Either the *filename* or *"file-specification"* must be declared, but not both.

FILE = *filename* | *"file-specification"*

> declares the output file.
>
> > *filename* specifies the fileref of an external file.
> >
> > *"file-specification"* specifies the physical name of an external file, which is enclosed in quotation marks. The physical name is the name by which the operating environment recognizes the file.
>
> Either the *filename* or *"file-specification"* must be declared, but not both.

Optional Parameter(s)

KEY = *encryption*-key

> Declares the numeric encryption key. Default is 5. Range: non-negative integer less than 51.

DEBUG = Y | YES | NO | N

> debugging flag, set to YES or NO. Alternatively, you can submit Y or N. Default is NO.

See Also

%DECRYPT, %ENCRYPT

Example

Sample Program

```
%encrypt (infile = '!SASROOT\license.txt',
          file   = 'C:\temp\license.enc',
          key    = 5)
```

SAS Log

```
1      %encrypt (infile = '!SASROOT\license.txt',
2               file   = 'C:\temp\license.enc',
3               key    = 5)
NOTE: The file 'C:\temp\license.enc' is:
      File Name=C:\temp\license.enc,
      RECFM=V,LRECL=256

NOTE: 68 records were written to the file 'C:\temp\license.enc'.
```

```
        The minimum record length was 0.
        The maximum record length was 94.
NOTE: The MACRO %ENCRYPT used:
      real time              0.17 seconds
      cpu time                   unknown
```

SAS Listing

This sample program does not have any listing output.

%EXCEPTION

Purpose

This macro creates an exception report for a field in a given data set based on a given format.

Syntax

%EXCEPTION (VAR = *variable-name*, FORMAT = *SAS-format* <, DATA = *SAS-data-set*><, ID = *variable-name*> <, DEBUG = Y | YES | N | NO>)

Required Parameter(s)

VAR = *variable-name*

> identifies the key variable for breaking out the SAS data set into various parts. Only one variable can be declared.

FORMAT = *SAS-format*

> The FORMAT statement associates a format with the groupings of the exception variable. SAS uses the format to divide the various values of the variable into exception and non-exception reporting.

Optional Parameter(s)

DATA = *SAS-data-set*

> identifies the input SAS data set. If DATA is not declared, the most recently created data set is used.

ID = *variable-name*

> identifies the identifier variable for referencing records. Only one variable can be declared.

DEBUG = Y | YES | NO | N

> debugging flag, set to YES or NO. Alternatively, you can submit Y or N. Default is NO.

Example

Sample Program

```
proc format ;
   value numrange 18-25 = '(18 - 25)'
                  26-35 = '(26 - 35)'
                  36-45 = '(36 - 45)'
                  46-55 = '(46 - 55)'
                  56-65 = '(56 - 65)'
                  66-85 = '(66 - 85)' ;
run ;

data test ;
```

```
      label patno = 'Patient Number' ;
      do patno = 1 to 200 ;
         age = round(patno*ranuni(0), 5) ;
         if age < 120 then output ;
      end ;
run ;

%exception (data=test, id=patno, var=age, format=numrange.)
```

SAS Log

```
1     proc format ;
2        value numrange 18-25 = '(18 - 25)'
3                       26-35 = '(26 - 35)'
4                       36-45 = '(36 - 45)'
5                       46-55 = '(46 - 55)'
6                       56-65 = '(56 - 65)'
7                       66-85 = '(66 - 85)' ;
NOTE: Format NUMRANGE has been output.
8     run ;

NOTE: PROCEDURE FORMAT used:
      real time           0.06 seconds
      cpu time            0.01 seconds

9
10    data test ;
11       label patno = 'Patient Number' ;
12       do patno = 1 to 200 ;
13          age = round(patno*ranuni(0), 5) ;
14          if age < 120 then output ;
15       end ;
16    run ;
NOTE: The data set WORK.TEST has 180 observations and 2 variables.
NOTE: DATA statement used:
      real time           0.02 seconds
      cpu time            0.01 seconds
17
18    %exception (data=test, id=patno, var=age, format=numrange.)
NOTE: The MACRO %EXCEPTION used:
      real time           0.42 seconds
      cpu time            unknown
```

SAS Listing

```
                              The SAS System
              Frequency
AGE           Count   Percent  PATNO: Patient Number
ƒƒƒƒƒƒƒƒƒƒƒƒƒƒƒƒƒƒƒƒƒƒƒƒƒƒƒƒƒƒƒƒƒƒƒƒƒƒƒƒƒƒƒƒƒƒƒƒƒƒƒƒƒƒƒƒƒƒƒƒƒƒƒƒƒƒƒƒƒƒƒƒƒƒƒƒƒƒƒƒƒ
         0        5     2.78   1 2 3 4 16

         5       21    11.67   5 6 7 8 9 10 11 12 13 14 26 27 31 33 36 43 51 53 59 128 195

        10       19    10.56   15 17 18 23 29 35 38 44 48 54 64 65 77 90 121 124 126 132 141

        15       15     8.33   19 20 22 24 25 30 57 67 89 93 95 116 131 148 200

(18 - 25)        22    12.22   21 28 34 39 40 46 55 66 72 73 75 80
                                81 82 97 115 119 143 154 171 172 186

(26 - 35)        17     9.44   32 37 41 42 47 58 61 62 69 74 79 83 84 106 107 125 198

(36 - 45)        12     6.67   45 49 56 60 88 99 101 120 127 135 149 188

(46 - 55)         9     5.00   50 52 102 103 123 150 159 169 178

(56 - 65)        12     6.67   63 68 70 71 76 86 94 134 137 147 161 194
```

```
(66 - 85)         28    15.56   78 85 87 91 92 96 100 104 105 108 111 113 117 118 122
                                129 133 138 145 152 158 160 162 164 167 173 175 182
      90           3     1.67   139 142 155
      95           3     1.67   98 110 166
     100           4     2.22   112 130 185 190
     105           6     3.33   109 114 153 156 168 189
     110           1     0.56   181
     115           3     1.67   163 174 180
```

%FILECAT

Purpose
This macro concatenates two files together and writes them out to a third output file

Syntax
%FILECAT (INFILE1 = *filename* | *"file-specification"*, INFILE1 = *filename* | *"file-specification"*, INFILE1 = *filename* | *"file-specification"*)

Required Parameter(s)
INFILE1 = *filename* | *"file-specification"*

INFILE2 = *filename* | *"file-specification"*

FILE = *filename* | *"file-specification"*

    declares the input files *(*INFILE1= *and* INFILE2=*) and output file (*FILE=*)*.

        filename specifies the fileref of an external file.

        "file-specification" specifies the physical name of an external file, which is enclosed in quotation marks. The physical name is the name by which the operating environment recognizes the file.

    Either the *filename* or *"file-specification"* must be declared, but not both.

Notes
For longer files, the FILE= option will also need to take any SAS file options such as LRECL=. When possible, seek an operating system approach to concatenation of files instead of using this macro.

%FILEIN

Purpose
This macro reads in a quoted comma delimited file to a SAS dataset

Syntax
%FILEIN (INFILE = *filename* | *'file-specification'*<, OUT = *SAS-data-set*> <, SAMPLE = *sample*>)

Required Parameter(s)
INFILE = *filename* | *"file-specification"*

> declares the input files (INFILE1= and INFILE2=) and output file (FILE=).
>
>> *filename* specifies the fileref of an external file.
>>
>> *"file-specification"* specifies the physical name of an external file, which is enclosed in quotation marks. The physical name is the name by which the operating environment recognizes the file.
>
> Either the *filename* or *"file-specification"* must be declared, but not both.

Optional Parameter(s)
OUT = *SAS-data-set*

> identifies the output SAS data set. If OUT is not declared, the next available logical SAS data set name is used.

SAMPLE = *sample*

> declares the number of records to read to attempt to logically assign variable lengths and formats such as date, time, and datetime values.

DEBUG = Y | YES | NO | N

> debugging flag, set to YES or NO. Alternatively, you can submit Y or N. Default is NO.

See Also
%XLS2SAS, %SAS2XLS, %FILEIN, %FILEOUT, PROC IMPORT, PROC EXPORT

Notes
This macro remains available but will no longer be supported because you can use PROC IMPORT to complete the same tasks.

Example

Sample Program
```
data _null_ ;
   file 'myfile.txt' notitles noprint ;
   put 'var1,var2,var3,var4' ;
   put '1.234,500,characterstring,01JAN2004' ;
   put '1.234,500,char,01JAN2004' ;
   put '1.234,500,char,01JAN2004' ;
   put '1.234,500,char,01JAN2004' ;
run ;

%filein (infile='myfile.txt', out=test)

proc print data=test ;
run ;
```

SAS Log

```
1    %filein (infile='myfile.txt', out=test)
WARNING: Macro %FILEIN is no longer supported because PROC IMPORT will complete the job.
         Use at your own risk.
NOTE: The data set WORK.TEST has 4 observations and 0 variables.
NOTE: The MACRO %FILEIN used:
      real time            0.15 seconds
      cpu time             unknown
2
3    proc print data=test ;
4    run ;

NOTE: No variables in data set WORK.TEST.
NOTE: PROCEDURE PRINT used:
      real time            0.01 seconds
      cpu time             0.01 seconds
```

SAS Listing

This sample program does not have any listing output.

%FILENOTE

Purpose

This macro creates a standard SAS File Creation Note. It does not actually "create" the file, but prepares the note for the file as if it has been created.

Syntax

%FILENOTE (*filename* | *'file-specification'* <, MIN = *minimum-line-size*> <, MAX = *maximum-line-size*> <, N = *number-of-records*>

Required Parameter(s)

filename | *'file-specification'*

    declares the file.

        filename specifies the fileref of an external file.

        "file-specification" specifies the physical name of an external file, which is enclosed in quotation marks. The physical name is the name by which the operating environment recognizes the file.

    Either the *filename* or *"file-specification"* must be declared, but not both.

Optional Parameter(s)

MIN = *minimum-line-size*

    declares the minimum expected line size of the input file.

MAX = *maximum-line-size*

    declares the maximum expected line size of the input file

N = *number-of-records*

    declares the number of records for the file. If this can be known from another SAS step, it should be done and entered here to save processing time.

DEBUG = Y | YES | NO | N

> debugging flag, set to YES or NO. Alternatively, you can submit Y or N. Default is NO.

See Also
%DATANOTE, %FILENOTE, %TIMENOTE, %INFO

Notes
FILENAME value can be in either SAS FILENAME or FILE SPECIFICATION format, but must be a valid format. This macro does not check for an invalid FILENAME or FILE SPECIFICATION description such as any unbalanced quotation marks. Do not expect the macro to work with different device types such as GTERM, PIPE, NAMEPIPE, TAPE, etc.

Example

Sample Program
%filenote ('!SASROOT\autoexec.sas') ;

SAS Log
```
1    %filenote ('!SASROOT\autoexec.sas') ;
NOTE: The file '!SASROOT\autoexec.sas' is:
      File Name=c:\sasv8\autoexec.sas,
      RECFM=V,LRECL=256

NOTE: 168 records were written to the file '!SASROOT\autoexec.sas'.
      The minimum record length was 0.
      The maximum record length was 106.
```

SAS Listing
This sample program does not have any listing output.

%FILEOUT

Purpose
This macro writes out a quoted comma delimited file from a SAS dataset

Syntax
%FILEOUT (FILE = *filename* | *'file-specification'*, VAR = *variable-list* <, DATA = *SAS-data-set*> <, HEADER = Y | YES | NO | N> <, OPTIONS = *file-print-options*> <, DEBUG = Y | YES | NO | N>)

Required Parameter(s)
filename | *'file-specification'*

> declares the file.
>
> > *filename* specifies the fileref of an external file.

"file-specification" specifies the physical name of an external file, which is enclosed in quotation marks. The physical name is the name by which the operating environment recognizes the file.

Either the *filename* or *"file-specification"* must be declared, but not both.

VAR = *variable-list*

declares the list of variables to write to the output file.

Optional Parameter(s)

DATA = *SAS-data-set*

declares the input SAS data set. If one is not declared, the most recent SAS data set will be used.

HEADER = Y | YES | NO | N

declares if a header record containing the variable names should be written on the first record.

OPTIONS = *file-print-options*

declares any PRINT options for the processing (such as LRECL=*value*). See the SAS PRINT statement for full details.

DEBUG = Y | YES | NO | N

debugging flag, set to YES or NO. Alternatively, you can submit Y or N. Default is NO.

See Also

%XLS2SAS, %SAS2XLS, %FILEIN, %FILEOUT, PROC IMPORT, PROC EXPORT

Notes

This macro remains available but will no longer be supported because you can use PROC EXPORT to complete the same tasks.

Example

Sample Program

```
data test ;
   do i = 1 to 5 ;
      ranuni1 = ranuni(0) ;
      color = 'red' ;
      output ;
   end ;
run ;

%fileout (data=test, file='fileouttest.csv', var=_all_, header=yes)
```

SAS Log

```
1    data test ;
2       do i = 1 to 5 ;
3          ranuni1 = ranuni(0) ;
4          color = 'red' ;
5          output ;
6       end ;
7    run ;

NOTE: The data set WORK.TEST has 5 observations and 3 variables.
```

```
NOTE: DATA statement used:
      real time           0.01 seconds
      cpu time            0.01 seconds


8
9    %fileout (data=test, file='fileouttest.csv', var=_all_, header=yes)
NOTE: The file 'fileouttest.csv' is:
      File Name=C:\Perl\bin\fileouttest.csv,
      RECFM=V,LRECL=256

NOTE: 6 records were written to the file 'fileouttest.csv'.
      The minimum record length was 15.
      The maximum record length was 18.
NOTE: The MACRO %FILEOUT used:
      real time              0.40 seconds
      cpu time                  unknown
WARNING: Macro %FILEOUT is no longer supported because PROC EXPORT will complete the job.
         Use at your own risk.
```

SAS Listing

This sample program does not have any listing output.

%FINDFILE

Purpose

This macro finds a file somewhere in a given drive or folder

Syntax

%FINDFILE (FILE = *'file-specification'*, ROOT = *root-drive-and-directory-path*, OUT = *SAS-data-set* <, DEBUG = YES | Y | NO | N>)

Required Parameter(s)

FILE = *'file-specification'*

> declares the file. *"file-specification"* specifies the physical name of an external file, which is enclosed in quotation marks. The physical name is the name by which the operating environment recognizes the file.
>
> Only *"file-specification"* may be declared. The macro does not recognize a SAS *filename*.

ROOT = *root-drive-and-directory-path*

> declares the root drive and operating system directory path to search for the named file.

OUT = *SAS-data-set*

> declares the output SAS data set to contain any and all occurrences of the named file and full path. If the named file appears more than once in the *root-drive-and-directory-path* declared in ROOT =, then the output data set will have multiple records.

Optional Parameter(s)

DEBUG = Y | YES | NO | N

> debugging flag, set to YES or NO. Alternatively, you can submit Y or N. Default is NO.

See Also
%COMMAND, %DOSPATH, %DIRECTORY, %CURRENTPATH, %FINDFILE, %SYSVARS, %DATAPATH, %DATAMEM, %MEM

Example

Sample Program
```
%findfile (file=excel.exe, root=C, out=out)

proc print data=out ;
run ;
```

SAS Log
```
1    %findfile (file=excel.exe, root=C, out=out)
NOTE: File "excel.exe" found at location "C:\PROGRAM FILES\MICROSOFT OFFICE\OFFICE10\EXCEL.EXE"
NOTE: The data set WORK.OUT has 1 observations and 1 variables.
NOTE: The MACRO %FINDFILE used:
      real time              0.59 seconds
      cpu time               unknown

2
3    proc print data=out ;
4    run ;

NOTE: There were 1 observations read from the data set WORK.OUT.
NOTE: PROCEDURE PRINT used:
      real time              0.00 seconds
      cpu time               0.00 seconds
```

SAS Listing

```
                          The SAS System

              Obs                     filename

               1     C:\PROGRAM FILES\MICROSOFT OFFICE\OFFICE10\EXCEL.EXE
```

%FORMAT

Purpose
This macro reads a *cntlin* dataset into a format catalog. It will work for one START variable and multiple LABEL variables. The name of each format corresponds to the name of the variable. If it is a character START variable, a dollar sign is automatically placed in front of the variable name.

Syntax
%FORMAT (CNTLIN = *SAS-data-set*, START = *start-variable*, LABEL = *label-variable-1* <...*label-variable-n*> <,CNTLOUT = *SAS-data-set*> <, LIBRARY = *SAS-library*> <, DEBUG = Y | YES | NO | N>)

Required Parameter(s)
CNTLIN = *SAS-data-set*

    declares the input SAS data set.

START = *start-variable*

declares the "start" variable, or the key or ID variable for creating the format.

LABEL = *label-variable-1 <...label-variable-n>*

declares the one or more variables to build SAS Format combinations from the START variable. All variables declared in the LABEL = statement must have names of seven characters or less, and the variable name must end in a letter or underscore.

Optional Parameter(s)

CNTLOUT = *SAS-data-set*

declares the CNTLOUT SAS data set from the process of creating the SAS Formats.

LIBRARY = *SAS-library*

declares the SAS LIBRARY to write the created formats to—default is WORK.

DEBUG = Y | YES | NO | N

debugging flag, set to YES or NO. Alternatively, you can submit Y or N. Default is NO.

Notes

Label variable names must NOT start or end with a number and must be seven or less characters long.

Example

Sample Program

```
data keyvals ;
   length char $10 ;
   do key = 1 to 10 ;
      num  = ranuni(0) * 1000 ;
      char = put(num, 10.) ;
      output ;
   end ;
run ;

%format (cntlin=keyvals, start=key, label=num char)

data _null_ ;
   do key = 1 to 10 ;
      put key= key= num. key= char. ;
   end ;
run ;
```

SAS Log

```
1    data keyvals ;
2       length char $10 ;
3       do key = 1 to 10 ;
4          num  = ranuni(0) * 1000 ;
5          char = put(num, 10.) ;
6          output ;
7       end ;
8    run ;

NOTE: The data set WORK.KEYVALS has 10 observations and 3 variables.
NOTE: DATA statement used:
      real time           0.02 seconds
      cpu time            0.01 seconds
```

```
9
10   %format (cntlin=keyvals, start=key, label=num char)
NOTE: format NUM has been output.
NOTE: format CHAR has been output.
NOTE: The MACRO %FORMAT used:
      real time           0.39 seconds
      cpu time                 unknown

11
12   data _null_ ;
13     do key = 1 to 10 ;
14       put key= key= num. key= char. ;
15     end ;
16   run ;

key=1 key=414.52543596 key=415
key=2 key=232.36196965 key=232
key=3 key=633.38826673 key=633
key=4 key=635.91556001 key=636
key=5 key=875.32486947 key=875
key=6 key=733.64118847 key=734
key=7 key=586.39034144 key=586
key=8 key=301.81380841 key=302
key=9 key=326.31937988 key=326
key=10 key=641.45295771 key=641
NOTE: DATA statement used:
      real time           0.01 seconds
      cpu time            0.01 seconds
```

SAS Listing

This sample program does not have any listing output.

%GOOD2BAD

Purpose

This macro creates trashed, messed-up data based on the values of an input data set. It is useful in creating (or at least creating the beginnings of) a testing SAS data set.

Syntax

%GOOD2BAD (OUT = *SAS-data-set*, N = *number-of-records* <, DATA = *SAS-data-set*> <, VAR = *variable-list*> <, ID = *variable-list*> <, DEBUG = Y | YES | NO | N>)

Required Parameter(s)

OUT = *SAS-data-set*

    identifies the output SAS data set.

N = *number-of-records*

    identifies the total number of records to write to the output SAS data set. *RANGE: N > 0, Integer*.

Optional Parameter(s)

DATA = *SAS-data-set*

    Identifies the input data set. If DATA is not declared, the most recently created data set is used.

VAR = *variable-list*

Identifies the variable or variables in the SAS data set to make adjustments to

ID = *variable-list*

Identifies the variable or variables in the SAS data set to not make any adjustments to and to treat as key variables

DEBUG = Y | YES | NO | N

debugging flag, set to YES or NO. Alternatively, you can submit Y or N. Default is NO.

Example

Sample Program

```
%good2bad (data=sashelp.retail, out=retail, n=10000)

proc print data=retail ;
run ;
```

SAS Log

```
1    %good2bad (data=sashelp.retail, out=retail, n=10000)
NOTE: The data set WORK.RETAIL has 10000 observations and 5 variables.
NOTE: The MACRO %GOOD2BAD used:
      real time           0.45 seconds
      cpu time            unknown

2
3    proc print data=retail ;
4    run ;

NOTE: There were 10000 observations read from the data set WORK.RETAIL.
NOTE: At least one W.D format was too small for the number to be printed. The decimal may be
      shifted by the "BEST" format.
NOTE: PROCEDURE PRINT used:
      real time           0.14 seconds
      cpu time            0.14 seconds
```

SAS Listing

```
                              The SAS System

         Obs    SALES    DATE       YEAR          MONTH        DAY

          1     $220     80Q1       1980.00       1.0000       1.000
          2     $-0      60Q1       1980.00       1.79769E308  1.000
          3     $257     80Q2       1980.00       4.0000       1.000
          4     $257       .       -1.7977E308    4.0000       1.000
          5     $258     80Q3       1980.00       7.0000       1.000
          6       .        .        1980.00      -0.0000      -0.000
          7     $295     80Q4       1980.00      10.0000       1.000
          8       .      59Q4       1980.00       0.7083       0.403
          9     $247     81Q1       1981.00       1.0000       1.000
         10     $0       81Q1       1981.00       0.0390       1.000
         11     $292     81Q2       1981.00       4.0000       1.000
         12     $0       81Q2        592.87       0.0000       1.000
         13     $286     81Q3       1981.00       7.0000       1.000
         14       .      61Q4       1.79769E308   0.0024       0.361
         15     $323     81Q4       1981.00      10.0000       1.000
```

%HTML2TXT

Purpose
This macro takes an html file and writes out the text to another file.

Syntax
%HTML2TXT (INFILE = *filename* | *'file-specification'*, FILE = *file-name* | *'file-specification'* <, ENGINE = IE | SAS> <, LRECL = *logical-record-length*> <, DEBUG = Y | YES | NO | N>)

Required Parameter(s)
INFILE = *filename* | *"file-specification"*

> declares the input HTML file.
>
>> *filename* specifies the fileref of an external file.
>>
>> *"file-specification"* specifies the physical name of an external file, which is enclosed in quotation marks. The physical name is the name by which the operating environment recognizes the file.
>
> Either the *filename* or *"file-specification"* must be declared, but not both.

FILE = *filename* | *"file-specification"*

> declares the output file.
>
>> *filename* specifies the fileref of an external file.
>>
>> *"file-specification"* specifies the physical name of an external file, which is enclosed in quotation marks. The physical name is the name by which the operating environment recognizes the file.
>
> Either the *filename* or *"file-specification"* must be declared, but not both.

Optional Parameter(s)
ENGINE = IE | SAS

> Declares the HTML interpretation engine. If running in MS-Windows operating system and you have access to Microsoft Internet Explorer®, select ENGINE = IE for the most efficient and accurate translation. For other operating systems or for systems without Internet Explorer, select ENGINE = SAS. The default is SAS.

LRECL = *logical-record-length*

> declares the logical record length of the incoming file. The default is 256. *Range LRECL > 0, Integer.*

DEBUG = Y | YES | NO | N

> debugging flag, set to YES or NO. Alternatively, you can submit Y or N. Default is NO.

See Also
%HTML2TXT, %TRIMFILE, %WORDWRAP

Example

Sample Program
```
filename html url 'http://www.spikeware.net/home.html' ;
filename text 'c:\temp\home2.txt' ;

%html2txt (infile=html, file=text, engine=ie, lrecl=1000)
```

SAS Log
```
1    filename html url 'http://www.spikeware.net/home.html' ;
2    filename text 'c:\temp\home2.txt' ;
3
4    %html2txt (infile=html, file=text, engine=ie, lrecl=1000)
NOTE: The file TEXT is:
      File Name=c:\temp\home2.txt,
      RECFM=V,LRECL=256

NOTE: 53 records were written to the file TEXT.
      The minimum record length was 0.
      The maximum record length was 256.
NOTE: The MACRO %HTML2TXT used:
      real time               11.39 seconds
      cpu time                unknown
```

SAS Listing
This sample program does not have any listing output.

%LFOOT

Purpose
Creates a left-justified footnote statement

Syntax
%LFOOT (*footnote-number, footnote*)

Required Parameter(s)
footnote-number

>Declares the order of the footnote (footnote1, footnote2, … footnote10). Range: 1 – 10, integer.

footnote (unquoted)

>the footnote text. May not contain commas or special characters.

Optional Parameter(s)
>None.

Example

Sample Program
```
data view1 /view=view1 ;
   do i = 1 to 10 ;
      output ;
   end ;
```

```
run ;

title1 'This is my title' ;
title2 'Scroll down to view the left-justified footnote' ;
%lfoot (1, This is my left-justified footnote)
proc print data=view1 ;
run ;
```

SAS Log

```
1     data view1 /view=view1 ;
2        do i = 1 to 10 ;
3           output ;
4        end ;
5     run ;

NOTE: DATA STEP view saved on file WORK.VIEW1.
NOTE: A stored DATA STEP view cannot run under a different operating system.
NOTE: DATA statement used:
      real time           0.05 seconds
      cpu time            0.00 seconds


6
7     title1 'This is my title' ;
8     title2 'Scroll down to view the left-justified footnote' ;
9     %lfoot (1, This is my left-justified footnote)
10    proc print data=view1 ;
11    run ;

NOTE: View WORK.VIEW1.VIEW used:
      real time           0.10 seconds
      cpu time            0.00 seconds

NOTE: There were 10 observations read from the data set WORK.VIEW1.
NOTE: PROCEDURE PRINT used:
      real time           0.26 seconds
      cpu time            0.01 seconds
```

SAS Listing

```
                         This is my title
                Scroll down to view the left-justified footnote

                              Obs        i

                               1         1
                               2         2
                               3         3
                               4         4
                               5         5
                               6         6
                               7         7
                               8         8
                               9         9
                              10        10



This is my left-justified footnote
```

%LINESOFCODE

Purpose
This macro creates an administrative report on all SAS programs in a given PC file folder

Syntax
%LINESOFCODE (DIR = *'root-drive-and-directory-path'* <, DEBUG = Y | YES | NO | N>)

Required Parameter(s)
ROOT = *root-drive-and-directory-path*

    declares the root drive and operating system directory path to search for the named file.

Optional Parameter(s)
DEBUG = Y | YES | NO | N

    debugging flag, set to YES or NO. Alternatively, you can submit Y or N. Default is NO.

Example

Sample Program
```
title1 'Lines of Code Report' ;
%linesofcode(dir=C:\spikeware\rds)
```

SAS Log
```
1    title1 'Lines of Code Report' ;
2    %linesofcode(dir=C:\spikeware\rds)
NOTE: The MACRO %LINESOFCODE used:
      real time           25.81 seconds
      cpu time            unknown
```

SAS Listing

```
                        Lines of Code Report

                        The UNIVARIATE Procedure
                   Variable:  COUNT   (Frequency Count)

                                Moments

         N                        241    Sum Weights              241
         Mean               141.651452   Sum Observations       34138
         Std Deviation      84.1378512   Variance          7079.17801
         Skewness           3.54422029   Kurtosis          18.6581438
         Uncorrected SS        6534700   Corrected SS      1699002.72
         Coeff Variation    59.3978035   Std Error Mean    5.41979544


                       Basic Statistical Measures

             Location                    Variability

         Mean     141.6515     Std Deviation           84.13785
         Median   119.0000     Variance                    7079
         Mode      64.0000     Range                  706.00000
                               Interquartile Range     64.00000
```

NOTE: The mode displayed is the smallest of 2 modes with a count of 11.

```
                    Tests for Location: Mu0=0

        Test            -Statistic-      -----p Value------

        Student's t    t   26.13594     Pr > |t|     <.0001
        Sign           M      120.5     Pr >= |M|    <.0001
        Signed Rank    S    14580.5     Pr >= |S|    <.0001


                       Quantiles (Definition 5)

                       Quantile      Estimate

                       100% Max         769
                       99%              540
                       95%              269
                       90%              226
                       75% Q3           159
                       50% Median       119
                       25% Q1            95
                       10%               75
                       5%                66
                       1%                64
                       0% Min            63
```

Lines of Code Report

```
                       The UNIVARIATE Procedure
                    Variable:  COUNT  (Frequency Count)

                          Extreme Observations

         -------------------------Lowest-------------------------

              Value    program                                   Obs

                 63    time.sas                                  213
                 64    today.sas                                 215
                 64    sqrtsmall.sas                             198
                 64    sqrtmaceps.sas                            197
                 64    sqrtbig.sas                               196


                          Extreme Observations

         -------------------------Highest------------------------

              Value    program                                   Obs

                393    compare.sas                                36
                408    xls2sas.sas                               236
                540    pareto.sas                                142
                622    slide.sas                                 191
                769    document.sas                               64


                            Frequency Counts

                 Percents                Percents                Percents
      Value Count  Cell  Cum   Value Count  Cell  Cum   Value Count  Cell  Cum

         63     1   0.4   0.4     91     3   1.2  19.5    117     3   1.2  48.1
         64    11   4.6   5.0     92     4   1.7  21.2    118     2   0.8  49.0
         66     1   0.4   5.4     93     3   1.2  22.4    119     5   2.1  51.0
```

Value	Count	Cell	Cum	Value	Count	Cell	Cum	Value	Count	Cell	Cum
67	2	0.8	6.2	94	2	0.8	23.2	121	2	0.8	51.9
69	2	0.8	7.1	95	5	2.1	25.3	122	9	3.7	55.6
71	1	0.4	7.5	96	3	1.2	26.6	123	1	0.4	56.0
72	1	0.4	7.9	98	4	1.7	28.2	124	3	1.2	57.3
73	4	1.7	9.5	99	3	1.2	29.5	125	5	2.1	59.3
74	1	0.4	10.0	101	2	0.8	30.3	126	2	0.8	60.2
75	1	0.4	10.4	102	2	0.8	31.1	128	2	0.8	61.0
80	1	0.4	10.8	103	11	4.6	35.7	129	2	0.8	61.8
81	1	0.4	11.2	104	1	0.4	36.1	132	1	0.4	62.2
82	1	0.4	11.6	105	4	1.7	37.8	133	3	1.2	63.5
83	1	0.4	12.0	106	1	0.4	38.2	135	1	0.4	63.9
84	1	0.4	12.4	107	4	1.7	39.8	136	3	1.2	65.1
85	3	1.2	13.7	108	3	1.2	41.1	137	3	1.2	66.4
87	1	0.4	14.1	109	1	0.4	41.5	139	1	0.4	66.8
88	5	2.1	16.2	110	2	0.8	42.3	140	4	1.7	68.5
89	2	0.8	17.0	111	2	0.8	43.2	141	2	0.8	69.3
90	3	1.2	18.3	115	9	3.7	46.9	143	1	0.4	69.7

Lines of Code Report

The UNIVARIATE Procedure
Variable: COUNT (Frequency Count)

Frequency Counts

Value	Count	Cell	Cum	Value	Count	Cell	Cum	Value	Count	Cell	Cum
144	2	0.8	70.5	183	2	0.8	82.2	246	1	0.4	92.9
146	2	0.8	71.4	186	2	0.8	83.0	256	1	0.4	93.4
148	2	0.8	72.2	190	1	0.4	83.4	257	1	0.4	93.8
151	1	0.4	72.6	193	4	1.7	85.1	265	1	0.4	94.2
153	1	0.4	73.0	202	1	0.4	85.5	267	1	0.4	94.6
154	2	0.8	73.9	203	1	0.4	85.9	269	1	0.4	95.0
155	1	0.4	74.3	206	1	0.4	86.3	279	1	0.4	95.4
158	1	0.4	74.7	207	2	0.8	87.1	282	1	0.4	95.9
159	1	0.4	75.1	208	1	0.4	87.6	283	1	0.4	96.3
166	1	0.4	75.5	211	1	0.4	88.0	302	1	0.4	96.7
168	1	0.4	75.9	216	1	0.4	88.4	335	1	0.4	97.1
169	1	0.4	76.3	219	2	0.8	89.2	364	1	0.4	97.5
172	6	2.5	78.8	225	1	0.4	89.6	382	1	0.4	97.9
174	2	0.8	79.7	226	1	0.4	90.0	393	1	0.4	98.3
175	1	0.4	80.1	227	2	0.8	90.9	408	1	0.4	98.8
177	1	0.4	80.5	236	2	0.8	91.7	540	1	0.4	99.2
178	1	0.4	80.9	238	1	0.4	92.1	622	1	0.4	99.6
181	1	0.4	81.3	239	1	0.4	92.5	769	1	0.4	100.0

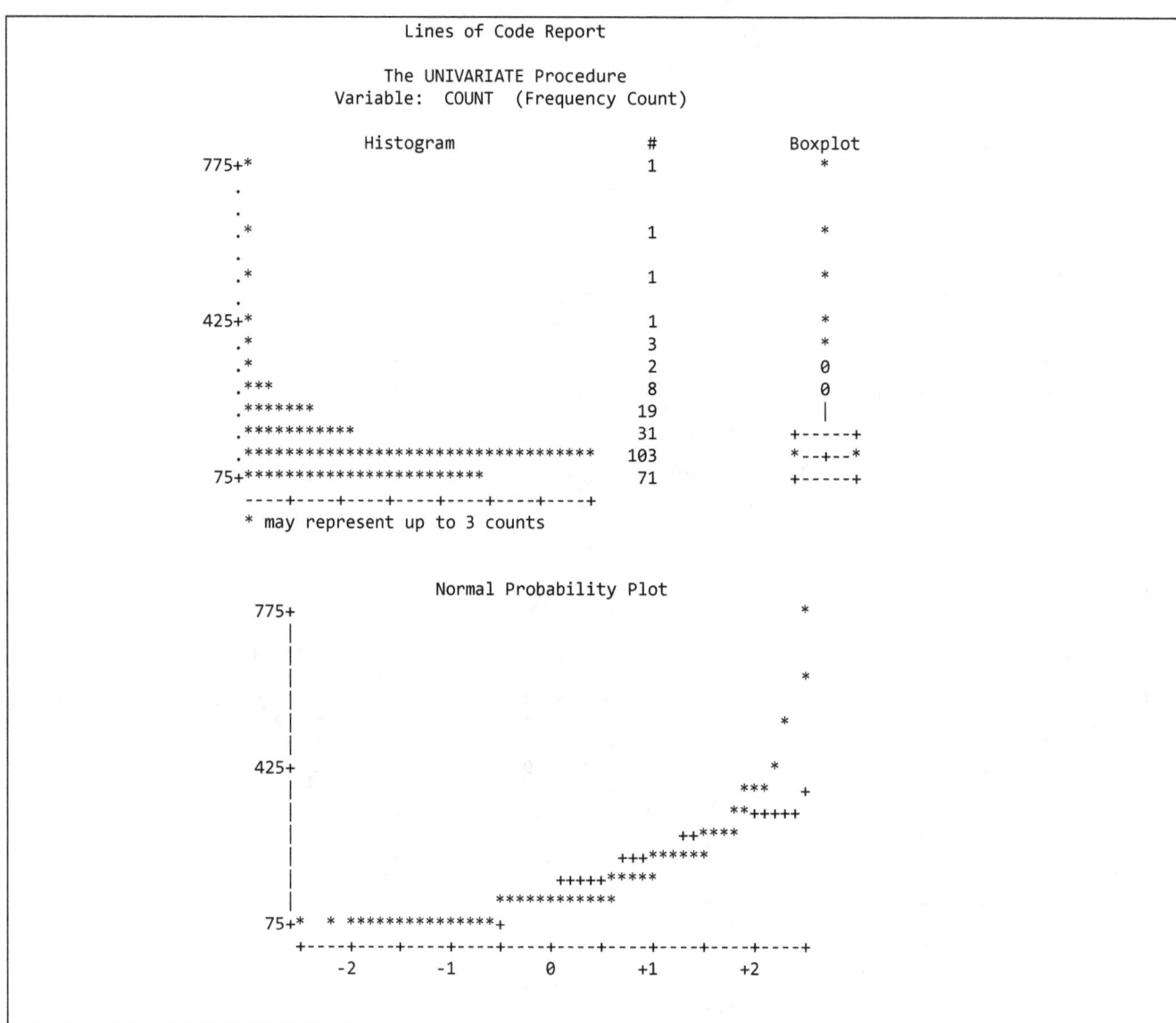

```
                    Lines of Code Report

           SAS Program              Lines of
           name                     Code

           _age.sas                       75
           _c2f.sas                       69
           _city.sas                      73
           _f2c.sas                       69
           _pctchange.sas                 87
           _propername.sas               183
           _state.sas                     73
           _zip.sas                       74
           abs.sas                        98
           airy.sas                       98
           arcos.sas                     105
           arsin.sas                     105
           atan.sas                       96
           band.sas                      141
           betainv.sas                   140
           big.sas                        64
           bigsort.sas                   219
           blshift.sas                   146
           bnot.sas                      126
           bor.sas                       140
           breakout.sas                  257
           brshift.sas                   148
           bxor.sas                      140
           byte.sas                       99
           cdf.sas                       172
           ceil.sas                       85
           cexist.sas                     83
           character.sas                 111
           checkall.sas                  227
           checkrec.sas                  238
           cinv.sas                      124
           cnonct.sas                    141
           collate.sas                   143
           comb.sas                      128
           command.sas                   190
           compare.sas                   393
           compound.sas                  122
           constant.sas                  175
           contents.sas                  181
           cos.sas                        95
           cosh.sas                       95
           css.sas                       115
           currentpath.sas                85
           cv.sas                        115
           daccdb.sas                    137
           daccdbsl.sas                  137
           daccsl.sas                    122
           daccsyd.sas                   122
           dairy.sas                      92
           data.sas                       81
```

```
                   Lines of Code Report

                                    Lines of
          SAS Program name            Code

               datamem.sas             172
               datanote.sas             92
               datapath.sas            183
               date.sas                 64
               datetime.sas             73
               decrypt.sas             158
               depdb.sas               136
               depdbsl.sas             137
               depsl.sas               122
               depsyd.sas              122
               dequote.sas              66
               digamma.sas              90
               directory.sas           193
               document.sas            769
               document_rtf.sas        269
               dospath.sas             211
               doubles.sas             246
               e.sas                    64
               encrypt.sas             159
               erf.sas                  98
               erfc.sas                 95
               euler.sas                64
               exception.sas           267
               exist.sas                93
               exp.sas                  93
               fact.sas                119
               fexist.sas               85
               filecat.sas              98
               filedt.sas               92
               fileexist.sas            82
               filein.sas              186
               filenote.sas            219
               fileout.sas             206
               fileread.sas            105
               filescan.sas            216
               findfile.sas            155
               finv.sas                153
               fipname.sas             133
               fipnamel.sas            133
               fipstate.sas            133
               floor.sas                94
               fnonct.sas              168
               format.sas              265
               fread.sas               104
               fuzz.sas                 91
               gaminv.sas              121
               gamma.sas               103
               getvar.sas              108
               getvarc.sas             117
               getvarn.sas             117
```

```
              Lines of Code Report        1

           SAS Program          Lines of
           name                 Code

           good2bad.sas              239
           html2txt.sas              364
           ibessel.sas               139
           iefbr14.sas                67
           indexc.sas                 84
           indexw.sas                 94
           info.sas                  124
           int.sas                    90
           intck.sas                 128
           intnx.sas                 129
           intrr.sas                 125
           irr.sas                   125
           jbessel.sas               118
           kurtosis.sas              122
           lfoot.sas                  80
           lgamma.sas                103
           linesofcode.sas           225
           log.sas                   103
           log10.sas                 103
           log2.sas                  103
           logpdf.sas                172
           logsdf.sas                172
           maceps.sas                 64
           maketitle.sas             227
           manifest.sas              202
           max.sas                   115
           mean.sas                  107
           mem.sas                   146
           min.sas                   115
           mort.sas                  132
           mput.sas                  108
           n.sas                     107
           name.sas                   95
           netpv.sas                 148
           nmiss.sas                 107
           normal.sas                102
           npv.sas                   135
           numeric.sas               111
           obscnt.sas                110
           ordinal.sas               129
           outlier.sas               256
           pareto.sas                540
           pdf.sas                   172
           perm.sas                  115
           pgmtest.sas               282
           pi.sas                     64
           poisson.sas               109
           popopts.sas               208
           poptitle.sas              236
           prefix.sas                 89
```

```
                    Lines of Code Report

           SAS Program          Lines of
           name                 Code

           probbeta.sas              136
           probbnml.sas              144
           probbnrm.sas              125
           probchi.sas               140
           probf.sas                 154
           probgam.sas               123
           probhypr.sas              174
           probit.sas                103
           probnegb.sas              144
           probnorm.sas               95
           probt.sas                 126
           pushopts.sas              151
           pushtitle.sas             125
           ranbin.sas                136
           ranbinary.sas             107
           rancau.sas                101
           ranexp.sas                103
           rangam.sas                121
           range.sas                 117
           rank.sas                   72
           rannor.sas                103
           ranpoi.sas                118
           rantri.sas                119
           ranuni.sas                101
           reccnt.sas                154
           repeat.sas                125
           reverse.sas                71
           round.sas                 110
           sample.sas                302
           sas2xls.sas               279
           sas2xml.sas               335
           saving.sas                124
           scramble.sas              207
           sdf.sas                   172
           shuffle.sas               193
           sign.sas                   92
           sin.sas                    96
           sinh.sas                   96
           skewness.sas              122
           sleep.sas                 207
           slide.sas                 622
           small.sas                  64
           sortall.sas               186
           sortlist.sas              203
           sqrt.sas                  102
           sqrtbig.sas                64
           sqrtmaceps.sas             64
           sqrtsmall.sas              64
           std.sas                   115
           stderr.sas                115
```

```
                    Lines of Code Report

              SAS Program       Lines of
              name              Code

              stemleaf.sas           236
              stfips.sas              88
              stname.sas              88
              stnamel.sas             88
              string.sas              73
              suffix.sas              91
              sum.sas                106
              sysmsg.sas              67
              sysvars.sas            178
              taghelp.sas            193
              tan.sas                 99
              tanh.sas                99
              time.sas                63
              timenote.sas           193
              today.sas               64
              translate.sas           93
              tranwrd.sas             91
              trigamma.sas           103
              trimfile.sas           283
              uniform.sas            103
              unique.sas             166
              univ.sas               382
              uss.sas                115
              var.sas                115
              varcnt.sas             108
              varfmt.sas             119
              varinfmt.sas           119
              varlabel.sas           122
              varlen.sas             119
              varlist.sas            105
              varnum.sas             103
              vartype.sas            122
              wakeup.sas             169
              wordcnt.sas            177
              wordwrap.sas           174
              xls2sas.sas            408
              xml2sas.sas            226
              zipfips.sas             90
              zipname.sas             88
              zipnamel.sas            88
              zipstate.sas            89
                                ==========
                                    34,138
```

%MAKETITLE

Purpose

This macro creates titles and footnotes from a title and footnote data set.

Syntax

%MAKETITLE (DATA = *SAS-data-set* <, DEBUG = Y | YES | NO | N>)

Required Parameter(s)

DATA = *SAS-data-set*

declares the input SAS data set containing the TITLE and FOOTNOTE information.

Optional Parameter(s)
DEBUG = Y | YES | NO | N

debugging flag, set to YES or NO. Alternatively, you can submit Y or N. Default is NO.

See Also
%PUSHTITLE, %POPTITLE, %MAKETITLE

Notes
This macro is depreciated. It has been replaced by POPTITLE.

Example

Sample Program
```
footnote1 "footnote" ;
footnote2 "second footnote" ;
footnote4 "fourth footnote" ;
proc contents data=sashelp.vtitle out=contents ;
run ;

proc append base=macro.title data=sashelp.vtitle ;
run ;

title1 ;
footnote1 ;
proc print data=macro.title ;
run ;

%maketitle (data=macro.title);

proc print data=macro.title ;
run ;
```

SAS Log
```
1      footnote1 "footnote" ;
2      footnote2 "second footnote" ;
3      footnote4 "fourth footnote" ;
4      proc contents data=sashelp.vtitle out=contents ;
5      run ;

NOTE: The data set WORK.CONTENTS has 3 observations and 40 variables.
NOTE: PROCEDURE CONTENTS used:
      real time           0.25 seconds
      cpu time            0.06 seconds


6
7      proc append base=macro.title data=sashelp.vtitle ;
8      run ;

NOTE: Appending SASHELP.VTITLE to MACRO.TITLE.
NOTE: BASE data set does not exist. DATA file is being copied to BASE file.
NOTE: There were 5 observations read from the data set SASHELP.VTITLE.
NOTE: The data set MACRO.TITLE has 5 observations and 3 variables.
NOTE: PROCEDURE APPEND used:
      real time           0.04 seconds
      cpu time            0.00 seconds
```

```
9
10   title1 ;
11   footnote1 ;
12   proc print data=macro.title ;
13   run ;

NOTE: There were 5 observations read from the data set MACRO.TITLE.
NOTE: PROCEDURE PRINT used:
      real time           0.02 seconds
      cpu time            0.01 seconds


14
15   %maketitle (data=macro.title);
NOTE: TITLES and FOOTNOTES adjusted according to data set MACRO.TITLE.
NOTE: The MACRO %MAKETITLE used:
      real time           0.36 seconds
      cpu time                 unknown

16
17   proc print data=macro.title ;
18   run ;

NOTE: There were 5 observations read from the data set MACRO.TITLE.
NOTE: PROCEDURE PRINT used:
      real time           0.01 seconds
      cpu time            0.01 seconds
```

SAS Listing

```
                           The SAS System

                         The CONTENTS Procedure

    Data Set Name: SASHELP.VTITLE              Observations:        .
    Member Type:   VIEW                        Variables:           3
    Engine:        SQLVIEW                     Indexes:             0
    Created:       9:41 Thursday, November 9, 2000   Observation Length:  272
    Last Modified: 9:41 Thursday, November 9, 2000   Deleted Observations: 0
    Protection:                                Compressed:          NO
    Data Set Type:                             Sorted:              NO
    Label:


              -----Alphabetic List of Variables and Attributes-----

           #    Variable   Type   Len   Pos   Flags   Label
           ƒƒƒƒƒƒƒƒƒƒƒƒƒƒƒƒƒƒƒƒƒƒƒƒƒƒƒƒƒƒƒƒƒƒƒƒƒƒƒƒƒƒƒƒƒƒƒƒƒƒƒƒƒƒ
           2    number     Num     8     8    P--     Title Number
           3    text       Char  256    16    P--     Title Text
           1    type       Char    1     0    P--     Title Location

                                footnote
                             second footnote

                              fourth footnote
```


```
              Obs    type    number    text

               1      T        1      The SAS System
               2      F        1      footnote
```

```
3    F    2    second footnote
4    F    3
5    F    4    fourth footnote
```

```
                    The SAS System
        Obs    type    number    text

        1      T       1         The SAS System
        2      F       1         footnote
        3      F       2         second footnote
        4      F       3
        5      F       4         fourth footnote

                       footnote
                    second footnote

                    fourth footnote
```

%MANIFEST

Purpose
This macro prints all values of any variable. It is designed to fit as many columns of that variable on a single page.

Syntax
%MANIFEST (VAR = *variable* <, DATA = *SAS-data-set*> <, DEBUG = Y | YES | NO | N>)

Required Parameter(s)
VAR = *variable*
> declares the variable to complete the report on. Only one variable may be declared.

Optional Parameter(s)
DATA = *SAS-data-set*
> declares the input SAS data set. If no data set is declared, the most recent data set is used.

DEBUG = Y | YES | NO | N
> debugging flag, set to YES or NO. Alternatively, you can submit Y or N. Default is NO.

Example

Sample Program
```
data manifest ;
   do i = 1 to 1000 ;
      printvar = round(ranuni(0)*100, .01) ;
      output ;
   end ;
run ;

title1 'SPIKEware Rapid Decision Support SAS Macro Package v3.2 demo' ;
```

```
title2 '%MANIFEST prints lots of columns on one page for each variable declared' ;
%manifest (data=manifest, var=printvar i)
```

SAS Log

```
1    data manifest ;
2       do i = 1 to 1000 ;
3          printvar = round(ranuni(0)*100, .01) ;
4          output ;
5       end ;
6    run ;

NOTE: The data set WORK.MANIFEST has 1000 observations and 2 variables.
NOTE: DATA statement used:
      real time           0.04 seconds
      cpu time            0.00 seconds


7
8    title1 'SPIKEware Rapid Decision Support SAS Macro Package v3.2 demo' ;
9    title2 '%MANIFEST prints lots of columns on one page for each variable declared' ;

10   %manifest (data=manifest, var=printvar i)


NOTE: The MACRO %MANIFEST used:
      real time           0.97 seconds
      cpu time            unknown
```

SAS Listing

```
                SPIKEware Rapid Decision Support SAS Macro Package v3.2 demo
            %MANIFEST prints lots of columns on one page for each variable declared
                           %MANIFEST Report on variable printvar
33.21   66.52   34.28   80.19   22.94   30.93   53.65   24.88   73.54
24.97   64.59   79.96   27.57   84.62   74.66   46.1    50.74   95.93
21.26   3.97    59.72   75.74   8.14    57.47   73.34   43.63   97.59
33.97   36.1    40.95   14.7    48.72   85.17   57.97   47.22   76.74
93.56   30.93   94.71   91.89   66.08   58.13   75.33   27.15   17.92
48.08   80.57   65.34   24.37   78.98   51.09   73.96   25      2.28
71.8    69.83   86.87   75.24   0.37    62.88   75.07   26.11   12.54
80.41   56.13   20.41   71.99   71.59   77.93   40.73   79.03   30.3
41.48   61.77   53.81   24.67   66.01   64.82   72.06   73.36   88.26
67.35   77.09   32.67   67.56   91.84   53.1    1.97    10.83   85.25
64.55   94.92   31.32   29.11   31.67   96.99   37.87   78.22   47.83
48.04   19.59   93.87   91.71   10.54   97.27   56.65   13.65   20.49
92.59   12.71   87.43   83.75   49.84   95.54   56.86   79.76   59.46
6.28    22.62   78.54   34.5    75.93   95.75   13.41   35.8    64.68
69.51   97.13   96.87   28.87   96.08   2.94    64.51   34.2    70.81
33.41   97.51   91.02   0.15    11.2    99.61   24.08   13.5    22.65
63.06   25      63.93   57.25   97.11   90.22   4.35    88.18   34.61
25.09   7.28    19.69   4.44    11.21   17.24   17.45   52.52   82.5
25.09   44.35   15.13   54.92   9.47    8.54    14.09   68.44   99.16
89.79   56.83   92.46   37.89   59.78   60.44   5.21    14.28   99.78
77.4    19.71   9.89    59.98   20.21   40.23   54.18   96.29   65.89
94.14   6       2.4     80.51   17.04   65.69   33.96   73.21   22.94
20.44   35.67   41.67   40.11   7.01    67.21   67.94   95.38   55.73
44.33   36.23   33.48   37.15   81.57   36.03   8.23    26.43   46.76
43.78   78.57   18.86   2.94    59      24.77   20.93   64.94   87.46
53.31   64.81   56.96   4.21    65.69   5.19    64.29   22.55   29.08
86.36   71.2    11.27   14.14   87.59   47.43   41.16   10.14   54.68
55.87
```

%OUTLIER

Purpose
This macro creates a second output data set from an input data set and screens the data (removes records) based on removing any outlier records that occur outside a given number of standard deviations from the mean. The outlier screen can be passed through a number of times.

Syntax
%OUTLIER (OUT = *SAS-data-set*, VAR = *variable* <, DATA = *SAS-data-set*> <, PASS = *passes*> <, MULT = *standard-deviation-multiplier*> <,EXCEPT = *SAS-data-set*> <DEBUG = Y | YES | NO | N>)

Required Parameter(s)
OUT = *SAS-data-set*
> declares the output SAS data set.

VAR = *variable*
> declares the variable for completion of the outlier screen. Only one variable may be declared.

Optional Parameter(s)
DATA = *SAS-data-set*
> declares the input SAS data set. If no data set is declared, the most recent data set is used.

EXCEPT = *SAS-data-set*
> declares the output SAS data set that will contain the exceptions that are deleted from the input data by the outlier screen.

PASS = *passes*
> declares the number of passes through the data to complete the outlier screening. Range: PASS > 0, integer.

MULT = *standard-deviation-multiplier*
> declares the multiplier for the range outside the standard deviation to screen outliers. Range: MULT > 0.

DEBUG = Y | YES | NO | N
> debugging flag, set to YES or NO. Alternatively, you can submit Y or N. Default is NO.

Notes
An outlier is a data point that is located far from the rest of the data. Given a mean and standard deviation a statistical distribution expects data points to fall within a specific range. Those that do not are called outliers. The default setting is a 2-Pass, 3-std outlier screen.

Visit http://www.graphpad.com/articles/outlier.htm to read a good article on detecting outliers by Dr. Harvey Motulsky.

Example

Sample Program

```
data test1 (drop = i j k l) ;
   do i = 1 to 960 ;
      testvar = ranuni(0) ;
      output ;
   end ;

   do j = 1 to 10 ;
      testvar = ranuni(0) * 2 ;
      output ;
   end ;

   do k = 1 to 10 ;
      testvar = ranuni(0) * 10 ;
      output ;
   end ;

   do l = 1 to 4 ;
      testvar = ranuni(0) - 2 ;
      output ;
   end ;
run ;

%outlier (data=test1, out=out1, var=testvar, pass=3, mult=3, except=except)

title1 '%OUTLIER macro testing' ;
title2 'Exception Report:  Outliers Removed' ;
proc print data=except ;
run ;

title2 'Univariate report on variable before outlier screen' ;
proc univariate data=test1 ;
   var testvar ;
run ;

title2 'Univariate report on variable after outlier screen' ;
proc univariate data=out1 ;
   var testvar ;
run ;
```

SAS Log

```
1     data test1 (drop = i j k l) ;
2        do i = 1 to 960 ;
3           testvar = ranuni(0) ;
4           output ;
5        end ;
6
7        do j = 1 to 10 ;
8           testvar = ranuni(0) * 2 ;
9           output ;
10       end ;
11
12       do k = 1 to 10 ;
13          testvar = ranuni(0) * 10 ;
14          output ;
15       end ;
16
17       do l = 1 to 4 ;
18          testvar = ranuni(0) - 2 ;
19          output ;
20       end ;
21    run ;
```

```
NOTE: The data set WORK.TEST1 has 984 observations and 1 variables.
NOTE: DATA statement used:
      real time           0.03 seconds
      cpu time            0.02 seconds


22
23    %outlier (data=test1, out=out1, var=testvar, pass=3, mult=3, except=except)

NOTE: Macro OUTLIER completed a 3-pass-3 outlier screen on WORK.TEST1 written to data set
WORK.OUT1
NOTE: 16 observations were removed from the outlier screen.
NOTE: The data set WORK.OUT1 has 968 observations and 1 variables.
NOTE: The MACRO %OUTLIER used:
      real time           0.76 seconds
      cpu time                 unknown

24
25    title1 '%OUTLIER macro testing' ;
26    title2 'Exception Report:  Outliers Removed' ;
27    proc print data=except ;
28    run ;

NOTE: There were 16 observations read from the data set WORK.EXCEPT.
NOTE: PROCEDURE PRINT used:
      real time           0.01 seconds
      cpu time            0.01 seconds


29
30    title2 'Univariate report on variable before outlier screen' ;
31    proc univariate data=test1 ;
32       var testvar ;
33    run ;

NOTE: PROCEDURE UNIVARIATE used:
      real time           0.08 seconds
      cpu time            0.01 seconds


34
35    title2 'Univariate report on variable after outlier screen' ;
36    proc univariate data=out1 ;
37       var testvar ;
38    run ;

NOTE: PROCEDURE UNIVARIATE used:
      real time           0.05 seconds
      cpu time            0.02 seconds
```

SAS Listing

```
                         %OUTLIER macro testing
                    Exception Report:  Outliers Removed

                         Obs        testvar

                          1         5.59804
                          2         9.74893
                          3         7.78714
                          4         4.01124
                          5         5.04629
                          6         8.27617
                          7         7.27105
                          8         9.66805
                          9         4.20496
                         10         1.80087
```

```
                                    11      1.93248
                                    12      1.57819
                                    13     -1.37671
                                    14     -1.06748
                                    15     -1.54332
                                    16     -1.41361
```

```
                              %OUTLIER macro testing
                   Univariate report on variable before outlier screen

                                The UNIVARIATE Procedure
                                   Variable: testvar

                                         Moments

        N                           984    Sum Weights                984
        Mean                   0.54861086   Sum Observations     539.833084
        Std Deviation          0.71041508   Variance             0.50468959
        Skewness               8.40511576   Kurtosis             92.9959967
        Uncorrected SS         792.268157   Corrected SS         496.109866
        Coeff Variation        129.493442   Std Error Mean       0.02264721


                              Basic Statistical Measures

              Location                          Variability

        Mean      0.548611       Std Deviation            0.71042
        Median    0.522106       Variance                 0.50469
        Mode         .           Range                   11.29225
                                 Interquartile Range      0.47950


                            Tests for Location: Mu0=0

         Test             -Statistic-      -----p Value------

         Student's t    t   24.22422       Pr > |t|     <.0001
         Sign           M        488       Pr >= |M|    <.0001
         Signed Rank    S     238429       Pr >= |S|    <.0001


                              Quantiles (Definition 5)

                         Quantile        Estimate

                         100% Max       9.74893428
                         99%            1.93247877
                         95%            0.96148135
                         90%            0.89763241
                         75% Q3         0.72533682
                         50% Median     0.52210608
                         25% Q1         0.24583498
                         10%            0.09342064
                         5%             0.05466290
                         1%             0.00471637
                         0% Min        -1.54331891
```

```
                              %OUTLIER macro testing
                   Univariate report on variable before outlier screen

                                The UNIVARIATE Procedure
                                   Variable: testvar
```

```
                        Extreme Observations

                 -------Lowest-------        -----Highest-----

                      Value      Obs           Value      Obs

                 -1.54331891     983         7.27105      977
                 -1.41360709     984         7.78714      973
                 -1.37671206     981         8.27617      976
                 -1.06748333     982         9.66805      978
                  0.00040427     623         9.74893      972
```

```
                          %OUTLIER macro testing
                Univariate report on variable after outlier screen

                              The UNIVARIATE Procedure
                                  Variable: testvar

                                        Moments

N                              968        Sum Weights              968
Mean                      0.49412273       Sum Observations    478.310805
Std Deviation             0.28391999       Variance             0.08061056
Skewness                 -0.0113988        Kurtosis            -1.1020498
Uncorrected SS            314.294654       Corrected SS         77.9504123
Coeff Variation           57.4594066       Std Error Mean       0.00912553


                            Basic Statistical Measures

              Location                        Variability

          Mean     0.494123        Std Deviation          0.28392
          Median   0.517691        Variance               0.08061
          Mode     .               Range                  1.28237
                                   Interquartile Range    0.46871


                           Tests for Location: Mu0=0

         Test              -Statistic-       -----p Value------

         Student's t      t   54.14727      Pr > |t|      <.0001
         Sign             M        484      Pr >= |M|     <.0001
         Signed Rank      S     234498      Pr >= |S|     <.0001


                             Quantiles (Definition 5)

                         Quantile       Estimate

                         100% Max       1.28277216
                         99%            0.99056966
                         95%            0.94908326
                         90%            0.88152781
                         75% Q3         0.71454249
                         50% Median     0.51769149
                         25% Q1         0.24583498
                         10%            0.09399950
                         5%             0.05762159
                         1%             0.01107190
                         0% Min         0.00040427
```

```
                     %OUTLIER macro testing
            Univariate report on variable after outlier screen

                        The UNIVARIATE Procedure
                           Variable:  testvar

                          Extreme Observations

          --------Lowest-------      ------Highest-----

               Value        Obs         Value        Obs

           0.000404270      623       0.996359      686
           0.000801841      499       0.996952      268
           0.001558296       17       0.997234      408
           0.003305480      312       0.998459      111
           0.003530075      635       1.282772      965
```

%PARETO

Purpose
This macro creates a Pareto Chart

Syntax:
%PARETO (DATA = *SAS-data-set*, X = *x-axis-variable*, Y = *y-axis-variable* <FILE = *'file-specification'* > <, SAS = *'file-specification'* > <, DEBUG = Y | YES | NO | N>)

Required Parameter(s)
DATA = *SAS-data-set*

> declares the input SAS data set. If no data set is declared, the most recent data set is used.

X = *x-axis-variable*

> declares the x-axis variable for the PARETO chart.

Y = *y-axis-variable*

> declares the y-axis variable for the PARETO chart.

Optional Parameter(s)
FILE = *"file-specification"*

> declares the output CSV file for creating an Microsoft Excel® graph. *"file-specification"* specifies the physical name of an external file, which is enclosed in quotation marks. The physical name is the name by which the operating environment recognizes the file.

SAS = *"file-specification"*

> declares the location of the SAS Software System® (sas.exe). *"file-specification"* specifies the physical name of an external file, which is enclosed in quotation marks. The physical name is the name by which the operating environment recognizes the file.

DEBUG = Y | YES | NO | N

> debugging flag, set to YES or NO. Alternatively, you can submit Y or N. Default is NO.

See Also
PROC PARETO (SAS\QC)

Notes
This macro creates a PARETO CHART as explained in the book _THE_80/20_PRINCIPLE_ by Richard Koch from Currency/Doubleday Press © 1998 pages 96-97. If you have a current license for SAS/GRAPH, then the SAS/GRAPH utilites are used. Otherwise, BASE SAS procedures are used. There is an option to create a comma-separated file for import into the SPIKEware Pareto Workbook for Microsoft Excel. If you do not wish to create this file, then simply leave that option blank. Further documentation is available on our website

Microsoft Power Point: http://www.spikeware.net/ftp/ppt/sw006.ppt

Microsoft Excel Template: http://www.spikeware.net/ftp/xlt/sw006.xlt

Adobe Acrobat Document: http://www.spikeware.net/ftp/pdf/sw006.pdf

Example

Sample Program
```
%pareto (data = sashelp.shoes,
         x    = product,
         y    = sales,
         file = 'C:\Temp\shoes.csv')
```

SAS Log
```
1      %pareto (data = sashelp.shoes,
2               x    = product,
3               y    = sales,
4               file = 'C:\Temp\shoes.csv')
NOTE: The file 'C:\Temp\shoes.csv' is:
      File Name=C:\Temp\shoes.csv,
      RECFM=V,LRECL=256

NOTE: 8 records were written to the file 'C:\Temp\shoes.csv'.
      The minimum record length was 13.
      The maximum record length was 23.
NOTE: The MACRO %PARETO used:
      real time           2.00 seconds
      cpu time                 unknown
```

SAS Graph Output

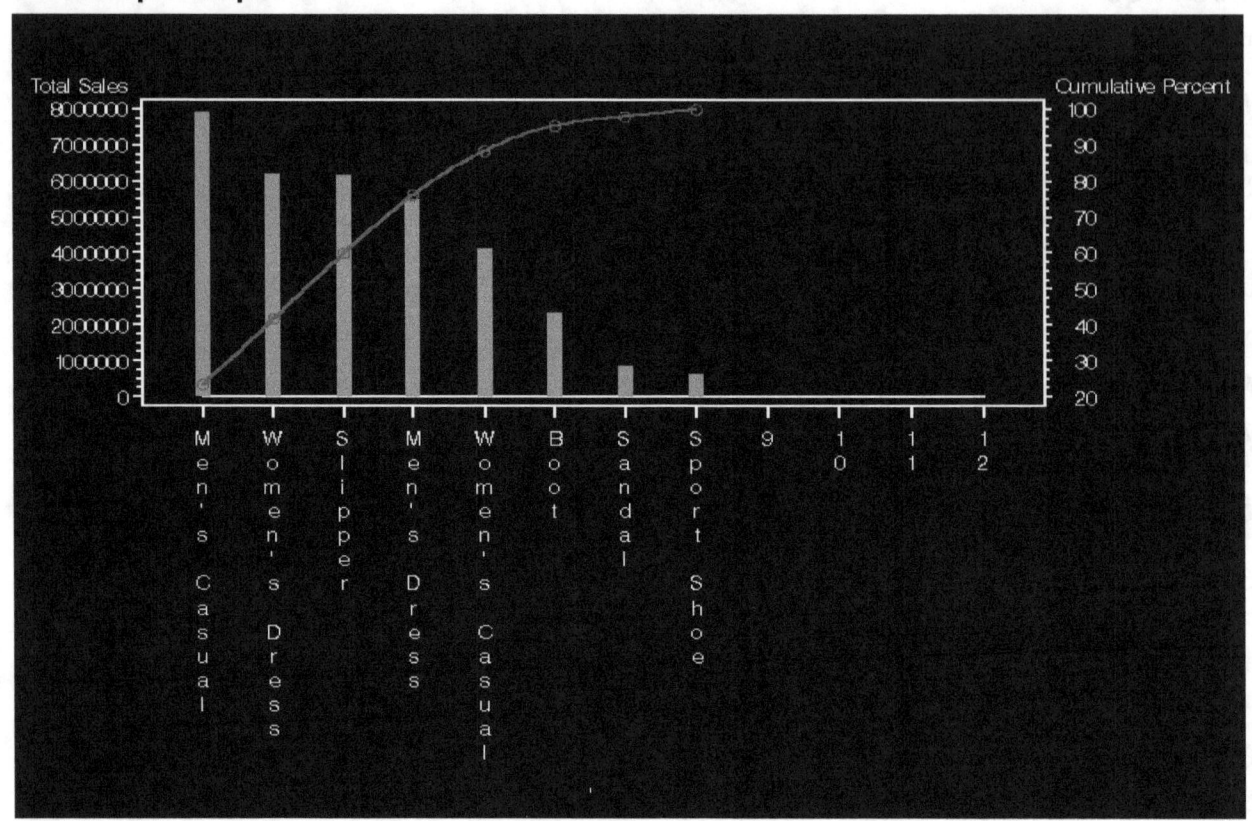

SAS Listing

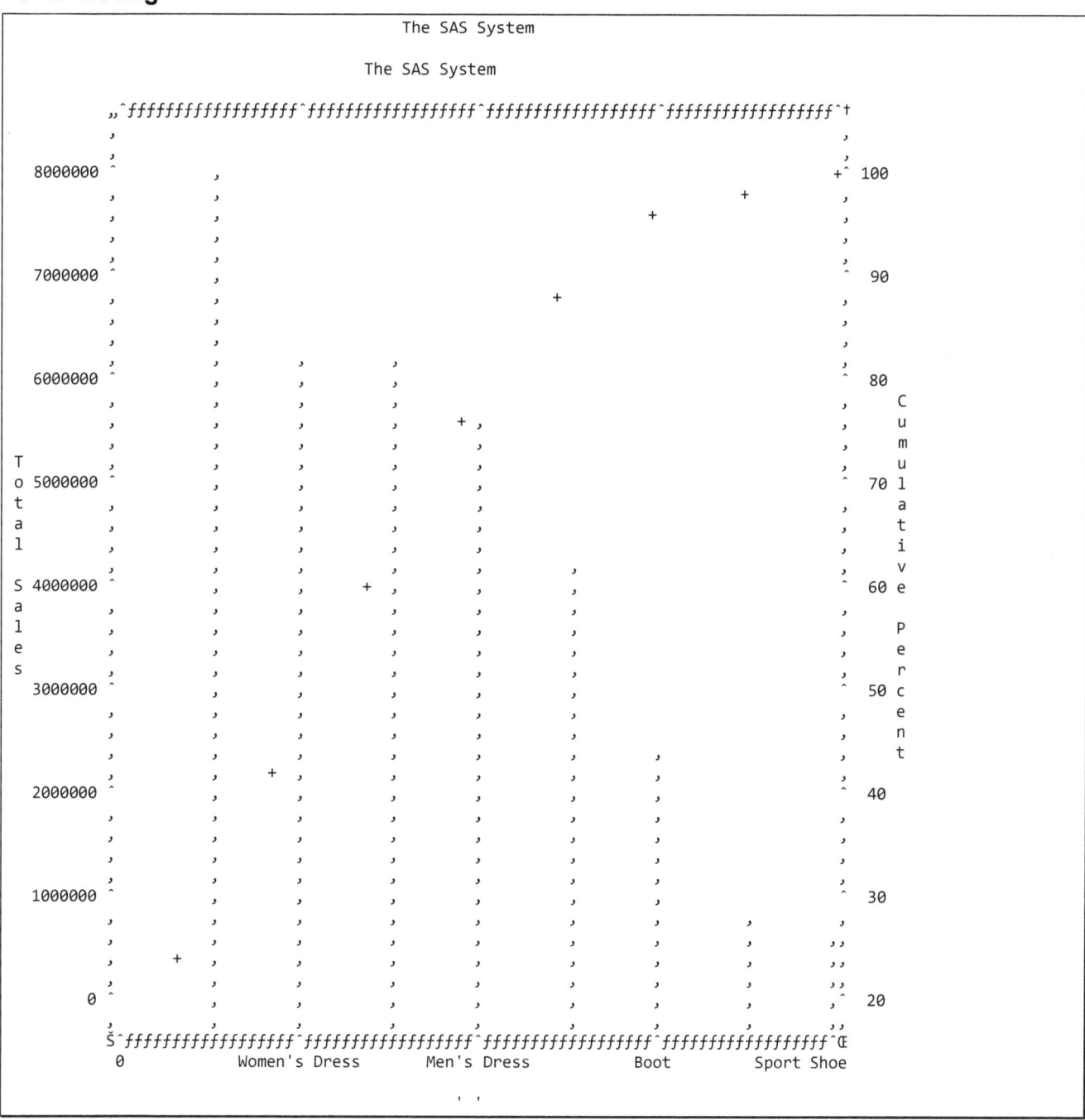

%PGMTEST

Purpose
Test and re-test a SAS program and report on the average run time of each procedure, data step, and RDS Macro.

Syntax
%PGMTEST (INCLUDE = *SAS-program* <, N = *iterations*> <,OUT = *SAS-data-set*> <, DEBUG = Y | YES | NO | N>)

Required Parameter(s)
INCLUDE = *SAS-program*

> declares the physical file name of the SAS program to test

Optional Parameter(s)
N = *iterations*

> declares the number of times to run the given program declared in INCLUDE =.

OUT = *SAS-data-set*

> declares the output SAS data set.

DEBUG = Y | YES | NO | N

> debugging flag, set to YES or NO. Alternatively, you can submit Y or N. Default is NO.

Notes
Thanks to Robert Patten for getting this program started with his paper 113-28 at SUGI 28 Coders Corner.

Example

Sample Program
```
%pgmtest (include = !SASROOT\core\sample\bpg42r01.sas)
```

SAS Log
```
1    %pgmtest (include = !SASROOT\core\sample\bpg42r01.sas)
NOTE: The MACRO %PGMTEST used:
      real time            5.63 seconds
      cpu time                  unknown
```

SAS Listing

```
                                        The SAS System

                              Min CPU   Mean CPU  Max CPU   Min Real  Mean Real Max Real
      Step                     Time      Time      Time      Time      Time      Time
      Number   SAS Note       (seconds) (seconds) (seconds) (seconds) (seconds) (seconds)

         1   SAS initialization used:   0.08      0.110     0.15      0.20      0.264     0.31
         2   DATA statement used:       0.00      0.008     0.02      0.01      0.016     0.02
         3   DATA statement used:       0.00      0.004     0.01      0.00      0.004     0.01
         4   PROCEDURE UNIVARIATE used: 0.01      0.026     0.05      0.05      0.128     0.35
         5   PROCEDURE PRINT used:      0.00      0.004     0.01      0.00      0.006     0.01
                                                 =========                     =========
                                                  0.152                         0.418
```

%POPOPTS

Purpose

This macro restores the SAS System Options from a SAS options holding SAS data set

Syntax

%POPOPTS (<DATA = *SAS-data-set*> <, DEBUG = Y | YES | NO | N>)

Required Parameter(s)

None.

Optional Parameter(s)

DATA = *SAS-data-set*

> declares the input SAS data set. If no data set is declared, the most recent data set is used. It is designed to accept the output data set from the macro %PUSHOPTS.

DEBUG = Y | YES | NO | N

> debugging flag, set to YES or NO. Alternatively, you can submit Y or N. Default is NO.

See Also

%PUSHOPTS, %POPOPTS

Example

Sample Program

```
%pushopts (out=options)
%popopts (data=options)
```

SAS Log

```
1          %pushopts (out=options)
NOTE: Current system options have been pushed to SAS data set WORK.OPTIONS.
NOTE: The data set WORK.OPTIONS has 224 observations and 4 variables.
NOTE: The MACRO %PUSHOPTS used:
      real time             0.16 seconds
      cpu time              unknown

2          %popopts (data=options)
```

```
NOTE: SAS System Options restored according to data set WORK.OPTIONS.
NOTE: The MACRO %POPOPTS used:
      real time              0.16 seconds
      cpu time               unknown
```

SAS Listing

This sample program does not have any listing output.

%POPTITLE

Purpose

This macro creates titles and footnotes from a title and footnote data set

Syntax

%POPTITLE (<DATA = *SAS-data-set*> <,DEBUG = Y | YES | NO | N>)

Required Parameter(s)

None.

Optional Parameter(s)

DATA = *SAS-data-set*

> declares the input SAS data set. If no data set is declared, the most recent data set is used. The data set given must be a valid "SAS TITLE Statement" data set, similar to the standard SAS view SASHELP.VTITLE. It is designed to accept the output data set from the macro %PUSHOPTS.

DEBUG = Y | YES | NO | N

> debugging flag, set to YES or NO. Alternatively, you can submit Y or N. Default is NO.

See Also

%PUSHTITLE, %POPTITLE, %MAKETITLE

Example

Sample Program

```
footnote1 "footnote" ;
footnote2 "second footnote" ;
footnote4 "fourth footnote" ;
proc contents data=sashelp.vtitle out=contents ;
run ;

%pushtitle (out=title) ;

title1 ;
footnote1 ;
proc print data=sashelp.shoes ;
run ;

%poptitle (data=title) ;

proc print data=sashelp.shoes ;
run ;
```

SAS Log

```
1    footnote1 "footnote" ;
2    footnote2 "second footnote" ;
3    footnote4 "fourth footnote" ;
4    proc contents data=sashelp.vtitle out=contents ;
5    run ;

NOTE: The data set WORK.CONTENTS has 3 observations and 40 variables.
NOTE: PROCEDURE CONTENTS used:
      real time           0.16 seconds
      cpu time            0.03 seconds


6
7    %pushtitle (out=title) ;
NOTE: The data set WORK.TITLE has 5 observations and 3 variables.
NOTE: The MACRO %PUSHTITLE used:
      real time           0.14 seconds
      cpu time            unknown

8
9    title1 ;
10   footnote1 ;
11   proc print data=sashelp.shoes ;
12   run ;

NOTE: There were 395 observations read from the data set SASHELP.SHOES.
NOTE: PROCEDURE PRINT used:
      real time           0.02 seconds
      cpu time            0.02 seconds


13
14   %poptitle (data=title) ;
NOTE: TITLES and FOOTNOTES adjusted according to data set WORK.TITLE.
NOTE: The MACRO %POPTITLE used:
      real time           0.20 seconds
      cpu time            unknown

15
16   proc print data=sashelp.shoes ;
17   run ;

NOTE: There were 395 observations read from the data set SASHELP.SHOES.
NOTE: PROCEDURE PRINT used:
      real time           0.00 seconds
      cpu time            0.00 seconds
```

SAS Listing

```
                               The SAS System

                            The CONTENTS Procedure

     Data Set Name: SASHELP.VTITLE              Observations:          .
     Member Type:   VIEW                        Variables:             3
     Engine:        SQLVIEW                     Indexes:               0
     Created:       9:41 Thursday, November 9, 2000    Observation Length:    272
     Last Modified: 9:41 Thursday, November 9, 2000    Deleted Observations:  0
     Protection:                                Compressed:            NO
     Data Set Type:                             Sorted:                NO
     Label:


                    -----Alphabetic List of Variables and Attributes-----

             #     Variable    Type    Len    Pos    Flags    Label
```

```
      fffffffffffffffffffffffffffffffffffffffffffffffffffffff
     2    number     Num     8     8    P--    Title Number
     3    text       Char  256    16    P--    Title Text
     1    type       Char    1     0    P--    Title Location


                              footnote
                          second footnote

                           fourth footnote
```

```
 Obs   Region   Product         Subsidiary     Stores      Sales     Inventory     Returns

  1    Africa   Boot            Addis Ababa      12       $29,761     $191,821       $769
  2    Africa   Men's Casual    Addis Ababa       4       $67,242     $118,036     $2,284
  3    Africa   Men's Dress     Addis Ababa       7       $76,793     $136,273     $2,433
  4    Africa   Sandal          Addis Ababa      10       $62,819     $204,284     $1,861
  5    Africa   Slipper         Addis Ababa      14       $68,641     $279,795     $1,771
  6    Africa   Sport Shoe      Addis Ababa       4        $1,690      $16,634        $79
  7    Africa   Women's Casual  Addis Ababa       2       $51,541      $98,641       $940
  8    Africa   Women's Dress   Addis Ababa      12      $108,942     $311,017     $3,233
  9    Africa   Boot            Algiers          21       $21,297      $73,737       $710
 10    Africa   Men's Casual    Algiers           4       $63,206     $100,982     $2,221
 11    Africa   Men's Dress     Algiers          13      $123,743     $428,575     $3,621
 12    Africa   Sandal          Algiers          25       $29,198      $84,447     $1,530
 13    Africa   Slipper         Algiers          17       $64,891     $248,198     $1,823
 14    Africa   Sport Shoe      Algiers           9        $2,617       $9,372       $168
 15    Africa   Women's Dress   Algiers          12       $90,648     $266,805     $2,690
```

```
                                    The SAS System

 Obs   Region   Product         Subsidiary     Stores      Sales     Inventory     Returns

  1    Africa   Boot            Addis Ababa      12       $29,761     $191,821       $769
  2    Africa   Men's Casual    Addis Ababa       4       $67,242     $118,036     $2,284
  3    Africa   Men's Dress     Addis Ababa       7       $76,793     $136,273     $2,433
  4    Africa   Sandal          Addis Ababa      10       $62,819     $204,284     $1,861
  5    Africa   Slipper         Addis Ababa      14       $68,641     $279,795     $1,771
  6    Africa   Sport Shoe      Addis Ababa       4        $1,690      $16,634        $79
  7    Africa   Women's Casual  Addis Ababa       2       $51,541      $98,641       $940
  8    Africa   Women's Dress   Addis Ababa      12      $108,942     $311,017     $3,233
  9    Africa   Boot            Algiers          21       $21,297      $73,737       $710

                                       footnote
                                    second footnote

                                    fourth footnote
```

%PUSHOPTS

Purpose
This macro pushes the options to a holding SAS data set

Syntax
%PUSHOPTS (OUT = *SAS-data-set* <, DEBUG = Y | YES | NO | N>)

Required Parameter(s)
OUT = *SAS-data-set*

> declares the output SAS data set. The output data set is designed to be acceptable as an input data set for the macro %POPOPTS.

Optional Parameter(s)
DEBUG = Y | YES | NO | N

debugging flag, set to YES or NO. Alternatively, you can submit Y or N. Default is NO.

See Also
%PUSHOPTS, %POPOPTS

Example:

Sample Program
```
%pushopts (out=options)
%popopts (data=options)
```

SAS Log
```
1          %pushopts (out=options)
NOTE: Current system options have been pushed to SAS data set WORK.OPTIONS.
NOTE: The data set WORK.OPTIONS has 224 observations and 4 variables.
NOTE: The MACRO %PUSHOPTS used:
      real time           0.16 seconds
      cpu time            unknown

2          %popopts (data=options)
NOTE: SAS System Options restored according to data set WORK.OPTIONS.
NOTE: The MACRO %POPOPTS used:
      real time           0.16 seconds
      cpu time            unknown
```

SAS Listing
This sample program does not have any listing output.

%PUSHTITLE

Purpose
This macro pushes the titles and footnotes to a holding SAS data set

Syntax
%PUSHTITLE (OUT = *SAS-data-set*, <,DEBUG = Y | YES | NO | N>)

Required Parameter(s)
OUT = *SAS-data-set*

> declares the output SAS data set. The output data set is designed to be acceptable as an input data set for the macro %POPTITLE.

Optional Parameter(s)
DEBUG = Y | YES | NO | N

> debugging flag, set to YES or NO. Alternatively, you can submit Y or N. Default is NO.

See Also
%PUSHTITLE, %POPTITLE

Example

Sample Program

```
footnote1 "footnote" ;
footnote2 "second footnote" ;
footnote4 "fourth footnote" ;
proc contents data=sashelp.vtitle out=contents ;
run ;

%pushtitle (out=title) ;

title1 ;
footnote1 ;
proc print data=sashelp.shoes ;
run ;

%poptitle (data=title) ;

proc print data=sashelp.shoes ;
run ;
```

SAS Log

```
1    footnote1 "footnote" ;
2    footnote2 "second footnote" ;
3    footnote4 "fourth footnote" ;
4    proc contents data=sashelp.vtitle out=contents ;
5    run ;

NOTE: The data set WORK.CONTENTS has 3 observations and 40 variables.
NOTE: PROCEDURE CONTENTS used:
      real time           0.16 seconds
      cpu time            0.03 seconds


6
7    %pushtitle (out=title) ;
NOTE: The data set WORK.TITLE has 5 observations and 3 variables.
NOTE: The MACRO %PUSHTITLE used:
      real time           0.14 seconds
      cpu time            unknown

8
9    title1 ;
10   footnote1 ;
11   proc print data=sashelp.shoes ;
12   run ;

NOTE: There were 395 observations read from the data set SASHELP.SHOES.
NOTE: PROCEDURE PRINT used:
      real time           0.02 seconds
      cpu time            0.02 seconds


13
14   %poptitle (data=title) ;
NOTE: TITLES and FOOTNOTES adjusted according to data set WORK.TITLE.
NOTE: The MACRO %POPTITLE used:
      real time           0.20 seconds
      cpu time            unknown

15
16   proc print data=sashelp.shoes ;
17   run ;

NOTE: There were 395 observations read from the data set SASHELP.SHOES.
```

```
NOTE: PROCEDURE PRINT used:
      real time           0.00 seconds
      cpu time            0.00 seconds
```

SAS Listing

```
                              The SAS System

                            The CONTENTS Procedure

     Data Set Name: SASHELP.VTITLE              Observations:         .
     Member Type:   VIEW                        Variables:            3
     Engine:        SQLVIEW                     Indexes:              0
     Created:       9:41 Thursday, November 9, 2000   Observation Length: 272
     Last Modified: 9:41 Thursday, November 9, 2000   Deleted Observations: 0
     Protection:                                Compressed:           NO
     Data Set Type:                             Sorted:               NO
     Label:


                    -----Alphabetic List of Variables and Attributes-----

           #    Variable    Type    Len    Pos    Flags    Label
           ƒƒƒƒƒƒƒƒƒƒƒƒƒƒƒƒƒƒƒƒƒƒƒƒƒƒƒƒƒƒƒƒƒƒƒƒƒƒƒƒƒƒƒƒƒƒƒƒƒƒƒƒƒƒƒƒƒƒƒ
           2    number      Num      8      8     P--      Title Number
           3    text        Char   256     16     P--      Title Text
           1    type        Char     1      0     P--      Title Location


                                  footnote
                               second footnote

                                fourth footnote
```

```
 Obs  Region  Product         Subsidiary    Stores      Sales    Inventory    Returns

  1   Africa  Boot            Addis Ababa      12     $29,761     $191,821       $769
  2   Africa  Men's Casual    Addis Ababa       4     $67,242     $118,036     $2,284
  3   Africa  Men's Dress     Addis Ababa       7     $76,793     $136,273     $2,433
  4   Africa  Sandal          Addis Ababa      10     $62,819     $204,284     $1,861
  5   Africa  Slipper         Addis Ababa      14     $68,641     $279,795     $1,771
  6   Africa  Sport Shoe      Addis Ababa       4      $1,690      $16,634        $79
  7   Africa  Women's Casual  Addis Ababa       2     $51,541      $98,641       $940
  8   Africa  Women's Dress   Addis Ababa      12    $108,942     $311,017     $3,233
  9   Africa  Boot            Algiers          21     $21,297      $73,737       $710
 10   Africa  Men's Casual    Algiers           4     $63,206     $100,982     $2,221
 11   Africa  Men's Dress     Algiers          13    $123,743     $428,575     $3,621
 12   Africa  Sandal          Algiers          25     $29,198      $84,447     $1,530
 13   Africa  Slipper         Algiers          17     $64,891     $248,198     $1,823
 14   Africa  Sport Shoe      Algiers           9      $2,617       $9,372       $168
 15   Africa  Women's Dress   Algiers          12     $90,648     $266,805     $2,690
```

```
                               The SAS System
 Obs  Region  Product         Subsidiary    Stores      Sales    Inventory    Returns

  1   Africa  Boot            Addis Ababa      12     $29,761     $191,821       $769
  2   Africa  Men's Casual    Addis Ababa       4     $67,242     $118,036     $2,284
  3   Africa  Men's Dress     Addis Ababa       7     $76,793     $136,273     $2,433
  4   Africa  Sandal          Addis Ababa      10     $62,819     $204,284     $1,861
  5   Africa  Slipper         Addis Ababa      14     $68,641     $279,795     $1,771
  6   Africa  Sport Shoe      Addis Ababa       4      $1,690      $16,634        $79
  7   Africa  Women's Casual  Addis Ababa       2     $51,541      $98,641       $940
  8   Africa  Women's Dress   Addis Ababa      12    $108,942     $311,017     $3,233
  9   Africa  Boot            Algiers          21     $21,297      $73,737       $710

                                  footnote
                               second footnote

                                fourth footnote
```

%SAMPLE

Purpose
This macro will create a random sample of a SAS dataset.

Syntax
%SAMPLE (OUT = *SAS-data-set*, NOBS = *observations* <, DATA = *SAS-data-set*> <, SEED = *random-number-seed*> <, DEBUG = Y | YES | NO | N>)

Required Parameter(s)
OUT = *SAS-data-set*

>   declares the output SAS data set.

NOBS = *observations*

>   declares the number of observations (or the sample size) in the output data set.

Optional Parameter(s)

DATA = *SAS-data-set*

>declares the input SAS data set. If no data set is declared, the most recent data set is used.

SEED = *random-number-seed*

>declares the random number seed for creating the random sample. Default is 0. Range: any real number.

DEBUG = Y | YES | NO | N

>debugging flag, set to YES or NO. Alternatively, you can submit Y or N. Default is NO.

See Also
%SAMPLE, %SHUFFLE

Example

Sample Program
```
%sample (data=sashelp.shoes, out=sample, nobs=20, seed=44)
```

SAS Log
```
3    %sample (data=sashelp.shoes, out=sample, nobs=20, seed=44)
NOTE: Macro SAMPLE used random number seed 44.
NOTE: The data set WORK.SAMPLE has 20 observations and 7 variables.
NOTE: The MACRO %SAMPLE used:
      real time             0.92 seconds
      cpu time              unknown
```

SAS Listing
This sample program does not have any listing output.

%SAS2XLS

Purpose
This macro reads a Microsoft Excel Spreadsheet into a SAS data set

Syntax
%SAS2XLS (FILE = *'file-specification'* <, DATA = *SAS-data-set*> <, VAR = *variable-list*> <,XLS = *'file-specification'*> <, DEBUG = Y | YES | NO | N>)

Required Parameter(s)

FILE = *'file-specification'*

>declares the output Microsoft Excel® file. *"file-specification"* specifies the physical name of an external file, which is enclosed in quotation marks. The physical name is the name by which the operating environment recognizes the file.

Optional Parameter(s)

DATA = *SAS-data-set*

declares the input SAS data set. If no data set is declared, the most recent data set is used.

VAR = *variable-list*

declares the list of variables to write to the output file.

XLS = *'file-specification'*

declares the location of the Microsoft Excel® executable file. *"file-specification"* specifies the physical name of an external file, which is enclosed in quotation marks. The physical name is the name by which the operating environment recognizes the file.

DEBUG = Y | YES | NO | N

debugging flag, set to YES or NO. Alternatively, you can submit Y or N. Default is NO.

See Also
%XLS2SAS, %SAS2XLS, %FILEIN, %FILEOUT, PROC IMPORT, PROC EXPORT

Notes
This macro takes an MS-Excel spreadsheet and reads it in to a SAS data set. Microsoft Excel is required and it will only function in Microsoft Windows Environment.

All variables read in are read in as character strings of the same length as defined in the LENGTH= option (default=200). The first row of the spreadsheet must contain the variable names. The macro will not read past a blank column and reads in the values as they are formatted in the MS-Excel spreadsheet (WYSIWYG).

MS-Excel has different file restrictions than SAS has. For example, a carriage-return character or a LRECL > 32767 will generate results that are unpredictable.

BENCHMARK: This macro used approximately 22 minutes of real-time to process a 63,535 record MS-Excel Spreadsheet of 256 columns. Each variable read in was of size $200 and the resulting SAS data set took up 3,285,574,656 bytes (3.2 Gb). A 10-record spreadsheet of 4 variables can be read in about 6 seconds.

If you have SAS/ACCESS Software for PC File Formats, you should use the procedures available (PROC IMPORT) in that package instead of this macro.

Example

Sample Program
```
%sas2xls (file=C:\Temp\shoes.xls, data=sashelp.shoes)
```

SAS Log
```
1    %sas2xls (file=C:\Temp\shoes.xls, data=sashelp.shoes)
NOTE: The file "C:\Temp\shoes.xls" is:
      DDE Session,
      SESSION=excel|shoes!r1c1:r396c7,RECFM=V,
      LRECL=32767
NOTE: 395 records were written to the file C:\Temp\shoes.xls
NOTE: The MACRO %SAS2XLS used:
      real time              6.70 seconds
      cpu time               unknown
```

SAS Listing
This sample program does not have any listing output.

MS-Excel File

	A	B	C	D	E	F	G
1	Region	Product	Subsidiary	Number of Stores	Total Sales	Total Inventory	Total Returns
2	Africa	Boot	Addis Ababa	12	$29,761	$191,821	$769
3	Africa	Men's Casual	Addis Ababa	4	$67,242	$118,036	$2,284
4	Africa	Men's Dress	Addis Ababa	7	$76,793	$136,273	$2,433
5	Africa	Sandal	Addis Ababa	10	$62,819	$204,284	$1,861
6	Africa	Slipper	Addis Ababa	14	$68,641	$279,795	$1,771
7	Africa	Sport Shoe	Addis Ababa	4	$1,690	$16,634	$79
8	Africa	Women's Casual	Addis Ababa	2	$51,541	$98,641	$940
9	Africa	Women's Dress	Addis Ababa	12	$108,942	$311,017	$3,233
10	Africa	Boot	Algiers	21	$21,297	$73,737	$710
11	Africa	Men's Casual	Algiers	4	$63,206	$100,982	$2,221
12	Africa	Men's Dress	Algiers	13	$123,743	$428,575	$3,621
13	Africa	Sandal	Algiers	25	$29,198	$84,447	$1,530
14	Africa	Slipper	Algiers	17	$64,891	$248,198	$1,823
15	Africa	Sport Shoe	Algiers	9	$2,617	$9,372	$168
16	Africa	Women's Dress	Algiers	12	$90,648	$266,805	$2,690
17	Africa	Boot	Cairo	20	$4,846	$18,965	$229
18	Africa	Men's Casual	Cairo	25	$360,209	$1,063,251	$9,424
19	Africa	Men's Dress	Cairo	5	$4,051	$45,962	$97
20	Africa	Sandal	Cairo	9	$10,532	$50,430	$598
21	Africa	Slipper	Cairo	9	$13,732	$54,117	$1,216
22	Africa	Sport Shoe	Cairo	3	$2,259	$20,815	$44

%SAS2XML

Purpose

This macro creates a simple XML file from a SAS data set.

Syntax

%SAS2XML (FILE = *filename* | *'file-specification'* <, DATA = *SAS-data-set*> <, XSL = *XSL-style-sheet,*> <, DEBUG = Y | YES | NO | N>)

Required Parameter(s)

FILE = *filename* | *'file-specification'*

>declares the output XML file

>>*filename* specifies the fileref of an external file.

>>*"file-specification"* specifies the physical name of an external file, which is enclosed in quotation marks. The physical name is the name by which the operating environment recognizes the file.

>Either the *filename* or *"file-specification"* must be declared, but not both.

Optional Parameter(s)

DATA = *SAS-data-set*

declares the input SAS data set. If no data set is declared, the most recent data set is used.

STYLESHEET = NONE | PRINT | *'file-specification'*

declares the location of the XML stylesheet. Default is PRINT.

PRINT specifies that the SPIKEware XML standard printing stylesheet will be used. This stylesheet is located at http://www.spikeware.net/xsl/print.xsl and requires an internet connection for proper viewing.

NONE specifies that no stylesheet will be applied

"file-specification" specifies the physical name of an external file, which is enclosed in quotation marks. The physical name is the name by which the operating environment recognizes the file.

DEBUG = Y | YES | NO | N

debugging flag, set to YES or NO. Alternatively, you can submit Y or N. Default is NO.

Notes

The XSL= option can declare a specific stylesheet by file location, can reference PRINT using http://www.spikeware.net/xsl/print.xsl as a standard stylesheet (this is the default), or leave it blank or use XSL=NONE for no XSL stylesheet at all.

Example

Sample Program

```
filename xml 'C:\temp\shoes.xml' ;
%sas2xml (data=sashelp.shoes, file=xml, xsl=none)
```

SAS Log

```
1     filename xml 'C:\temp\shoes.xml' ;
2     %sas2xml (data=sashelp.shoes, file=xml, xsl=none)
NOTE: The file XML is:
      File Name=C:\temp\shoes.xml,
      RECFM=V,LRECL=256

NOTE: 4031 records were written to the file XML.
      The minimum record length was 0.
      The maximum record length was 256.
NOTE: The MACRO %SAS2XML used:
      real time            0.77 seconds
      cpu time                  unknown
```

SAS Listing

This sample program does not have any listing output.

%SCRAMBLE

Purpose

This macro is used to generate a random password, compress a file protected by that password, and send that file via e-mail followed by another e-mail containing the password.

Syntax

%SCRAMBLE (INFILE = *filename* | *'file-specification'*, ZIP = *file-declaration*, TO = *e-mail-recipient* <, DEBUG = Y | YES | NO | N>)

Required Parameter(s)

INFILE = *filename* | *'file-specification'*

> *declares the input file*
>
> > *filename* specifies the fileref of an external file.
> >
> > *"file-specification"* specifies the physical name of an external file, which is enclosed in quotation marks. The physical name is the name by which the operating environment recognizes the file.
>
> Either the *filename* or *"file-specification"* must be declared, but not both.

ZIP = *file-declaration*

> declares the name of the ZIP file that will contain the compressed data (i.e. *file-declaration*.zip)

TO = *e-mail-recipient*

> declares the e-mail recipient of the zipped and password-protected file.

Optional Parameter(s)

DEBUG = Y | YES | NO | N

> debugging flag, set to YES or NO. Alternatively, you can submit Y or N. Default is NO.

Notes

The setup is for a Windows environment using PKZIP to compress and add passwords. You may need to make adjustments for your system. This is most certainly not the greatest way to password-protect and send files, but for basic security it works better than nothing.

%SHUFFLE

Purpose

This macro randomly shuffles the records of a SAS data set

Syntax

%SHUFFLE (OUT = *SAS-data-set* <, DATA = *SAS-data-set*> <, SEED = *random-number-seed*> <, DEBUG = Y | YES | NO | N>)

Required Parameter(s)

OUT = *SAS-data-set*

> declares the output SAS data set.

Optional Parameter(s)

DATA = *SAS-data-set*

declares the input SAS data set. If no data set is declared, the most recent data set is used.

SEED = *random-number-seed*

declares the random number seed for creating the random sample. Default is 0. Range: any real number.

DEBUG = Y | YES | NO | N

debugging flag, set to YES or NO. Alternatively, you can submit Y or N. Default is NO.

See Also
%SAMPLE, %SHUFFLE

Example

Sample Program
%shuffle (data=sashelp.shoes, out=shoes, seed=50)

SAS Log
```
8    %shuffle (data=sashelp.shoes, out=shoes, seed=50)
NOTE: Macro SHUFFLE used random number seed 50.
NOTE: The data set WORK.SHOES has 395 observations and 7 variables.
NOTE: The MACRO %SHUFFLE used:
      real time             0.54 seconds
      cpu time                   unknown
```

SAS Listing
This sample program does not have any listing output.

%SLIDE

Purpose
This macro creates a slide-bar chart to compare the results of individual observations of a SAS data set. There is an option to to place more data (i.e. date, character, etc.) below the printed form by creating a macro called %MORENULL and setting MORENULL=Y in the macro call.

Syntax
%SLIDE (ASCEND = *variable-list*, DESCEND = *variable-list* <, DATA = *SAS-data-set*> <, ID = *variable*> <, FORMAT = *SAS-format*> <, FORMCHAR = *'formatting-characters'* > <, MORENULL = Y | YES | NO | N> <, DEBUG = Y | YES | NO | N>)

Required Parameter(s)
ASCEND = *variable-list*
DESCEND = *variable-list*

declares the variable lists of ascending and descending variables groups. At least one set of ASCEND and DESCEND variables must be used.

Optional Parameter(s)

DATA = *SAS-data-set*

    declares the input SAS data set. If no data set is declared, the most recent data set is used.

ID = *variable*

    identifies the identifier variable for referencing records. Only one variable can be declared.

FORMAT = *SAS-format*

    The FORMAT statement associates a format with the substring of the check-all-that-apply variable. SAS uses the format to write the values of the variable that you specify

FORMCHAR = *'formatting-characters'*

    specifies any string or list of strings of characters up to 64 bytes long. If fewer than 64 bytes are specified, the string is padded with blanks on the right.

MORENULL = Y | YES | NO | N>

    Declares the use of a macro called MORENULL that will contain additional DATA _NULL_ statements for use within the report output.

DEBUG = Y | YES | NO | N

    debugging flag, set to YES or NO. Alternatively, you can submit Y or N. Default is NO.

Notes

All variable names used in calculations must be of 7 characters in length. Each variable will create a &var.1, &var.9, &var.n, and &var.x for the statistics, &var.f for the format, and &&&var.l for the label. Labels of variables scored cannot have a comma present. Special note: values for at least one of &ascend or &descend must be present.

Example

Sample Program

```
proc summary data=sashelp.shoes nway ;
   class region ;
   var stores sales inventory returns ;
   output out=shoes (drop = _type_ _freq_)
          sum=stores sales inv returns ;
run ;

%slide (data=shoes, ascend=stores sales inv, descend=returns, id=region)
```

SAS Log

```
1     proc summary data=sashelp.shoes nway ;
2        class region ;
3        var stores sales inventory returns ;
4        output out=shoes (drop = _type_ _freq_)
5               sum=stores sales inv returns ;
6     run ;

NOTE: There were 395 observations read from the data set SASHELP.SHOES.
NOTE: The data set WORK.SHOES has 10 observations and 5 variables.
NOTE: PROCEDURE SUMMARY used:
      real time           0.04 seconds
```

```
        cpu time              0.03 seconds

7
8    %slide (data=shoes, ascend=stores sales inv, descend=returns, id=region)
NOTE: The MACRO %SLIDE used:
      real time             0.90 seconds
      cpu time              unknown
```

SAS Listing

```
                                    The SAS System

                                     Slide Chart

ID: REGION = Africa                                                    page 1 of 10

                          %tile      |     Percentile Ranges    |
Variable       Result Rank Score     | 10th      Med      90th  | 10th    Med    90th

Ascending Values:
 Number of Stores   532.0    6   54  | 210.5    487.0    637.0  |           *
 Total Sales   $2,342,58    3   27   | 138E4    305E4    557E4  |    *
 Total Inventory $7,101,07  3   27   | 358E4    907E4    157E5  |                  *

Descending Values:
 Total Returns    $74,087   9   81   | 197E3    115E3    42491  |         *
```

This chart is completed with the SPIKEware Slide Chart Macro Utility.

%SORTALL

Purpose
This macro sorts all input datasets by the same variables.

Syntax
%SORTALL (BY = *variable-list* <, DATALIST = *SAS-data-set-1 SAS-data-set-2 ... SAS-data-set-N*> <OPTIONS = *options*> <, DEBUG = Y | YES | NO | N>)

Required Parameter(s)
BY = *variable-list*

>   declares the variables to sort by. Syntax is the same as the PROC SORT BY statement.

Optional Parameter(s)
DATALIST = *SAS-data-set-1 SAS-data-set-2 ...SAS-data-set-n*

>   identifies the one or more input SAS data sets for sorting. If not data sets are declared, the most recent data set is used.

OPTIONS = *options*

>   declares PROC SORT options.

DEBUG = Y | YES | NO | N

>   debugging flag, set to YES or NO. Alternatively, you can submit Y or N. Default is NO.

Notes
If no SAS dataset is specified, the last SAS dataset created is used.

Example

Sample Program
```
%sortall (datalist=adomsg adsmsg afmsg, by=msgid)
```

SAS Log
```
1    %sortall (datalist=adomsg adsmsg afmsg, by=msgid)
NOTE: Dataset WORK.ADOMSG contains 458 observations and 6 variables.
NOTE: Dataset WORK.ADSMSG contains 426 observations and 6 variables.
NOTE: Dataset WORK.AFMSG contains 1086 observations and 6 variables.
NOTE: All datasets are sorted by MSGID.
NOTE: The MACRO %SORTALL used:
      real time            0.14 seconds
      cpu time             unknown
```

SAS Listing
This sample program does not have any listing output.

%STEMLEAF

Purpose
This macro creates a standard STEM-LEAF diagram

Syntax
%STEMLEAF (VAR = *variable*, ROUND = *round-off-unit* <, DATA = *SAS-data-set*> <, OUT = *SAS-data-set*> <, DEBUG = Y | YES | NO | N>)

Required Parameter(s)
VAR = variable

    declares the numeric variable for the stem-leaf calculation

ROUND = round-off-unit

    declares the round-off-unit (see ROUND function). Rounds the STEM to the nearest round-off unit. Range: is numeric and nonnegative.

Optional Parameter(s)
DATA= SAS-data-set

    identifies the input SAS data set. If no data set is declared, the most recent data set is used.

OUT = SAS-data-set

    identifies the output SAS data set.

DEBUG = Y | YES | NO | N

    debugging flag, set to YES or NO. Alternatively, you can submit Y or N. Default is NO.

Example

Sample Program
```
title1 'Stem-Leaf plot of variable SALES in SASDATA.SHOES' ;
%stemleaf (data=sashelp.shoes, var=sales, round=1000, out=stemleaf)
```

SAS Listing
```
1    title1 'Stem-Leaf plot of variable SALES in SASDATA.SHOES' ;
2    %stemleaf (data=sashelp.shoes, var=sales, round=1000, out=stemleaf)
NOTE: The data set WORK.STEMLEAF has 167 observations and 2 variables.
NOTE: The MACRO %STEMLEAF used:
      real time           0.65 seconds
      cpu time            unknown
```

SAS Listing

```
            Stem-Leaf plot of variable SALES in SASDATA.SHOES

         Stem of sales
          (in 1000's)     Leaf of sales

               0          344567778999
               1          01111234556667899
               2          011222455668
               3          0002455
               4          0112678889
               5          11123667
               6          015
               7          8
               8          03345
               9          1279
              10          5
              11          13779
              12          123467
              13          79
              14          049
              15          003447899
              16          0223346
              17          0233479
              18          01111777
              19          1122569
              20          1488
              21          224444
              22          0179
              23          127
              24          479
              25          7
              26          48
              27          77
              28          2357
              29          014557
              30          1469
              31          35
              32          689
              33          02678
              34          569
              35          3
              36          1236
              37          1245
              38          4799
              39          34
              40          02
              41          39
              42          4667
              43          4
              44          179
              45          5
              48          025
              49          8
              50          1
```

%SYSVARS

Purpose

This macro gets all SYSTEM variables and writes to a SAS data set

Syntax
%SYSVARS (OUT = *SAS-data-set* <, DEBUG = Y | YES | NO | N>)

Required Parameter(s)
OUT = SAS-data-set

    identifies the output SAS data set.

Optional Parameter(s)
DEBUG = Y | YES | NO | N

    debugging flag, set to YES or NO. Alternatively, you can submit Y or N. Default is NO.

See Also
%COMMAND, %DOSPATH, %DIRECTORY, %CURRENTPATH, %FINDFILE, %SYSVARS, %DATAPATH, %DATAMEM, and %MEM

Example

Sample Program
```
%sysvars (out = system)
proc print data=system ;
run ;
```

SAS Log
```
1    %sysvars (out = system)
NOTE: The data set WORK.SYSTEM has 77 observations and 2 variables.
NOTE: The MACRO %SYSVARS used:
      real time            0.18 seconds
      cpu time                  unknown

2    proc print data=system ;
3    run ;
NOTE: There were 77 observations read from the data set WORK.SYSTEM.
NOTE: PROCEDURE PRINT used:
      real time            0.00 seconds
      cpu time             0.00 seconds
```

SAS Listing

```
  Obs    variable                value

   1     ADRegion                North America
   2     ALLUSERSPROFILE         C:\Documents and Settings\All Users
   3     APPDATA                 C:\Documents and Settings\q727909\Application Data
   4     Build                   QIC
   5     BuildLocation           USKAN
   6     BuildPath               \
   7     BuildRev                0011
   8     BuildServer             QKANSSMSAMR
   9     BuildShare              QICBUILD$
  10     BuildType               NETIMAGE
  11     BuildVer                2.0
  12     BusinessUnit            NONE
  13     CommonProgramFiles      C:\Program Files\Common Files
  14     ComponentGroup          AMR
  15     ComputerModel           HP d530 SFF(PB604A)
  16     ComputerModelSeries     HPD530
  17     COMPUTERNAME            USKANWD20272
  18     ComputerType            Desktop
  19     ComSpec                 C:\WINDOWS\system32\cmd.exe
  20     Country                 US
  21     DestinationLocation     USKAN
  22     DestinationServer       QKANSSMSAMR
  23     DestinationShare        QICBUILD$
  24     EISIMAGE                !sasext0\eis\sasmisc
  25     FT15F001                FT15F001.DAT
  26     HOMEDRIVE               M:
  27     HOMEPATH                \
```

%TIMENOTE

Purpose

This macro is designed to record the run time of another macro

Syntax

%TIMENOTE (MACRO = *string*, STARTTIME = *date-time-value* <, DEBUG = Y | YES | NO | N>)

Required Parameter(s)

MACRO = *string*

> declares the macro name to use in the NOTE statement.

STARTTIME = *date-time-value*

> declares the beginning date-time stamp in numerical value. This is easiest to calculate using the statement
>
>   %let starttime=%sysfunc(datetime()) ;

Optional Parameter(s)

DEBUG = Y | YES | NO | N

> debugging flag, set to YES or NO. Alternatively, you can submit Y or N. Default is NO.

See Also
%DATANOTE, %FILENOTE, %TIMENOTE, %INFO

Example

Sample Program

```
%*----------------------------------------------------------------------*
 | the TIMENOTE macro requires an input value in SAS date-time variable format |
 *----------------------------------------------------------------------* ;

%let starttime=%sysfunc(datetime()) ;

%*-------------------------------------------*
 | the first application shows a very short time |
 +-------------------------------------------+--------------------------*
 | note that both options STIMER and NOSTIMER are shown.  Because the macros |
 | are run at different times (albiet very close together) the resulting run |
 | times will differ.  The same will hold true for the second application.   |
 *--------------------------------------------------------------------* ;

options stimer ;
%timenote (macro=no-name, starttime=&starttime) ;

options nostimer ;
%timenote (macro=no-name, starttime=&starttime) ;

%*--------------------------------------*
 | the second application is artificially |
 | incremented--to show a longer time.    |
 *--------------------------------------* ;

data _null_ ;
   newstarttime = &starttime - 1134325.0435 ;
   call symput ('newstarttime', trim(left(put(newstarttime, best.)))) ;
run ;

options stimer ;
%timenote (macro=no-name, starttime=&newstarttime) ;

options nostimer ;
%timenote (macro=no-name, starttime=&newstarttime) ;
```

SAS Log

```
25   %*----------------------------------------------------------------------*
26    | the TIMENOTE macro requires an input value in SAS date-time variable format |
27    *----------------------------------------------------------------------* ;
28
29   %let starttime=%sysfunc(datetime()) ;
30
31   %*-------------------------------------------*
32    | the first application shows a very short time |
33    +-------------------------------------------+--------------------------*
34    | note that both options STIMER and NOSTIMER are shown.  Because the macros |
35    | are run at different times (albiet very close together) the resulting run |
36    | times will differ.  The same will hold true for the second application.   |
37    *--------------------------------------------------------------------* ;
38
39   options stimer ;
40   %timenote (macro=no-name, starttime=&starttime) ;
NOTE: The MACRO %NO-NAME used:
      real time             0.01 seconds
      cpu time              unknown
41
```

```
42    options nostimer ;
43    %timenote (macro=no-name, starttime=&starttime) ;
NOTE: The MACRO %NO-NAME used 0.07 seconds.
44
45    %*----------------------------------------*
46     | the second application is artificially |
47     | incremented--to show a longer time.    |
48     *----------------------------------------* ;
49
50    data _null_ ;
51       newstarttime = &starttime - 1134325.0435 ;
52       call symput ('newstarttime', trim(left(put(newstarttime, best.)))) ;
53    run ;


54
55    options stimer ;
56    %timenote (macro=no-name, starttime=&newstarttime) ;
NOTE: The MACRO %NO-NAME used:
      real time           315:05:25.20
      cpu time                  unknown
57
58    options nostimer ;
59    %timenote (macro=no-name, starttime=&newstarttime) ;
NOTE: The MACRO %NO-NAME used 13 days 3 hours 5 minutes and 25.25 seconds.
```

SAS Listing

This sample program does not have any listing output.

%TRIMFILE

Purpose

This macro trims all trailing blanks on a file and compresses blanks down to one blank only (see the COMPBL function in BASE SAS). The designed application is to trim/compress *.html files.

Syntax

%TRIMFILE (INFILE = *filename* | *'file-specification'*, FILE = *filename* | *'file-specification'* <, LEADING = Y | YES | NO | N > <, COMPBL = Y | YES | NO | N> <, LRECL = *logical-record-length*> <, OUTLRECL = *logical-record-length*> <, DEBUG = Y | YES | NO | N>)

Required Parameter(s)

INFILE = *filename* | *'file-specification'*

    declares the input file

        filename specifies the fileref of an external file.

        "file-specification" specifies the physical name of an external file, which is enclosed in quotation marks. The physical name is the name by which the operating environment recognizes the file.

    Either the *filename* or *"file-specification"* must be declared, but not both.

FILE = *filename* | *'file-specification'*

    declares the input file

        filename specifies the fileref of an external file.

"file-specification" specifies the physical name of an external file, which is enclosed in quotation marks. The physical name is the name by which the operating environment recognizes the file.

Either the *filename* or *"file-specification"* must be declared, but not both.

Optional Parameter(s)

LEADING = Y | YES | NO | N

    declares if leading blanks should be removed

COMPBL = Y | YES | NO | N

    declares if multiple blank spaces should be removed and compressed to one blank from within the text.

LRECL = *logical-record-length*

    declares the logical record length of the input file. The default is 256. *Range LRECL > 0, Integer.*

LRECL = *logical-record-length*

    declares the logical record length of the output file. The default is 256. *Range LRECL > 0, Integer.*

DEBUG = Y | YES | NO | N

    debugging flag, set to YES or NO. Alternatively, you can submit Y or N. Default is NO.

See Also

%HTML2TXT, %TRIMFILE, %WORDWRAP

Notes

leading = YES trims leading blanks

leading = NO does not trim leading blanks

compbl = YES compresses blanks

compbl = NO does not compress blanks

Example

Sample Program

```
%*----------------------------------------------------------*
 | create a file with lots of blanks and trailing blanks |
 *----------------------------------------------------------* ;

data _null_ ;
   file 'trimfile.txt' ;
   put 'This is the first line                 with many blanks.' ;
   put 'The second    line    also   has  many blanks    look for trailing blanks                         ';
   put 'The line after this one is blank--it will be compressed to a single blank space' ;
   put '                               ' ;
   put '          leading blanks on the last line' ;
run ;

%*----------------------------------------------------------*
 | this configuration is good for trimming *.html files |
 *----------------------------------------------------------* ;

%trimfile (infile='trimfile.txt', file='trimmed.txt')
```

```
%*----------------------------------*
 | this option leaves leading blanks |
 | it uses COMPBL functionality      |
 | it removes trailing blanks        |
 *----------------------------------* ;

%trimfile (infile='trimfile.txt', file='leading.txt', leading=no)

%*----------------------------------*
 | this option removes leading blanks |
 | it does not use COMPBL             |
 | it removes trailing blanks         |
 *----------------------------------* ;

%trimfile (infile='trimfile.txt', file='compbl.txt', compbl=no)

%*----------------------------------------*
 | this option removes trailing blanks only |
 | this is good for trimming SAS programs   |
 | or other files with trailing blanks      |
 *----------------------------------------* ;

%trimfile (infile='trimfile.txt', file='trail.txt', compbl=no, leading=no)

%*---------------------*
 | read from a web page |
 *---------------------* ;

filename html url 'http://www.spikeware.net:80/home.html' ;
filename text 'web.txt' ;

%trimfile (infile=html, file=text)


%*------------------------------------*
 | use a data _NULL_ to view the files |
 *------------------------------------* ;

data _null_ ;
   infile 'trimfile.txt' ;
   file print ;
   if _n_ = 1 then put 'ORIGINAL FILE: The "|" character is used to show the end of line' // ;
   input @1 line $1. ;
   put _infile_ '|' ;
run ;

data _null_ ;
   infile 'trimmed.txt' ;
   file print ;

   input @1 line $1. ;
   if _n_ = 1 then put 'TRIMMED (LEADING=YES, COMPBL=YES): The "|" character is used to show the end of line' //
     ;
   put _infile_ '|' ;
run ;

data _null_ ;
   infile 'leading.txt' ;
   file print ;

   input @1 line $1. ;
   if _n_ = 1 then put 'LEADING (LEADING=YES, COMPBL=NO): The "|" character is used to show the end of line' //
     ;
   put _infile_ '|' ;
run ;

data _null_ ;
```

```
    infile 'compbl.txt' ;
    file print ;

    input @1 line $1. ;
    if _n_ = 1 then put 'COMPBL (COMPBL=YES, LEADING=NO): The "|" character is used to show the end of line' // ;
    put _infile_ '|' ;
run ;

data _null_ ;
    infile 'trail.txt' ;
    file print ;

    input @1 line $1. ;
    if _n_ = 1 then put 'TRAIL (COMPBL=NO, LEADING=NO): The "|" character is used to show the end of line' // ;
    put _infile_ '|' ;
run ;

data _null_ ;
    infile 'web.txt' ;
    file print ;

    input @1 line $1. ;
    if _n_ = 1 then put 'Read directly from the internet: The "|" character is used to show the end of line' /
                       'NOTE:   The LRECL is 256, where the web page might be much higher' // ;
    put _infile_ '|' ;
run ;
```

SAS Log

```
1     %*-------------------------------------------------------*
2     | create a file with lots of blanks and trailing blanks |
3     *-------------------------------------------------------* ;
4
5     data _null_ ;
6        file 'trimfile.txt' ;
7        put 'This is the first line                   with many blanks.' ;
8        put 'The second      line    also   has   many blanks    look for trailing blanks
8    !                        ';
9        put 'The line after this one is blank--it will be compressed to a single blank space' ;

10       put '                                       ' ;
11       put '               leading blanks on the last line' ;
12    run ;

NOTE: The file 'trimfile.txt' is:
      File Name=C:\Perl\bin\trimfile.txt,
      RECFM=V,LRECL=256

NOTE: 5 records were written to the file 'trimfile.txt'.
      The minimum record length was 31.
      The maximum record length was 101.
NOTE: DATA statement used:
      real time           0.03 seconds
      cpu time            0.01 seconds


13
14    %*------------------------------------------------------*
15    | this configuration is good for trimming *.html files |
16    *------------------------------------------------------* ;
17
18    %trimfile (infile='trimfile.txt', file='trimmed.txt')
NOTE: The file 'trimmed.txt' is:
      File Name=C:\Perl\bin\trimmed.txt,
      RECFM=V,LRECL=256

NOTE: 5 records were written to the file 'trimmed.txt'.
      The minimum record length was 0.
```

```
             The maximum record length was 79.
NOTE: The MACRO %TRIMFILE used:
      real time              0.19 seconds
      cpu time               unknown

19
20   %*---------------------------------*
21    | this option leaves leading blanks |
22    | it uses COMPBL functionality      |
23    | it removes trailing blanks        |
24    *---------------------------------* ;
25
26   %trimfile (infile='trimfile.txt', file='leading.txt', leading=no)
NOTE: The file 'leading.txt' is:
      File Name=C:\Perl\bin\leading.txt,
      RECFM=V,LRECL=256

NOTE: 5 records were written to the file 'leading.txt'.
      The minimum record length was 0.
      The maximum record length was 79.
NOTE: The MACRO %TRIMFILE used:
      real time              0.08 seconds
      cpu time               unknown

27
28   %*----------------------------------*
29    | this option removes leading blanks |
30    | it does not use COMPBL             |
31    | it removes trailing blanks         |
32    *----------------------------------* ;
33
34   %trimfile (infile='trimfile.txt', file='compbl.txt', compbl=no)
NOTE: The file 'compbl.txt' is:
      File Name=C:\Perl\bin\compbl.txt,
      RECFM=V,LRECL=256

NOTE: 5 records were written to the file 'compbl.txt'.
      The minimum record length was 0.
      The maximum record length was 79.
NOTE: The MACRO %TRIMFILE used:
      real time              0.09 seconds
      cpu time               unknown

35
36   %*------------------------------------------*
37    | this option removes trailing blanks only  |
38    | this is good for trimming SAS programs    |
39    | or other files with trailing blanks       |
40    *------------------------------------------* ;
41
42   %trimfile (infile='trimfile.txt', file='trail.txt', compbl=no, leading=no)

NOTE: The file 'trail.txt' is:
      File Name=C:\Perl\bin\trail.txt,
      RECFM=V,LRECL=256

NOTE: 5 records were written to the file 'trail.txt'.
      The minimum record length was 0.
      The maximum record length was 79.
NOTE: The MACRO %TRIMFILE used:
      real time              0.17 seconds
      cpu time               unknown

43
44   %*---------------------*
45    | read from a web page |
46    *---------------------* ;
47
```

```
48    filename html url 'http://www.spikeware.net:80/home.html' ;
49    filename text 'web.txt' ;
50
51    %trimfile (infile=html, file=text)
NOTE: The file TEXT is:
      File Name=C:\Perl\bin\web.txt,
      RECFM=V,LRECL=256

NOTE: 124 records were written to the file TEXT.
      The minimum record length was 1.
      The maximum record length was 256.
NOTE: The MACRO %TRIMFILE used:
      real time             0.73 seconds
      cpu time              unknown

52
53
54    %*-------------------------------------*
55     | use a data _NULL_ to view the files |
56    *-------------------------------------* ;
57
58    data _null_ ;
59       infile 'trimfile.txt' ;
60       file print ;
61       if _n_ = 1 then put 'ORIGINAL FILE: The "|" character is used to show the end of line' //
61 !  ;
62       input @1 line $1. ;
63       put _infile_ '|' ;
64    run ;

NOTE: The infile 'trimfile.txt' is:
      File Name=C:\Perl\bin\trimfile.txt,
      RECFM=V,LRECL=256

NOTE: 9 lines were written to file PRINT.
NOTE: 5 records were read from the infile 'trimfile.txt'.
      The minimum record length was 31.
      The maximum record length was 101.
NOTE: DATA statement used:
      real time             0.08 seconds
      cpu time              0.00 seconds


65
66    data _null_ ;
67       infile 'trimmed.txt' ;
68       file print ;
69
70       input @1 line $1. ;
71       if _n_ = 1 then put 'TRIMMED (LEADING=YES, COMPBL=YES): The "|" character is used to show
71 !  the end of line' // ;
72       put _infile_ '|' ;
73    run ;

NOTE: The infile 'trimmed.txt' is:
      File Name=C:\Perl\bin\trimmed.txt,
      RECFM=V,LRECL=256

NOTE: 8 lines were written to file PRINT.
NOTE: 5 records were read from the infile 'trimmed.txt'.
      The minimum record length was 1.
      The maximum record length was 79.
NOTE: DATA statement used:
      real time             0.01 seconds
      cpu time              0.01 seconds

74
```

```
75    data _null_ ;
76       infile 'leading.txt' ;
77       file print ;
78
79       input @1 line $1. ;
80       if _n_ = 1 then put 'LEADING (LEADING=YES, COMPBL=NO): The "|" character is used to show
80 ! the end of line' // ;
81       put _infile_ '|' ;
82    run ;

NOTE: The infile 'leading.txt' is:
      File Name=C:\Perl\bin\leading.txt,
      RECFM=V,LRECL=256

NOTE: 8 lines were written to file PRINT.
NOTE: 5 records were read from the infile 'leading.txt'.
      The minimum record length was 1.
      The maximum record length was 79.
NOTE: DATA statement used:
      real time           0.01 seconds
      cpu time            0.01 seconds


83
84    data _null_ ;
85       infile 'compbl.txt' ;
86       file print ;
87
88       input @1 line $1. ;
89       if _n_ = 1 then put 'COMPBL (COMPBL=YES, LEADING=NO): The "|" character is used to show
89 ! the end of line' // ;
90       put _infile_ '|' ;
91    run ;

NOTE: The infile 'compbl.txt' is:
      File Name=C:\Perl\bin\compbl.txt,
      RECFM=V,LRECL=256

NOTE: 8 lines were written to file PRINT.
NOTE: 5 records were read from the infile 'compbl.txt'.
      The minimum record length was 1.
      The maximum record length was 79.
NOTE: DATA statement used:
      real time           0.01 seconds
      cpu time            0.01 seconds


92
93    data _null_ ;
94       infile 'trail.txt' ;
95       file print ;
96
97       input @1 line $1. ;
98       if _n_ = 1 then put 'TRAIL (COMPBL=NO, LEADING=NO): The "|" character is used to show the
98 ! end of line' // ;
99       put _infile_ '|' ;
100   run ;

NOTE: The infile 'trail.txt' is:
      File Name=C:\Perl\bin\trail.txt,
      RECFM=V,LRECL=256

NOTE: 8 lines were written to file PRINT.
NOTE: 5 records were read from the infile 'trail.txt'.
      The minimum record length was 1.
      The maximum record length was 79.
NOTE: DATA statement used:
      real time           0.00 seconds
```

```
      cpu time              0.00 seconds

101
102  data _null_ ;
103    infile 'web.txt' ;
104    file print ;
105
106    input @1 line $1. ;
107    if _n_ = 1 then put 'Read directly from the internet:  The "|" character is used to show
107! the end of line' /
108                     'NOTE:  The LRECL is 256, where the web page might be much higher' //
108! ;
109    put _infile_ '|' ;
110  run ;

NOTE: The infile 'web.txt' is:
      File Name=C:\Perl\bin\web.txt,
      RECFM=V,LRECL=256

NOTE: 155 lines were written to file PRINT.
NOTE: 124 records were read from the infile 'web.txt'.
      The minimum record length was 1.
      The maximum record length was 256.
NOTE: DATA statement used:
      real time             0.00 seconds
      cpu time              0.00 seconds
```

SAS Listing

ORIGINAL FILE: The "|" character is used to show the end of line

```
This is the first line               with many blanks.|
The second    line    also   has   many blanks    look for trailing blanks
    |
The line after this one is blank--it will be compressed to a single blank space|
                       |
         leading blanks on the last line|
```

TRIMMED (LEADING=YES, COMPBL=YES): The "|" character is used to show the end of line

```
This is the first line with many blanks.|
The second line also has many blanks look for trailing blanks|
The line after this one is blank--it will be compressed to a single blank space|
 |
leading blanks on the last line|
```

LEADING (LEADING=YES, COMPBL=NO): The "|" character is used to show the end of line

```
This is the first line               with many blanks.|
The second    line    also   has   many blanks    look for trailing blanks|
The line after this one is blank--it will be compressed to a single blank space|
 |
leading blanks on the last line|
```

COMPBL (COMPBL=YES, LEADING=NO): The "|" character is used to show the end of line

```
This is the first line with many blanks.|
The second line also has many blanks look for trailing blanks|
The line after this one is blank--it will be compressed to a single blank space|
```

```
|
          leading blanks on the last line|
```

TRAIL (COMPBL=NO, LEADING=NO): The "|" character is used to show the end of line

```
This is the first line                   with many blanks.|
The second    line    also   has   many blanks    look for trailing blanks|
The line after this one is blank--it will be compressed to a single blank space|
|
          leading blanks on the last line|
```

%UNIV

Purpose
This macro completes a statistical analysis of many variables and prints the output on one page. Basically, it is a PROC UNIVARIATE with an output that looks like PROC MEANS.

Syntax
%UNIV (<DATA = *SAS-data-set*> <, OUT = *SAS-data-set*> <, VAR = *variable-list*> <FORMAT = *SAS-format*> <, ROUND = *round-off-unit*> <BY = *by-variables*> <STATS = _ALL_ | _STD_ | *statistics*> <, DEBUG = Y | YES | NO | N>)

Required Parameter(s)
There are no required parameters.

Optional Parameter(s)
DATA = *SAS-data-set*

    identifies the input SAS data set. If no data set is declared, the most recent data set is used.

OUT = *SAS-data-set*

    identifies the output SAS data set.

FORMAT = *SAS-format*

    The FORMAT statement associates a format with the substring of the check-all-that-apply variable. SAS uses the format to write the values of the variable that you specify

ROUND = round-off-unit

    declares the round-off-unit (see ROUND function). Rounds the statistical measure to the nearest round-off unit. Range: is numeric and nonnegative.

BY = *variable-list*

    declares the list of by-variables for processing.

VAR = *variable-list*

    declares the list of numeric variables for completion of statistical measures

STATS = _ALL_ | _STD_ | *statistics*

    declares the statistical measures to display

ALL displays all statistical measures available in the list of *statistics* keywords.

STD displays the standard statistical measures. They are: n, mean, std, cv, sum, min, p10, p25, p50, p75, p90, max.

statistics displays specific statistical measures by keyword. The keywords are: n, nobs, nmiss, mean, mode, sum, std, cv, css, uss, qrange, msign, normal, stdmean, probn, probm, probs, signrank, t, kurtosis, skewness, range, qrange, sumwgt, min, p1, p5, p10, p25, p50, p75, p90, p95, p99, max.

DEBUG = Y | YES | NO | N

debugging flag, set to YES or NO. Alternatively, you can submit Y or N. Default is NO.

Example

Sample Program
```
%univ (data=sashelp.shoes)
```

SAS Log
```
1    %univ (data=sashelp.shoes)
NOTE: The MACRO %UNIV used:
      real time              0.80 seconds
      cpu time               unknown
```

SAS Listing

Variable name	Variable description	Number non-missing values	Mean value	Standard deviation	Coefficient of variation
Stores	Number of Stores	395	11.65	8.87	76.18
Sales	Total Sales	395	85700.17	129107.23	150.65
Inventor	Total Inventory	395	250898.86	351514.63	140.10
Returns	Total Returns	395	2967.32	4611.74	155.42

Variable name	Sum of all values	Minimum value	10th %tile	25th %tile	50th %tile	75th %tile	90th %tile	Maximum value
Stores	4601	1	2	3	10	18	25	41
Sales	33851566	325	2617	15312	38912	108936	229372	1298717
Inventor	99105051	374	15889	43155	118849	336513	625925	2881005
Returns	1172092	10	120	578	1438	3698	7447	57362

%WORDWRAP

Purpose
This macro reads in a file and removes hard carriage returns inside of paragraphs. A paragraph break must originally be noted as a blank line.

Syntax
%WORDWRAP (INFILE = *"filename"*, file = *"filename"*, <,DEBUG = YES | Y | NO | N>)

Required Parameter(s)

INFILE = *"filename"|file-specification*

> specifies the quoted filename or unquoted file specification of the input file.

FILE = *"filename"|file-specification*

> specifies the quoted filename or unquoted file specification of the output file.

Options

DEBUG = Y | YES | NO | N

> debugging flag, set to YES or NO. Alternatively, you can submit Y or N. Default is NO.

See Also

%HTML2TXT, %TRIMFILE, %WORDWRAP

Notes

This macro is designed to read in a text file and remove hard-breaks in the paragraphs that often occur when copying text files. Blank lines are treated as a paragraph break while all other lines are combined to place one paragraph on an entire line of the text file.

Example

Sample Program

```
filename in1  'C:\sasv8\license.txt' ;
filename out1 'C:\temp\out.txt' ;
%wordwrap (infile=in1, file=out1)
```

SAS Log

```
1    filename in1  'C:\sasv8\license.txt' ;
2    filename out1 'C:\temp\out.txt' ;
3    %wordwrap (infile=in1, file=out1)
NOTE: The file OUT1 is:
      File Name=C:\temp\out.txt,
      RECFM=V,LRECL=700

NOTE: 26 records were written to the file OUT1.
      The minimum record length was 0.
      The maximum record length was 700.
NOTE: The MACRO %WORDWRAP used:
      real time           0.27 seconds
      cpu time            unknown
```

SAS Listing

This sample program does not have any listing output.

%XLS2SAS

Purpose

This macro reads a Microsoft Excel Spreadsheet into a SAS data set

Syntax
%XLS2SAS (INFILE = *"filename"*, OUT = *SAS-data-set* <,ROW = *rows*> <,COL = *columns*> <,SHEET = *worksheet*> <,LENGTH = *length*> <,XLS = *"filename"*> <,DEBUG = YES | Y | NO | N>)

Required Parameter(s)
INFILE = *"filename"*

> specifies the complete path and filename of the output PC file, spreadsheet, or delimited external file. If the name does not include special characters (like the backslash in a path), lowercase characters, or spaces, you can omit the quotes.

OUT = *SAS-data-set*

> idetifies the output SAS data set with either a one- or two-level SAS name (library and member name). If the specified SAS data set does not exist, the macro creates it. If you specify a one-level name, the macro uses the WORK library.

Options
ROW = *rows*

> a positive integer less than or equal to 63,536 that declares the maximum number of rows in the spreadsheet to read in. The default is 63536.

COL = *columns*

> a positive integer less than or equal to 256 that declares the maximum number of columns in the spreadsheet to read in The default is 256.

SHEET = *worksheet*

> A text string that declares the worksheet (or tab) to read in. The default is SHEET1.

LENGTH = *length*

> a positive integer less than or equal to 32,737 that declares the maximum variable length when reading in variables from each cell. This value is fixed for all columns in the spreadsheet. The default is 200.

XLS = *"filename"*

> specifies the complete path and filename of Microsoft Excel. This can be set up in the initial installation of the macro.

DEBUG = Y | YES | NO | N

> debugging flag, set to YES or NO. Alternatively, you can submit Y or N. Default is NO.

See Also
%XLS2SAS, %SAS2XLS, %FILEIN, %FILEOUT, PROC IMPORT, PROC EXPORT

Notes
This macro takes a Microsoft Excel spreadsheet and reads it in to a SAS data set. Microsoft Excel is required and this macro will only function in Microsoft Windows Environment. All variables read in are read in as character strings of the same length as defined in the LENGTH= option (default=200).

The first row of the spreadsheet must contain the variable names.

The macro will not read past a blank column and reads in the values as they are formatted in the MS-Excel spreadsheet (WYSIWYG). MS-Excel has different file restrictions than SAS has. For example, a carriage-return character or a LRECL > 32767 will generate results that are unpredictable.

BENCHMARK: This macro used approximately 22 minutes of real-time to process a 63,535 record MS-Excel Spreadsheet of 256 columns. Each variable read in was of size $200 and the resulting SAS data set took up 3,285,574,656 bytes (3.2 Gb). A 10-record spreadsheet of 4 variables can be read in about 6 seconds.

If you have SAS/ACCESS Software for PC File Formats, you should use the procedures available (PROC IMPORT) in that package instead of this macro.

Example

Sample Program

```
%xls2sas (infile=C:\Temp\shoes.xls,
          out=shoes,
          sheet=shoes)

proc print data=shoes label ;
run ;
```

SAS Log

```
1     %xls2sas (infile=C:\Temp\shoes.xls,
2               out=shoes,
3               sheet=shoes)
NOTE: The infile "C:\Temp\shoes.xls" is:
      DDE Session,
      SESSION=excel|shoes!r1c1:r395c7,RECFM=V,
      LRECL=32767
NOTE: 395 records were read from the infile C:\Temp\shoes.xls
NOTE: The data set WORK.SHOES has 394 observations and 7 variables.
NOTE: The MACRO %XLS2SAS used:
      real time          6.39 seconds
      cpu time           unknown

4
5     proc print data=shoes label ;
6     run ;

NOTE: There were 394 observations read from the data set WORK.SHOES.
NOTE: PROCEDURE PRINT used:
      real time          0.09 seconds
      cpu time           0.03 seconds
```

SAS Listing

Obs	Region	Product	Subsidiary	Number of Stores	Total Sales	Total Inventory	Total Returns
1	Africa	Boot	Addis Ababa	12	$29,761	$191,821	$769
2	Africa	Men's Casual	Addis Ababa	4	$67,242	$118,036	$2,284
3	Africa	Men's Dress	Addis Ababa	7	$76,793	$136,273	$2,433
4	Africa	Sandal	Addis Ababa	10	$62,819	$204,284	$1,861
5	Africa	Slipper	Addis Ababa	14	$68,641	$279,795	$1,771
6	Africa	Sport Shoe	Addis Ababa	4	$1,690	$16,634	$79
7	Africa	Women's Casual	Addis Ababa	2	$51,541	$98,641	$940
8	Africa	Women's Dress	Addis Ababa	12	$108,942	$311,017	$3,233
9	Africa	Boot	Algiers	21	$21,297	$73,737	$710
10	Africa	Men's Casual	Algiers	4	$63,206	$100,982	$2,221
11	Africa	Men's Dress	Algiers	13	$123,743	$428,575	$3,621
12	Africa	Sandal	Algiers	25	$29,198	$84,447	$1,530

%XML2SAS

Purpose
This macro reads in a SPIKEware XML data file into a SAS data set.

Syntax
%XML2SAS (INFILE = , OUT = *SAS-data-set* <, DEBUG = Y | YES | NO | N>)

Required Parameter(s)
INFILE = *filename* | *'file-specification'*

> declares the input XML file
>
>> *filename* specifies the fileref of an external file.
>>
>> *"file-specification"* specifies the physical name of an external file, which is enclosed in quotation marks. The physical name is the name by which the operating environment recognizes the file.
>
> Either the *filename* or *"file-specification"* must be declared, but not both.

OUT = *SAS-data-set*

> declares the output SAS data set.

Optional Parameter(s)
DEBUG = Y | YES | NO | N

> debugging flag, set to YES or NO. Alternatively, you can submit Y or N. Default is NO.

Example

Sample Program
```
filename xml "c:\temp\shoes.xml" ;
%xml2sas (out=shoes, infile=xml)
```

SAS Log
```
7    filename xml "c:\temp\shoes.xml" ;
8    %xml2sas (out=shoes, infile=xml)
NOTE: The data set WORK.SHOES has 395 observations and 7 variables.
NOTE: The MACRO %XML2SAS used:
      real time            0.48 seconds
      cpu time             unknown
```

SAS Listing
This sample program does not have any listing output.

Methods

%_AGE

Purpose
This macro is designed to function INSIDE a SAS data step. It will calculate the age in years given a start and end date.

Syntax
age = %_age(birth_date, today) ;

> *birth_date* is a valid SAS date
>
> *today* is optional, representing the date the age is measured. If no value is given, the current date is used.

See Also
%_CITY, %_STATE, %_ZIP, %_PROPERNAME, %_F2C, %_C2F, %_AGE, %_PCTCHANGE

Example

Sample Program
```
data _null_ ;
   birth = '01jan1960'd ;
   age = %_age(birth) ;
   put age= ;
run ;
```

SAS Log
```
1          data _null_ ;
2             birth = '01jan1960'd ;
3             age = %_age(birth) ;
4             put age= ;
5          run ;

age=46
```

SAS Listing
This sample program does not have any listing output.

%_C2F

Purpose
This macro is designed to function INSIDE a SAS data step. It will convert Degrees Celsius to Degrees Fahrenheit

Syntax
degf = %_c2f(degrees_celsius) ;

degrees_celsius is the temperature in Celsius

See Also
%_CITY, %_STATE, %_ZIP, %_PROPERNAME, %_F2C, %_C2F, %_AGE, %_PCTCHANGE

Notes
reference http://www.usatoday.com/weather/wtempcf.htm

Example

Sample Program
```
data _null_ ;
   degf = %_c2f(100) ;
   put degf= ;
run ;
```
SAS Log

```
1          data null ;
2             degf = %_c2f(100) ;
3             put degf= ;
4          run ;
```

degf=212

SAS Listing
This sample program does not have any listing output.

%_CITY

Purpose
This macro is designed to function INSIDE a SAS data step. It will take a standard City_state_ZIP variable and pull out the CITY

Syntax
city = %_city (csz) ;

csz is the city, state and zip combined variable. The macro will work with two-character state codes and/or full state names as well as five and nine-digit ZIP codes. CITY and STATE must be separated by a comma.

See Also
%_CITY, %_STATE, %_ZIP, %_PROPERNAME, %_F2C, %_C2F, %_AGE, %_PCTCHANGE

Example

Sample Program
```
Data _null_ ;
   city_state_ZIP1 = 'Chicago, IL   60606
   city_state_ZIP2 = 'New York, New York 10005-3701
   city1 = %_city(city_state_ZIP1
   city2 = %_city(city_state_ZIP2
```

```
   put city1= city2
run ;
```

SAS Log

```
1          data _null_ ;
2             city_state_ZIP1 = 'Chicago, IL  60606' ;
3             city_state_ZIP2 = 'New York, New York 10005-3701' ;
4             city1 = %_city(city_state_ZIP1) ;
5             city2 = %_city(city_state_ZIP2) ;
6             put city1= city2= ;
7          run ;

city1=Chicago city2=New York
```

SAS Listing

This sample program does not have any listing output.

%_F2C

Purpose

This macro is designed to function INSIDE a SAS data step. It will convert Degrees Fahrenheit to Degrees Celsius

Syntax

degc = %_f2c(degrees_fahrenheit) ;

degrees_fahrenheit is the temperature in Fahrenheit

See Also

%_CITY, %_STATE, %_ZIP, %_PROPERNAME, %_F2C, %_C2F, %_AGE, %_PCTCHANGE

Notes

reference http://www.usatoday.com/weather/wtempcf.htm

Example

Sample Program

```
data _null_ ;
   degc = %_f2c(32) ;
   put degc ;
run ;
```

SAS Log

```
1          data _null_ ;
2             degc = %_f2c(32) ;
3             put degc= ;
4          run ;

degc=0
```

SAS Listing

This sample program does not have any listing output.

%_PCTCHANGE

Purpose
This macro is designed to function INSIDE a SAS data step. It will calculate the percent change between two points.

Syntax
change = %_pctchange(start, end, mult) ;

    START (numeric) is the starting point for comparison.

    END (numeric) is the ending point for comparison.

    MULT (any) is a flag to multiply the result by 100 or not. A 0 or NULL STRING will return the value as a decimal, any other string will return the value multiplied by 100.

See Also
%_CITY, %_STATE, %_ZIP, %_PROPERNAME, %_F2C, %_C2F, %_AGE, %_PCTCHANGE

Notes
This simple calculation could be done without a macro but for the sake of consistency we created one anyway. With this macro, percent change will be calculated the same way every time.

Example

Sample Program
```
data _null_ ;
   start = 1 ;
   end   = 2 ;

   change = %_pctchange (start, end) ;
   put change= ;

   change = %_pctchange (start, end, 1) ;
   put change= ;
run ;
```

SAS Log
```
1          data _null_ ;
2             start = 1 ;
3             end   = 2 ;
5             change = %_pctchange (start, end) ;
6             put change= ;
8             change = %_pctchange (start, end, 1) ;
9             put change= ;
10         run ;

change=1
change=100
```

SAS Listing
This sample program does not have any listing output.

%_PROPERNAME

Purpose
This macro is designed to function INSIDE a SAS data step. It will transform the input variable values to mixed case for proper nouns. It is not 100% accurate, as macgyver becomes MacGyver, but mack will become MacK. Make edits to meet your needs based on your database.

Syntax
name = %_propername (varname, length) ;

varname is the variable name (or quoted string) to adjust to proper name style mixed case

length is the maximum length of resulting string

See Also
%_CITY, %_STATE, %_ZIP, %_PROPERNAME, %_F2C, %_C2F, %_AGE, %_PCTCHANGE

Notes
This macro operates within a data step. The following data step variables are reseved for use within the data step: *WORDCOUNT, LENGTH, I, SCAN*, and *_NEWSTRING*. This macro is depreciated in SAS9. If you are using SAS9, use the new data step function PROPERNAME.

Example

Sample Program
```
data _null_ ;
   mcdonald = "paul david mcdonald" ;
   %_propername (mcdonald, 40) ;

   goodnight = 'dr. jim goodnight' ;
   %_propername (goodnight, 40) ;

   obrien = "Miles O'Brien" ;
   %_propername (obrien, 40) ;

   hyphen = 'john rhys-davies' ;
   %_propername (hyphen, 40) ;

   howell = 'thurston howell iii' ;
   %_propername (howell, 40) ;

   phd = 'julius irving, phd' ;
   %_propername (phd, 40) ;

   put mcdonald= goodnight= obrien= hyphen= howell= phd= ;
run ;
```

SAS Log
```
1     data _null_ ;
2        mcdonald = "paul david mcdonald" ;
3        %_propername (mcdonald, 40) ;
NOTE: Data step macro %_PROPERNAME uses reserved data step variables _WORDCOUNT_, _LENGTH_, _I_,
_SCAN_, and _NEWSTRING_ in processing.
4
5        goodnight = 'dr. jim goodnight' ;
```

```
6          %_propername (goodnight, 40) ;
NOTE: Data step macro %_PROPERNAME uses reserved data step variables _WORDCOUNT_, _LENGTH_, _I_,
_SCAN_, and _NEWSTRING_ in processing.
7
8          obrien = "Miles O'Brien" ;
9          %_propername (obrien, 40) ;
NOTE: Data step macro %_PROPERNAME uses reserved data step variables _WORDCOUNT_, _LENGTH_, _I_,
_SCAN_, and _NEWSTRING_ in processing.
10
11         hyphen = 'john rhys-davies' ;
12         %_propername (hyphen, 40) ;
NOTE: Data step macro %_PROPERNAME uses reserved data step variables _WORDCOUNT_, _LENGTH_, _I_,
_SCAN_, and _NEWSTRING_ in processing.
13
14         howell = 'thurston howell iii' ;
15         %_propername (howell, 40) ;
NOTE: Data step macro %_PROPERNAME uses reserved data step variables _WORDCOUNT_, _LENGTH_, _I_,
_SCAN_, and _NEWSTRING_ in processing.
16
17         phd = 'julius irving, phd' ;
18         %_propername (phd, 40) ;
NOTE: Data step macro %_PROPERNAME uses reserved data step variables _WORDCOUNT_, _LENGTH_, _I_,
_SCAN_, and _NEWSTRING_ in processing.
19
20         put mcdonald= goodnight= obrien= hyphen= howell= phd= ;
21     run ;

mcdonald=Paul David McDonald goodnight=Dr. Jim Goodnight obrien=Miles O'Brien
hyphen=John Rhys-Davies howell=Thurston Howell III phd=Julius Irving, PhD
NOTE: DATA statement used:
      real time           0.13 seconds
      cpu time            0.05 seconds
```

SAS Listing

This sample program does not have any listing output.

%_STATE

Purpose

This macro is designed to function INSIDE a SAS data step. It will take a standard City_state_ZIP variable and pull out the STATE

Syntax

state = %_state (_csz_) ;

> csz is the city, state and zip combined variable. The macro will work with two-character state codes and/or full state names as well as five and nine-digit ZIP codes. CITY and STATE must be separated by a comma.

See Also

%_CITY, %_STATE, %_ZIP, %_PROPERNAME, %_F2C, %_C2F, %_AGE, %_PCTCHANGE

Example

Sample Program

```
data _null_ ;
   city_state_ZIP1 = 'Chicago, IL  60606' ;
```

```
      city_state_ZIP2 = 'New York, New York 10005-3701' ;
      state1 = %_state(city_state_ZIP1) ;
      state2 = %_state(city_state_ZIP2) ;
      put state1= state2= ;
run ;
```

SAS Log

```
1         data _null_ ;
2             city_state_ZIP1 = 'Chicago, IL  60606' ;
3             city_state_ZIP2 = 'New York, New York 10005-3701' ;
4             state1 = %_state(city_state_ZIP1) ;
5             state2 = %_state(city_state_ZIP2) ;
6             put state1= state2= ;
7         run ;

state1=IL state2=New York
```

SAS Listing

This sample program does not have any listing output.

%_ZIP

Purpose

This macro is designed to function INSIDE a SAS data step. It will take a standard City_state_ZIP variable and pull out the zip code

Syntax

zip = %_zip (_csz_) ;

> *csz* is the city, state and zip combined variable. The macro will work with two-character state codes and/or full state names as well as five and nine-digit ZIP codes. CITY and STATE must be separated by a comma.

See Also

%_CITY, %_STATE, %_ZIP, %_PROPERNAME, %_F2C, %_C2F, %_AGE, %_PCTCHANGE

Example

Sample Program

```
data _null_ ;
   length zip1 zip2 $1 ;
   city_state_ZIP1 = 'Chicago, IL  60606' ;
   city_state_ZIP2 = 'New York, New York 10005-3701' ;
   zip1 = %_zip(city_state_ZIP1) ;
   zip2 = %_zip(city_state_ZIP2) ;
   put zip1= zip2= ;
run ;
```

SAS Log

```
1         data _null_ ;
2             length zip1 zip2 $10 ;
3             city_state_ZIP1 = 'Chicago, IL  60606' ;
4             city_state_ZIP2 = 'New York, New York 10005-3701' ;
5             zip1 = %_zip(city_state_ZIP1) ;
6             zip2 = %_zip(city_state_ZIP2) ;
```

```
7              put zip1= zip2= ;
8         run ;

zip1=60606 zip2=10005-3701
```

SAS Listing

This sample program does not have any listing output.

FAQ

Frequently asked questions on the Rapid Decision Support SAS Macro Package.

General Questions

Q: What is the difference between a "Function", a "Macro", and a "Method"?

A: First, all are technically "macros" because they use the SAS Macro language. FUNCTIONS and METHODS are specific kinds of SAS Macros. A FUNCTION is specifically designed to return a string from a given set of arguments. A METHOD is specifically designed to function inside a data step. All other macros are simply called "Macros".

Q: How can I learn about the setup, usage, and operation of a macro?

A: The macros are all designed to go in a given macro library. The README.TXT has general setup instructions. However, some macros do require extra work for your site. A simple way to check is to complete a search for the string "###" (three pound signs) which marks any code that may need modification due to site-specific issues. Documentation is included in the comments for every such occurrence.

Installation/Usage

Q: How do I install the macros?

A: We recommend creating a folder in the !SASROOT directory called MACROS (for example: c:\program files\SAS Institute\SAS\V8\Macros) and placing all macros in folders there. We also recommend keeping the macros separate from their source, such as RDS Macros in a folder called "RDS" and other macros in other folders.
The RDS\Administrator package includes a file called AUTOEXEC.SAS that should be copied to your !SASROOT directory. See your site SAS Administrator for support.

Q: I am having trouble with one of the macros. How can I troubleshoot?

A: Macro FUNCTIONS and METHODS require different approaches to troubleshooting. Because FUNCTIONS and METHODS are set up for specific applications, they should be handled individually. Regular "MACROS" (the "all-other" category) can provide a jump-start for troubleshooting by entering the option DEBUG=YES when calling the macro. This will turn on several options that will assist with troubleshooting and will not automatically delete any data sets or views created by the macro.

Licensing

Q: Can I change or modify the macros?

A: Yes. Feel free to change or modify the macros as you see fit. Any changes or modifications (including syntax, purpose, notes, etc) should be noted in the header.

Q: Are there any limits to the modifications I can make?

A: It would violate the license agreement to remove the header information including the licensing section and references to SPIKEware. We have devoted many, many hours to the development of these tools--some have been developed and tested for more than ten years. We have made these tools freely available in exchange for keeping our name and contact information with the programs.

Q: Can I distribute the macros to others?

A: Yes, under the following terms: 1) The recipient agrees to the terms of the license, 2) Any modifications are noted in the headers and disclosed to the recipient, 3) there is no charge for the programs. The official wording is "you can redistribute it and/or modify it under the terms of the GNU

Lesser General Public License as published by the Free Software Foundation--either version 2.1 of the License, or (at your option) any later version."

Applications

Q: How secure are %ENCRYPT, %DECRYPT, and %SCRAMBLE?

A: %ENCRYPT, %DECRYPT, and %SCRAMBLE are designed for very simple encryption. They would not slow down any serious hackers.

Non-SAS Components

Q: Where can I learn more about the Windows batch files?

A: Each Windows Batch File has its own comments and instructions in the code like the SAS Macros. The batch files also contain installation instructions and support. Type batchfile /? to learn more.

Q: Why have you included several PDF files?

A: Because they may be helpful and contain information developed through the lifetime of the Rapid Decision Support system.